The Parents' Guide to Kids' Movies

Also by Jo Berry

The Ultimate DVD Easter Egg Guide
Chick Flicks (with Angie Errigo)

The Parents' Guide to Kids' Movies

JO BERRY

First published in Great Britain in 2006 by Orion
an imprint of Orion Books Ltd
Orion House, 5 Upper St Martin's Lane, London WC2H 9EA

A CIP catalogue record for this book is available from the British Library

ISBN 0 75287 487 X

Typeset in Great Britain by Geoff Green Book Design, Cambridge

Printed and bound by Clays Ltd, St Ives plc

Contents

●●

MAR   2007

Dedication

To Danny.
While you were sleeping, my beautiful angel …
Love, Mummy.

With thanks

To Steve – thank you for your help, patience and love.

And thanks also to Marta, without whom this book would never have been finished, Marianne Gray for being lovely and helpful, and the NCT Girls (aka Jacks, As, Trudi, Noreen, Yvette, Anastasia and Rebecca) for their revealing input. And big hugs to Nicki, Ian and Elliot, Sarah, Jessie and Robbie, Alex and Laurie, Ndidi, Karen, Jane and Paul and, last but not least, Jenny and Grandpa Peter.

Introduction

• •

The idea for this review book of kids and family movies first came about after I heard about a dad who picked up his eleven-year-old son from a sleepover at a friend's house only to discover the host's father had allowed the boys to watch Quentin Tarantino's blood-soaked, '18'-certificate *Kill Bill* on DVD the night before. To add insult to injury, the host father's excuse was 'I couldn't think of anything else they would want to watch.'

This (admittedly lame) excuse made me scratch my head in puzzlement. Without really thinking I came up with over 100 films boys that age would probably like, including more than a few that were just as cool as a Tarantino movie, but lacking the gore and eyebrow-raising language that can chill a parent to the bone.

This book is for that father, so next time his son's friends sleep over he doesn't come off as the country's most irresponsible movie-chooser. And it's also for all those parents, relatives and guardians who have sat in front of the TV with their adorable tot, grinding their teeth in frustration as said babe insists they watch the same DVD for the 101st time. Now you can jump to the chapter of films that most suit your child's taste (for example, if you've just sat through *Cinderella* again, check out all the other princess-y alternatives in the Fairy Tales, Fantasies and Legends section) and you'll have a few anti-Cinders suggestions handy for the next time you're at your local DVD store.

In the reviews, I have made a point of mentioning scary moments, upsetting scenes (and, of course, the ultimate horror – bad acting) to help you and your family decide what movies to watch on TV or DVD. However, there are a few things about me you need to know. I am a mum. I am a film critic. I am not, however, a child psychologist. And most importantly of all, I am NOT your child's parent. Only you know what scares your little one, what upsets him/her, and what you do or don't want him to see on screen. All parents make different decisions (just ask *Kill Bill* Dad) – what is considered appropriate by one person may not be by the next. For example, a friend of mine was so freaked out by *Sooty and Sweep* as a child, she now won't let her ten-year-old boy see any movies featuring puppets (meaning the poor guy missed out on the deliciously daft Muppet movies), while I sat with my son Danny to watch Sesame Street's *The Adventures of Elmo in Grouchland* (a classic, I may add) when he was just a few months old. Different strokes, as they say.

As well as being a parental guide, hopefully this book will remind you of long-forgotten films from your own childhood that you may want to show your own kids (or watch on your own), suggest new movies that the family may like, help you decide what's worth catching on TV, and also help make a trip to the DVD store less overwhelming as you stand among the aisles searching for inspiration.

In the end, though, I hope you find this book enjoyable as well as informative. Remember, movies are wonderful things – they can make you laugh, cry or hide behind the sofa. They can be educational or inspirational. And, best of all, they can be fun.

So sit back, grab the popcorn and the kids, and let the fun begin!

JO BERRY, MARCH 2006

Available on DVD

The majority of movies featured in this guide are available on DVD (or, if they are recent cinema releases, will be later this year). Unavailability on DVD here in the UK (Region 2) is highlighted in the text (those unavailable here, but available on import/US/Region 1, are indicated for those of you with multi-region players). For this, and information on film classification see the appendices.

Each review features the most recent British classification, followed by the US and Australian rating. For full information on the criteria for classification, see p.

Adaptations

••

Many a movie featured in this book is based on a children's novel or short story. The chapter Fairy Tales, Fantasies and Legends contains all those classic bedtime stories like *Snow White*, *Cinderella* and *Beauty and the Beast*, while Animals, surprise surprise, includes movies based on books about creatures great and small. This chapter is the place to find movie adaptations of well-known novels, children's classics and family favourites that in the most part are just as famous in the written-word versions that came first as in the subsequent movies.

Perhaps a child discovering a movie like *The Chronicles of Narnia* may be inspired to pick up the CS Lewis book on which it is based, while another may enjoy comparing *Willy Wonka and the Chocolate Factory* or *Charlie and the Chocolate Factory* with the original Roald Dahl book they know so well. And if you have (or are) an older child, check out the Cheat Sheet guide at the end of the section to see which movie adaptations of common GCSE and A-level literature are worth watching and which have no resemblance to the texts whatsoever. (Note that the featured Cheat Sheet films aren't recommended for younger children – after all, in *Hamlet*, for example, virtually the entire cast has died in an unpleasant manner by the end.)

THE ADVENTURES OF HUCK FINN

Starring Elijah Wood, Courtney B Vance, Robbie Coltrane (1993)

Mark Twain's classic story set in the American South before the civil war is fun rather than faithful to the novel, as Elijah Wood's Huck runs away from his alcoholic father and journeys down the Mississippi on a raft with escaped slave Jim (Vance). Some of the characters from the

James Bond – Secret Agent, Boyhood Hero?

While author Ian Fleming may have written *Chitty Chitty Bang Bang* with kids in mind, it's safe to say his most famous creation – James Bond, agent 007 – was aimed at older readers. However, the adventures of a dashing hero, complete with memorable bad guys, fascinating gadgets and exotic locations, mean the books have long been favourites with little boys (one assumes they skip the icky sex scenes to get to the fighting parts). But, bearing in mind they're not aimed at kids, which movies based on Fleming's Bond books are the best for younger viewers?

The simple answer would be the first, Sean Connery ones. Beginning with *Dr No*, they're fun, exciting adventures (without being too violent) that are sexy without being explicit (assuming characters with names like Pussy Galore will fly right over junior heads). Choose from *Dr No* (1962), *From Russia With Love* (1963), *Goldfinger* (1964), *Thunderball* (1965), *You Only Live Twice* (1967) and *Diamonds Are Forever* (1971). Ignore Connery's 1983 return to the role, *Never Say Never Again* – not because it is more explicit or violent, just because it's plain awful.

The one film to feature George Lazenby as Bond, *On Her Majesty's Secret Service* (1969), isn't bad either, and the Roger Moore movies romp along at a fair old pace – while *Live and Let Die* (1973) has some sinister moments, things get sillier in later adventures such as 1979's *Moonraker* (the film-makers' attempt to cash in on *Star Wars*) and *Octopussy* (1983). (The best Bond film to feature Roger Moore is 1977's *The Spy Who Loved Me*, featuring one of the best openings to a movie ever – the ski chase that ends with Bond flying off the edge, only for his Union Jack parachute to pop open.)

If your little viewer is under twelve, it's probably best to stop right there. Timothy Dalton, who first starred as Bond in *The Living Daylights* (1987), played him as a man on the edge who's even more sinister than the bad guys he's supposed to be catching, and the film-makers also made the action for his films grittier and less kiddie-friendly to keep up with other modern-day thrillers. And while Pierce Brosnan (from 1995's *GoldenEye* to 2002's *Die Another Day*) made the most dashing Bond since Connery, the recent Bond movies have been made to compete with action movies like *Die Hard* and *Mission: Impossible*, so are more violent, more political (which kids will find boring) and dripping with sex (remember Famke Janssen's Xenia Onatopp, who could crush men to death with her thighs?). They're fine for grown-up boys, though…

book hardly get a look-in here, and events that fans of the novel may remember are sometimes dealt with too swiftly by *The Mummy* director Stephen Sommers, but Vance, Wood and co-stars Coltrane and Jason Robards are all enjoyable to watch, and this is a simple, Disney version that may work best as an introduction to the novel for younger viewers.

In fact, no movie version has done the book justice, but the 1939 version, *The Adventures of Huckleberry Finn*, with Mickey Rooney as Huck, remains the closest to the text. Rooney is perfect as the young boy, and there is great support from a cast that includes Rex Ingram as Jim, Walter Connolly as 'The King' and Victor Kilian as Pap Finn. Unfortunately it's not available on DVD at present. ★★★☆☆

ALICE IN WONDERLAND

Voices by Kathryn Beaumont, Richard Haydn, Sterling Holloway (1951)

Lewis Carroll's episodic fantasy stories have been translated onto the screen more than twenty times (including a Bollywood version and a Japanese TV series), but Disney's animated version – while not as classic as, say, *Bambi* – remains the best, perhaps because a cartoon is the only way to bring such quirky characters as Tweedledum and Tweedledee to life.

Using parts of both Carroll's *Alice's Adventures in Wonderland* and *Through the Looking-Glass*, it is, of course, the story of young Alice (Beaumont), who tumbles down a rabbit hole after the White Rabbit and ends up in a surreal world filled with odd creatures such as the grinning Cheshire Cat, the Mad Hatter, the March Hare and the Queen of Hearts. Packed with eccentric scenes as Alice has a series of

Getting Biblical

There have, of course, been hundreds of movies based on different parts of the Bible, and stories linked to that era, from *Ben-Hur* and *The Ten Commandments* to Mel Gibson's blood-soaked *The Passion of the Christ*. None of them are aimed at tots, of course, but there are a few biblical stories that have been animated and are ideal for younger viewers – most notably 1998's *The Prince of Egypt* and 2000's *The Miracle Maker*.

THE MIRACLE MAKER

Voices by Ralph Fiennes, Julie Christie, Ian Holm (2000)

The story of Jesus is simply and effectively told here, using stop-motion animation with marionettes and featuring the voice of Fiennes as Jesus. It's a very reverent adaptation, spanning Christ's life, crucifixion and resurrection, which should offend no one but may be a bit dull for younger viewers. The vocal cast also includes Richard E Grant as John the Baptist, Ian Holm as Pontius Pilate, William Hurt as Jairus and Miranda Richardson as Mary Magdalene. ★★★☆☆

THE PRINCE OF EGYPT

Voices by Val Kilmer, Ralph Fiennes, Michelle Pfeiffer (1998)

An Old Testament tale was reworked for this animated movie featuring an all-star voice cast (also including Sandra Bullock, Patrick Stewart, Helen Mirren and Steve Martin). After being found in a basket on the river, the baby Moses is raised by the Queen of Egypt alongside her own son, Rameses (Fiennes). Years later the brothers are divided when Moses (Kilmer) realises his roots and flees to the desert, where he understands his true heritage is to lead the Hebrews to a free land. It's stunning to look at, and while the film's opening explains it is 'true to the essence, values and integrity' of the story, rather than a film that's 100% faithful to the text, it is nonetheless moving stuff. ★★★★☆

adventures, it's colourful, fun and as surreal as Disney is ever likely to get (just check out the Mad Hatter's bonkers tea party). It isn't as good as the books, partly because so much had to be left out otherwise the movie would last a week, but it works as a cute introduction to them. (And if you or your kids want more, check out the 1999 TV miniseries, starring Whoopi Goldberg, Miranda Richardson and Gene Wilder, and the one many parents remember, 1972's musical *Alice's Adventures in Wonderland*, with Fiona Fullerton, Michael Crawford and Peter Sellers.)
★★★☆☆

ANNE OF GREEN GABLES

Starring Anne Shirley, Tom Brown (1934)

The best version of Lucy Maud Montgomery's much-loved novel is actually the Emmy award-winning US/Canadian TV miniseries from 1985 and its sequel, *Anne of Avonlea*, but if you can't get your hands on those, this sweet 1934 movie that occasionally pops up on TV is the next best thing. Anne Shirley (played by actress Dawn O'Day, who changed her name to Anne Shirley after making the film) is the red-headed, spirited orphan adopted by farmer Matthew Cuthbert (OP Heggie) and his sister Marilla (Helen Westley). They were actually expecting a boy, to help them on their farm, but they soon warm to the imaginative and talkative girl and she settles into life on the farm and at school, where she meets new best friend Diana and young Gilbert Blythe (Brown).

It's lovely stuff that should appeal to girls who like old-fashioned stories such as *Little House on the Prairie* and *Little Women*. Sweetly nostalgic fare (not one for cynics), and Anne Shirley is just right as the girl who charms and infuriates those around her in equal measure.
★★★★☆

AROUND THE WORLD IN 80 DAYS

Starring David Niven, Cantinflas (1956)

Forget the awful 2004 version and entertain the entire family with this Oscar-winning (it won five, including Best Picture) romp around the world, as based on Jules Verne's novel. A dapper David Niven stars as Victorian Englishman Phileas Fogg, who bets that with those newfangled steamships and railways he will be able to travel around the world in eighty days, accompanied by his valet Passepartout (Mexican actor/singer Cantinflas, who does his own bullfighting in the film).

Fun from beginning to end, the film is packed with exotic locations, flashy costumes (over 30,000 of them) and a cast of thousands, including cameos from John Gielgud, Noel Coward, Marlene Dietrich, Frank Sinatra, Shirley MacLaine (looking like she has been dipped in gravy for her turn as an Indian princess), Peter Lorre, George Raft and John Mills. Kids, of course, won't recognise any of them, but they'll be too enchanted by this Technicolor adventure of balloons, boats and trains to notice. ★★★★☆

AROUND THE WORLD IN 80 DAYS

Starring Steve Coogan, Jackie Chan (2004)

Comedian Coogan stars as Phileas Fogg, the 19th-century inventor who is challenged by nefarious Lord Kelvin (Jim Broadbent) to circumnavigate the globe in eighty days. If he manages it, he will become the new head of the Royal Academy of Science. If he fails, he must promise never to invent anything again. To complicate his adventures, Phileas is accompanied by Passepartout (Chan), who is using the trip for his own ends, while Kelvin has put a bumbling policeman (Ewen Bremner in a thankless role) on Phileas's trail, with instructions to stop him at all costs. And there are Chinese assassins after them, too.

Based on Jules Verne's classic novel, this remake sadly lacks both excitement and humour as Phileas trots round the globe with surprising ease (obstacles like the Pacific Ocean and the Himalayas are glossed over as our hero flits across continents). While the original 1956 film (starring the far more charismatic David Niven) featured exotic locations cinema audiences had never visited, seeing Coogan and Chan romp around fake sets of Paris, London, San Francisco and China is about as exciting as watching an old repeat of *Wish You Were Here?*. And while fifties cinemagoers were treated to cameos from John Gielgud, Frank Sinatra and Buster Keaton, all we get in this 21st-century version is a teeth-grindingly awful turn from Arnold Schwarzenegger as Prince Hapi, and an assortment of 'so-what' contributions from Richard Branson, Macy Gray, Luke and Owen Wilson (in one of the few moments that's amusing) and Kathy Bates.

Apparently, studio bigwigs wanted Hugh Grant or Johnny Depp for the lead, both of whom have the acting personality and skill to improve this limp piece of film-making. Instead, Coogan – devoid of comic material and forced to play it like the romantic lead he clearly isn't – fades into the scenery, leaving Chan to kick some butts and inject into an otherwise lifeless movie a few rare moments of energy that may entertain younger kids. ★★☆☆☆

THE BORROWERS

Starring Jim Broadbent, John Goodman, Celia Imrie (1997)

While British TV viewers will always have a soft spot for the 1992 BBC TV series with Ian Holm, this big-screen version made five years later is delightful too. It's based on Mary Norton's charming children's books about a family of little people who secretly live under the floor-boards or behind the walls in the houses of humans (or 'human beans' as the Borrowers call us), surviving by 'borrowing' cast-off bits of string, buttons, scraps and crumbs to furnish their miniature home and feed themselves.

A mix of comedy, adventure and brilliant special effects from *Garfield* director Peter Hewitt, this follows the teeny tiny Clock family, led by dad Pod (Broadbent) and mum Homily (Imrie), as their nice little world is disrupted when the owner of the house in which they live dies, and mean American lawyer Ocious P Potter (Goodman, on fine comic form) arrives to flatten it and build apartments on the land. It's thoroughly entertaining, thanks to some great performances from Broadbent ('we may be small but heaven help anyone who thinks he might squish us'), Imrie and a supporting cast of comic actors such as Hugh Laurie, Ruby Wax and *The Fast Show*'s Mark Williams – a must-see slice of hilarity for all ages. Fans of Hewitt's earlier movie, *Bill & Ted's Bogus Journey*, should keep their eyes peeled for Bill himself, aka Alex Winter, who makes a brief cameo appearance. ★★★★☆

THE CAT IN THE HAT 🔺 PG PG

Starring Mike Myers, Alec Baldwin, Dakota Fanning (2003)

Oh dear, oh dear, oh dear. It's probably a good thing that genius author Dr Seuss wasn't alive to see this mean film version of one of his best-loved books. He certainly wouldn't be pleased that his story of a cat running amok in a house while babysitting two children has been turned into a rude adventure centring around a scene-chewing (and not in a good way) Mike Myers as the feline. And parents of young children won't be impressed either, as many of the jokes seem to be aimed at young teens who think anything involving vomit is hilarious.

It must have been difficult to adapt Seuss's slim tome (it's less than 2000 words long) for the screen, especially as the Cat himself is so unlikeable, but despite millions being spent on the splashy, colourful (and, well, tacky) design and the too-good-for-this cast (Kelly Preston, Baldwin and Fanning), there's really nothing to recommend about this film. Save your money and buy the book instead! ★☆☆☆☆

CHARLIE AND THE CHOCOLATE FACTORY

Starring Johnny Depp, Freddie Highmore (2005)

Director Tim Burton's occasionally dark reworking of Roald Dahl's classic kids' book is as much a treat as 1971's *Willy Wonka and the Chocolate Factory*, which was based on the same tome. It is, of course, the tale of Charlie Bucket (Highmore), a boy who lives with his parents and grandparents in a tiny ramshackle house that sits in the shadow of eccentric Willy Wonka's chocolate factory. The family is so poor that all Charlie gets for his birthday is a solitary chocolate bar, but this year there is the possibility of that bar containing something extra special – a golden ticket that entitles the holder to a tour of the factory. There are only five golden tickets though, and Wonka bars are shipped all over the world, so will Charlie win the prize of his dreams?

Like many of Burton's films – *Edward Scissorhands*, *Beetlejuice* and *Batman* among them – this is a darkly visual feast, from the Buckets' creaky little home to Wonka's amazing factory, packed with sugary delights, chocolate rivers, squirrels who quality-check the nuts (a scene involving them whisking away one of the naughtier children may upset little viewers but delight older ones) and, of course, the Oompa-Loompas – those odd little men who work in the sweet factory (actually played by one actor, Deep Roy). All the cast are terrific (including David Kelly as Grandpa Joe, James Fox, Christopher Lee), but unsurprisingly it is Depp, as Wonka himself, who steals the show, delivering a performance that is sometimes creepy, sometimes innocent, partly crazed and utterly fantastic. ★★★★☆

CHARLOTTE'S WEB

Voices by Debbie Reynolds, Henry Gibson (1973)

Get the hankies out for this sweet cartoon adaptation of the weepie novel by EB White (who also wrote *Stuart Little*) about the friendship between a pig, Wilbur (Gibson), and the spider, Charlotte (Reynolds), who helps to save him from slaughter by writing a message in her web about how special he is.

Cute without being sickly, this keeps pretty much to the original story and should delight even the smallest children (though, without wishing to spoil the ending, some may get upset as a major character dies) with its simple animation (by the animators at Hanna-Barbera, best known for *The Flintstones*), songs and charming characters. A new film version of the story, starring Dakota Fanning and featuring the voices of Julia Roberts (as Charlotte), Oprah Winfrey, John Cleese and Robert Redford, is due for release in time for Christmas 2006. ★★★★☆

THE CHRONICLES OF NARNIA: THE LION, THE WITCH AND THE WARDROBE

Starring Tilda Swinton, Georgie Henley (2005)

CS Lewis's mythical children's story (the first in the Narnia series) has been made for the screen before (a 1988 TV adaptation) but this is the most spectacular version you're likely to see, as directed by *Shrek*'s Andrew Adamson. Filmed in New Zealand (which gives it a similar epic feel to *The Lord of the Rings*), it's the story of four children evacuated to a sprawling country house during the Second World War, who discover a wardrobe that leads to the magical world of Narnia.

It's little Lucy (an adorable turn by Henley) who first discovers the snowbound world when she hides among the fur coats in the wardrobe, but soon her selfish brother Edmund (Skandar Keynes), sceptical sister Susan (Anna Popplewell) and oldest brother Peter (William Moseley) are also exploring the strange land of talking animals and whispering trees, frozen in ice by the White Witch (a spectacularly mean turn from Swinton). According to Narnian legend, only four humans can end her evil reign, and those four are the children, who have to be protected by creatures such as Mr and Mrs Beaver (voiced by Ray Winstone and Dawn French), Mr Tumnus (James McAvoy) and the regal lion Aslan (voiced by Liam Neeson).

A beautiful mix of live action and animated creatures, this is a terrific telling of Lewis's tale that should impress everyone and possibly inspire kids to read the other books in the series. There are some scary scenes – the wolves chasing the children are particularly nasty and there's a battle scene that boys will probably love but smaller children may be frightened by – and atheist older viewers may be turned off by the religious undertones that were present in Lewis's stories (Aslan the lion perhaps represents Jesus), but all in all this is an impressive and entertaining adaptation of a classic book. ★★★★☆

COURAGE MOUNTAIN

Starring Juliette Caton, Joanna Clarke, Charlie Sheen (1990)

The *Heidi* story is reworked here to the point that original author Johanna Spyri doesn't get a mention. It's something of a sequel to the original tale, as now-teenage Heidi (Caton) is sent to boarding school in Italy, only for the First World War to break out. Soon the Italian army has commandeered her school and the children are rounded up and taken to a harsh orphanage where they decide to escape, travelling across the Alps back to Heidi's grandfather in Switzerland. Meanwhile, Gramps has heard what has happened and has sent Heidi's love, Peter (Sheen), off to rescue her.

Like a junior *Sound of Music* without the songs, this romps along with some nice performances from the children and boasts some superb scenery as the gang head towards Switzerland with the bad guy (Yorgo Voyagis's orphanage owner) in hot pursuit. There's just enough suspense, (chaste) romance and adventure to keep little girls entertained throughout, though older viewers may question Sheen's casting (he's twenty-five playing eighteen, and doesn't drop the American accent) and the less plausible plot points. ★★★☆☆

DANNY THE CHAMPION OF THE WORLD

Starring Jeremy Irons, Robbie Coltrane (1989)

Originally made for TV but released at cinemas in the UK, this adaptation of Roald Dahl's story teams actor Jeremy Irons with his son Samuel, who plays the Danny of the title (Sam's granddad, Cyril Cusack, pops up as the local doctor). It's 1955, and Samuel and his widowed dad (Irons) live in a caravan on a small piece of land, but their way of life comes under threat from mean businessman Victor Hazell (Coltrane), who wants the land for himself. So when Hazell decides to hold a lavish pheasant shoot for the local gentry, Sam and his dad see an opportunity to get rid of him once and for all.

With a cast that also includes Jimmy Nail, Jean Marsh from *Upstairs Downstairs*, Michael Hordern and Lionel Jeffries, this is an old-fashioned British film that's sweet and nice rather than exciting or adventure-packed. ★★★☆☆

DAVID COPPERFIELD

Starring WC Fields, Basil Rathbone (1935)

There have been over a dozen film and TV versions of Dickens's novel, the oldest a silent black and white short filmed in 1911. A 1999 BBC TV version, with a young Daniel Radcliffe (aka Harry Potter), Bob Hoskins and Ian McKellen, is definitely worth a look, and there's also a passable TV film with Hugh Dancy, Paul Bettany and Sally Field made in 2000 (a 1993 animated film, with Sheena Easton, Julian Lennon and Michael York is so awful it's almost worth seeing). But the best made-for-cinema version remains the 1935 film, directed by George Cukor and starring WC Fields as Micawber, a role he would always be associated with.

It's the story, of course, of poor unfortunate David, whose father died before he was born and whose mother goes on to remarry Murdstone (Rathbone), a man who rules the house with an iron fist. When his mother dies, David is sent to work in London and crosses paths with a variety of interesting characters, including Micawber (Fields, who replaced Charles Laughton in the part), the scheming Uriah Heep (Roland Young) and the young Dora (Maureen O'Sullivan).

While it would be impossible to include every character and event from Dickens's weighty novel, Cukor manages to keep much of the book intact, and delivers a classic adaptation brimming with impressive costumes and sets, and memorable performances. ★★★★☆

A FAR OFF PLACE

Starring Reese Witherspoon, Ethan Embry (1993)

Laurens Van der Post's books *A Far Off Place* and *A Story Like the Wind* were turned into this moving and beautifully filmed kids-in-peril adventure set in Africa. Game warden's daughter Nonnie (Witherspoon) and sulky Harry (Embry) see their parents massacred by poachers, and so team up to trek over 1000 miles across the Kalahari desert with the help of a young bushman. There's a bad guy in hot pursuit who wants them dead as they are the only witnesses to the murders, but the movie is really about the kids learning about their surroundings and the magic that their bush guide Xhabbo brings to the journey.

While fans of the books may be annoyed that the stories' hero has morphed from a boy into a then 14-year-old Witherspoon, this otherwise remains pretty true to the tales, which does mean that it is violent in places – a herd of elephants are killed for their tusks which are hacked off with chainsaws, for example – and not suitable for younger or sensitive viewers. ★★★★☆

FIVE CHILDREN AND IT

Starring Kenneth Branagh, **the voice of** Eddie Izzard (2004)

At a time when most family films are packed with computer trickery, the old-fashioned, live-action *Five Children and It* comes as a breath of fresh, if somewhat nostalgic, air and is a sweet adventure that should enchant small children while reminding their grown-up companions of the films we used to love as tots, such as *The Railway Children* and other long-ago delights like *Bedknobs and Broomsticks*.

Based on the much-loved E Nesbit children's book, the film follows five brothers and sisters as they are evacuated during the First World War, sent to stay with their eccentric uncle (Kenneth Branagh), his hideous young son Horace (Alexander Pownall) and the dotty housekeeper (Zoe Wanamaker) at their run-down mansion by the sea. It's there the siblings – led by precocious Robert (Freddie Highmore) – find a secret beach that's home to a Psammead, an 8000-year-old sand fairy they call 'It'. 'It' (voiced by Eddie Izzard) can grant their wishes, but he's a pesky creature, so each one tends to backfire before it fizzles out at the end of the day.

With fun cameo performances from John Sessions and Norman Wisdom, this is a cute little traditional film rather than an exciting one packed with lasers and creatures (although there is a CGI dinosaur and, of course, 'It' himself). In fact, what special effects there are – the kids wish to fly and sprout angelic wings, for example – are decidedly creaky, but that's actually part of the movie's charm. Some of Izzard's characterisations may seem a bit modern for the historical setting too, but as a Sunday-afternoon diversion that has its heart in the right place, this is just what you and your little ones would wish for. ★★★☆☆

GULLIVER'S TRAVELS

Starring Richard Harris, Catherine Schell (1977)

Jonathan Swift's novel has been animated (1939's cute cartoon, the first American animated feature not made by Disney), made into an adventure with effects by stop-motion genius Ray Harryhausen (1960's *The 3 Worlds of Gulliver*) and turned into a lavish miniseries (1996, with Ted Danson in the lead), and there is also this film version, a mix of live action and animation. Unfortunately, it's a bit of a disappointment – especially to fans of the book – as it misses out whole journeys that Gulliver memorably takes (including the visit to the floating island of Laputa).

It's 1699, and Gulliver (Harris), a ship's surgeon, finds himself imprisoned by the people of Lilliput after his ship capsized at sea. To the little people of Lilliput, he's a giant, and they see his arrival as an opportunity to finally win a war against their neighbours.

While grown-ups may snigger at Harris trying to act against, well... nothing (the animation being drawn in later), kids won't be impressed by the dated animation or the slow storytelling. The 1996 miniseries is probably the best one to check out for anyone interested in a filmic version that actually stays close to the source material. ★★☆☆☆

HARRY POTTER AND THE CHAMBER OF SECRETS

Starring Daniel Radcliffe, Kenneth Branagh (2002)

The story of trainee wizard Harry's arrival at Hogwarts School was covered in 2001's *Harry Potter and the Philosopher's Stone*, so in this first follow-up based on JK Rowling's phenomenally successful second book, we get straight to the action and the film is much better for it. This time, Harry is warned by house-elf Dobby not to return to Hogwarts School, but he does, to find a new Defence Against the Dark Arts teacher, the suave Gilderoy Lockhart (Branagh), and some mysterious goings-on that are turning his fellow pupils to stone.

'We (Radcliffe and his young co-stars Rupert Grint and Emma Watson) joke that we'll all be on Zimmer-frames by *Harry Potter V* but I think probably we will all just have learnt to run faster so that we don't get caught as the series accelerates. The stories are clever and sharp and they test our minds.' HARRY POTTER himself, aka DANIEL RADCLIFFE

There's a flying car, giant spiders and a secret diary to keep viewers amused, and the computer-generated Dobby (voiced by Toby Jones) is a treat, but best of all is Kenneth Branagh's turn as the dim but dashing Lockhart. It's darker and more edgy than the original movie – even the Quidditch match seems a bit tense – but if your little one has already read the book, they won't be surprised or fazed by any of the scary bits.

★★★★☆

HARRY POTTER AND THE GOBLET OF FIRE

Starring Daniel Radcliffe, Ralph Fiennes (2005)

The fourth Harry Potter movie was the first to receive a '12' certificate (the previous three were 'PG's) in the UK owing to its dark themes and scary bits (young ones may be especially scared of the mermen who appear when Harry has to dive in the lake). Better than *Harry Potter and the Prisoner of Azkaban*, but still a little too long for younger viewers at nearly two and a half hours, this is the one in which the evil Voldemort returns in physical form. First, however, our magical hero Harry finds himself mysteriously entered in the Triwizard Tournament, an event in which students from three rival magic schools compete, putting their lives in danger to solve magical puzzles.

Dumbledore (Michael Gambon), Snape (Alan Rickman), and Harry's Hogwarts friends Ron (Rupert Grint) and Hermione (Emma Watson) all return – and there's even a hint of future romance for Harry – but it's the arrival of Voldemort (as played by a very menacing Ralph Fiennes, complete with bizarre fishlike face) that makes this an edge-of-the-seat and surprisingly gloomy instalment of the Potter story. ★★★★☆

HARRY POTTER AND THE PHILOSOPHER'S STONE 🎬 PG PG

Starring Daniel Radcliffe, Richard Harris (2001)

Director Chris Columbus – who inflicted Macaulay Culkin in *Home Alone* on the cinema-going public, but over a decade later should probably be finally forgiven for it – was the man burdened with the task of translating the most popular children's book in recent history to the big screen. Fans of trainee wizard Harry weren't disappointed by Columbus's lengthy (two and a half hours) but faithful adaptation of JK Rowling's first book, of course, as the director wisely tried to pack as much of the story into the script with the help of a cast that's a who's who of British talent, including Maggie Smith, Alan Rickman, Richard Harris, Fiona Shaw, John Cleese, John Hurt and Julie Walters.

As everyone who hasn't been living under a rock for the past few years knows, Harry (Radcliffe) is a young orphan who discovers he's a wizard and is whisked off to Hogwarts School of Witchcraft and Wizardry, where he befriends Ron (Rupert Grint) and Hermione (Emma Watson). The school is run by the wise Professor Dumbledore (Harris), one of the wizards who knows what happened to Harry's parents and why the boy himself may be in danger. The younger members of the cast may not be the greatest actors in the universe (though their skills have improved in the subsequent sequels), but they each have their own charms and fit nicely into their roles. Columbus, meanwhile, uses just the right amount of CGI effects to realise this magical world, from the detailed Quidditch match to Hogwarts itself. Known, like the book, as *Harry Potter and the Sorceror's Stone* in the US (one assumes that 'philosopher' sounded too clever and not magical enough). ★★★★☆

HARRY POTTER AND THE PRISONER OF AZKABAN 🅿🄶 PG PG

Starring Daniel Radcliffe, Gary Oldman, Michael Gambon (2004)

The third film of one of JK Rowling's magical adventures was the darkest thus far, as trainee wizard Harry learns more secrets about his past and discovers convicted murderer Sirius Black (Oldman) has escaped from the prison of Azkaban and could be coming to look for him.

The kiddie cast (Daniel Radcliffe as Harry, Rupert Grint as Ron and Emma Watson as Hermione) are now strapping teens (Harry can be seen playing with his magic wand under the covers, which grown-ups may find amusing on another level), so there's even a hint of pubescent angst in this slow but faithful adaptation from director Alfonso Cuarón (*A Little Princess*), who adds a darkness not present in the first two films (parents should note the soul-sucking Dementors posted outside Hogwarts to capture Sirius will frighten younger viewers as much as the Ringwraiths in *The Lord of the Rings*). Meanwhile, new cast members include an excellent David Thewlis as Professor Lupin, Michael Gambon as Dumbledore (taking over from Richard Harris who died in 2002) and the part-horse, part-eagle known as the Hippogriff, which is just one of the many special-effects marvels on display. ★★★★☆

'I'd like my baby daughter Gracie to see the *Harry Potter* films because she can see her daddy (David Thewlis) working as Professor Lupin. I'd prefer it if she were five or six before she saw that because he plays a wolf in the film. I don't particularly want to have to say to her: "Oh, by the way, your Daddy's not really a wolf!"' ANNA FRIEL

HEIDI

Starring Shirley Temple, Jean Hersholt (1937)

Depending on how young your little one is, she'll either think Shirley Temple as Heidi is the cutest thing she's ever seen or find this adaptation of Johanna Spyri's classic book unbearably twee (boys of all ages, no doubt, will be in the latter camp). So cynical older kids should give this a wide berth (and perhaps try the more modern 1990 adaptation, *Courage Mountain*, instead), and let little girls sit back and enjoy the story of Heidi, the tousle-haired poppet sent to live in the Swiss Alps with a grandfather (Hersholt) she has never known. Soon she warms the grumpy geezer's heart, but that's not the happy ending you think it is – her mean aunt then sells her to nasty Fräulein Rottenmeier (Mary Nash) and Grandpa has to go searching for her.

One of over twenty big and small screen versions of the Heidi story, this is still one of the best, with Temple on spirited form, and nice support from the grown-up cast. If your little one loves Temple here, other movies of hers worth looking out for are *Rebecca of Sunnybrook Farm* (1938), *The Little Princess* (1939) and *Little Miss Marker* (1934). ★★★★☆

A HIGH WIND IN JAMAICA ★★☆☆ u/c

Starring Anthony Quinn, James Coburn (1965)

A rollicking movie for kids that boasts pirates and a dangerous sea voyage, this is based on the novel by Richard Hughes. Emily (Deborah Baxter) and her siblings' parents don't think they are getting the proper British upbringing in Jamaica, where they live, so mum and dad decide they should return to England. However, during the journey their ship is boarded by pirates, and the children end up stowing away on the pirate ship, much to the consternation of Captain Chavez (Quinn) and his first mate Zac (Coburn), who soon get more than they bargained for.

A slower pirate adventure than, say, *Pirates of the Caribbean*, this is nonetheless an interesting adventure, thanks to some good performances (including a young Martin Amis in his only screen role as the eldest brother) and a plot twist that keeps your attention until the end. ★★★☆☆

HOLES

Starring Sigourney Weaver, Shia LaBeouf (2003)

Sigourney Weaver agreed to star in this movie because her daughter told her how much she loved the Louis Sachar novel on which it is based. And it was a good decision, as this is one of the best kids' films of recent years. After being falsely accused of stealing a pair of valuable trainers, young Stanley Yelnats (LaBeouf) is given the choice of going to jail or to Camp Green Lake. Since the camp doesn't sound too bad, Stanley opts for that, only to discover it's a camp in the desert (with no lake to be seen), where the children are forced to dig large holes in the dirt each day by the Warden (Weaver) and her creepy cohorts Mr Sir (Jon Voight) and Pendanski (Tim Blake Nelson). It seems that the Warden believes a treasure stolen by bandit queen Kissin' Kate Barlow (Patricia Arquette) many years before may be buried somewhere nearby and she is using the boys – who have nicknames like Armpit, Squid, ZigZag and X-Ray – to find it.

Aimed at the over-10s who will be thrilled by the complex plot as it flits between Stanley's misfortunes, flashbacks of the legend of Kissin' Kate and stories of Stanley's Latvian ancestors, this is funny, moving, smart and even bizarre, with superb performances by both the younger actors and the older cast (which includes Henry Winkler as Stanley's dad and Eartha Kitt). Kids will love it, and want to read the book if they haven't already, while grown-ups should take a look themselves as it's pretty darn brilliant. ★★★★☆

HOOK

Starring Robin Williams, Dustin Hoffman, Julia Roberts, Bob Hoskins (1991)

Widely considered to be director Steven Spielberg's lamest movie, this film poses the question: what if JM Barrie's famous creation Peter Pan grew up? Well, it seems he turns into a boring workaholic named Peter Banning (the normally hirsute Williams, who had to shave his arms and chest for the role) who has no recollection of his life in Neverland until his own children are kidnapped by Captain Hook (Hoffman, chewing the scenery with moustache-twirling glee) and he has to return to the magical land and reclaim his youthful spirit in order to be able to rescue them.

With a cast that includes Bob Hoskins as Smee, Maggie Smith as the grown-up Wendy, Julia Roberts (with very unfetching haircut) as Tinkerbell and, erm, Phil Collins as the inspector investigating Peter's missing children, you would expect this to be a treat. And there are some good bits (many involving Hoffman, and some impressive flying effects), but there are very bad ones too (the Lost Boys have been given a late 20th-century makeover, with punky haircuts and skateboards to zip around on). Saddest of all, though, is that, while packing his film with star power, Spielberg completely forgot to throw in some much-needed charm. ★★☆☆☆

THE HUNCHBACK OF NOTRE DAME

Voices by Demi Moore, Tom Hulce, Kevin Kline (1996)

This, Disney's 34th animated movie, is 'inspired' (i.e. don't expect it to be quite as tragic) by the classic Victor Hugo novel, but is probably best employed as entertainment and an introduction to literature for younger viewers than as an accurate interpretation of the novel for students. High above Paris, in the bell tower of Notre Dame cathedral, lives Quasimodo (Hulce), a hunchback banished there by his master, Judge Frollo. With only three stone statues – who come alive to dispense wisdom and wit – as his companions, he dreams of being a part of the city below, and decides to escape his tower to attend the Festival of Fools. It is there that he meets major babe Esmeralda (Moore), a gypsy dancer who incurs the wrath of evil Frollo, whose main aim is to rid the city of all gypsies, with the reluctant help of hunky army captain Phoebus (Kline).

Like the classics of Disney's past, the villain is deliciously depraved and rather scary, the girl high-spirited and the heroes (Phoebus and the rather adorable Quasi) steadfast and true. Packed with wit, colour, beautiful animation, great songs and set pieces, and spot-on characterisations from the well-known vocal cast, this is utterly delightful family entertainment. (Some scenes, involving the sinister Frollo and his abuse of local gypsies, and the generally dark tone, may be too much for very young viewers.) ★★★★☆

I CAPTURE THE CASTLE R PG

Starring Romola Garai, Rose Byrne, Bill Nighy (2003)

Based on the Dodie Smith (*101 Dalmatians*) novel of the same name, this sweet drama focuses on the teenage life and first romances of young Cassandra (Garai), who lives with her eccentric family in an almost condemned castle in 1930s Suffolk. Her father (Nighy) is a writer who hasn't written anything for over a decade (which explains why they have no money and haven't paid their landlord for two years), while Cassandra's sister Rose (Byrne) spends her time wishing for a handsome and wealthy man to take her away from the crumbling walls and leaking pipes. Her prayers seem to be answered when two American brothers come to call, having inherited the nearby mansion, and Rose soon sets her sights on the eldest, Simon (Henry Thomas), despite his brother Neil's (Marc Blucas) obvious interest in her, and unaware that Cassandra has fallen for Simon herself.

A nice tale of growing up and growing wiser, this drama works well, thanks to the spot-on casting of Byrne, and especially Garai (who appeared in the BBC's *Daniel Deronda*), who is in virtually every scene and injects each one with memorable warmth. ★★★★☆

THE IRON GIANT U PG PG

Voices by Jennifer Aniston, Harry Connick Jr, Vin Diesel (1999)

A cracking sci-fi animated adventure based on poet laureate Ted Hughes's novella, this was directed by Brad Bird, who went on to make *The Incredibles*. Like that film, this is just as entertaining for adults as for the kids it is aimed at, thanks to slick animation, a spirited script and great vocal performances.

Set during the cold war, it's the story of young Hogarth (Eli Marienthal), who befriends a massive robot he finds near his home (voiced by Diesel) after the being has crashed down from outer space. Keeping his discovery secret from his mum (Aniston) with the help of a local scrap dealer (Connick Jr), Hogarth also has to hide the metal creature from a paranoid government agent (Christopher McDonald) who is on their trail. It's like *ET* but with many metal appendages, as boy and robot bond, and it's surprisingly moving too. A must-see for all ages. ★★★★☆

JAMES AND THE GIANT PEACH

Starring Joanna Lumley, Miriam Margolyes (1996)

A wickedly fun version of Roald Dahl's children's tale, this mixture of live action and stop-motion animation is just as funny for adults as for kids. Sent to live with his wicked aunts (Lumley and Margolyes) after his parents die, James (Paul Terry) dreams of running away to New York. When a mysterious man gives him a bag of magical glowing crocodile tongues that could answer his prayers, James accidentally spills them by an old peach tree. A giant peach grows and a starving James starts to eat it, only to find himself able to crawl inside, where he meets a group of unusual bugs (voiced by Simon Callow, Richard Dreyfuss, David Thewlis, Jane Leeves, Susan Sarandon and Margolyes).

From the moment James enters the peach, the film switches from live action (which is camp and pantomime-ish) to animation, and perks up considerably as the motley group roll down the hill, into the sea and on to America. The script successfully captures all the humour of Dahl's quirky book, as do the wonderful vocal characterisations from the star-studded cast, and the marvellous animation. A tasty treat. ★★★★☆

KIDNAPPED

Starring Peter Finch, James MacArthur (1960)

There have been numerous movie and TV versions of Robert Louis Stevenson's classic adventure, but the most kiddie-friendly is this Disney production. Orphaned David Balfour (MacArthur) is sold into shipboard slavery by his mean old uncle, but finds adventure on the high seas and in the rolling hills of Scotland when his ship is commandeered by Highlander Alan Breck Stewart (Finch), and the pair team up to evade the nasty Redcoats on their trail.

It's a luscious adaptation, complete with stunning Scottish scenery, that's a truly *Boy's Own* adventure. Of the other versions, there was a 1971 remake, starring Michael Caine as Breck, that's uneven but enjoyable, and decent TV adaptations from 1995 (with Armand Assante) and 2005 (a BBC series with Iain Glen as Breck). ★★★☆☆

LEMONY SNICKET'S A SERIES OF UNFORTUNATE EVENTS PG PG

Starring Jim Carrey, Meryl Streep (2004)

A dark, slightly sinister tale based on the first three children's books of the Lemony Snicket series. It's the gothic tale of the Baudelaire children, orphaned when a strange fire engulfs their home and kills their parents. Bookworm Klaus (Liam Aiken), inventor Violet (Emily Browning) and little Sunny (played by twins Kara and Shelby Hoffman) are sent to live with their sinister relative Count Olaf (Carrey), but it's not long before they discover the eccentric actor is only interested in their inheritance and will do anything, no matter how dastardly or deadly, to relieve them of it.

So begins that series of unfortunate events as the children try to escape his clutches and his various disguises while meeting some oddball friends of their late parents along the way – kindly Uncle Monty (Billy Connolly) and nervous Aunt Josephine (Streep), both of whom have secrets that may explain some mysterious occurrences over the years. As narrated by 'author' Lemony Snicket (played by a shadowy Jude Law, Snicket is actually the creation of writer Daniel Handler), this is a very Tim Burton-esque tale that delivers plenty of laughs but has a rather satisfyingly creepy underbelly. A twisted parable, it benefits from terrific performances from the child actors, and – while Carrey is allowed to go a little over the top in places – a wicked turn from the comic actor, complete with bizarre facial hair and manic posturing.

While you'll wish some of the other actors, like Connolly, Timothy Spall, Catherine O'Hara and Jennifer Coolidge, got more of a look in, the most delicious performance of all, especially for grown-ups, isn't from Carrey but from Meryl Streep, who reveals a previously untapped comic talent as the children's meek aunt. ★★★☆☆

LITTLE LORD FAUNTLEROY G u/c

Starring Ricky Schroder, Alec Guinness, Connie Booth (1980)

Frances Hodgson Burnett's classic kids' book was first made into a British movie in 1914, with H Agar Lyons (aka Dr Fu Manchu in the 1920s adventures), but the most entertaining version is this 1980 one, starring child star Ricky Schroder (now better known as 'Rick', and a former star of the very adult TV series *NYPD Blue*). He, all ruffled blond hair and cheeky-grinned, is Ceddie Errol, an American boy who is the only heir of the Earl of Dorincourt (Guinness). The Earl, getting on a bit, asks that Ceddie and his mum (Booth) come to live with him in England where the boy will become Lord Fauntleroy. Of course, it turns out that Dorincourt is a grumpy old man, but Ceddie soon melts his heart – just in time for a nasty American woman to come along and claim that it is actually her son who is next in line to inherit the estate.

It's sweet stuff and a nice adaptation of a children's favourite (actually originally made for US TV) featuring a cast of British talent, including Patrick Stewart, Rachel Kempson and Colin Blakely. ★★★☆☆

A LITTLE PRINCESS

Starring Liesel Matthews, Eleanor Bron, Liam Cunningham (1995)

First made as *The Little Princess* back in 1939 with Shirley Temple in the lead role, Frances Hodgson Burnett's book was transformed into a girlie movie delight by Alfonso Cuarón, the Mexican director who also made *Harry Potter and the Prisoner of Azkaban*.

When her father goes off to war, young Sara (Matthews) is sent to a private boarding school run by the nasty Miss Minchin (Bron). And when news comes that her father is missing in action, the young girl is forced to act as servant at the school, so she finds solace in an imaginary world, using her fantasies as an escape from reality. It's a lovely, often suspenseful tale, and is tackled superbly by Cuarón, who hasn't approached the film as if it is just for kids, instead directing and delivering a film that is just as enjoyable for grown-ups as younger viewers. A real treat. ★★★★☆

LITTLE WOMEN

Starring Katharine Hepburn, Joan Bennett (1933)

Louisa May Alcott's lovely girlie classic has been filmed many times, and there are two super movie versions well worth sampling. The most modern is the 1994 movie, with the impressive cast of Winona Ryder, Susan Sarandon, Gabriel Byrne, Christian Bale, Kirsten Dunst and Claire Danes, but the most engaging is George Cukor's 1933 film, a spirited, beautiful version that will simply thrill fans of the novel.

It's the story, as every girl knows, of the March sisters. With their father away during the American Civil War, they are struggling, with beloved mother Marmee (Spring Byington), to make ends meet, while the older girls find first love, first disappointment and even tragedy in their lives. Hepburn is simply perfect as tomboy Jo, while Frances Dee, Joan Bennett and Jean Parker all make good impressions as Meg, Amy and Beth. Lovely stuff. If you can't see this version, the 1949 adaptation with June Allyson, Elizabeth Taylor and Janet Leigh is an adorable, if sugary, alternative. ★★★★☆

LORD OF THE FLIES

Starring Balthazar Getty, Chris Furrh (1990)

This version of William Golding's novel doesn't remain too faithful to the text, but is an interesting boys' film nonetheless. A group of American boys from a military school (it was British prep school boys in the book) are stranded on an island following a plane crash and have to work together to survive. However, they split into two factions – the group who believe in decency and making things work, led by Ralph (Getty), and an opposing group led by Jack (Furrh) who start off as hunters but then become something far more sinister.

While the book was a fascinating look at children's descent into savagery, this is rather too glossy and slick to be convincing. The 1963 British black-and-white film is somewhat grittier, and there are good performances from the children, many of whom were new to acting. ★★★☆☆

THE LORD OF THE RINGS: THE FELLOWSHIP OF THE RING

Starring Ian McKellen, Elijah Wood, Viggo Mortensen, Orlando Bloom (2001)

The first part of director Peter Jackson's phenomenal movie trilogy is based, of course, on the first of JRR Tolkien's famous three books about the hobbits, elves and other creatures who populate the land known as Middle Earth. Hobbit (a small, hairy-footed creature) Frodo Baggins (Wood) is entrusted with a dangerous ring that can give the wearer great power. On the advice of wizard Gandalf (McKellen), Frodo and his friend Sam (Sean Astin) must leave their home and travel great distances to the one place, Mordor, where it can be destroyed, and they are accompanied by a fellowship elected to protect them: Gandalf, warriors Aragorn (Mortensen) and Boromir (Sean Bean), elf Legolas (Bloom) and dwarf Gimli (John Rhys-Davies).

Translating a much-loved series of books to the screen was a massive task for Jackson to undertake – as well as including all the details and minor plot points fans would demand, he had to keep it exciting and interesting for viewers who had never read the novels – and he managed it brilliantly, filming the three movies in one go, over sixteen months, against stunning New Zealand scenery. It's a classic quest, packed with epic moments and an impressive cast (also including Christopher Lee as Saruman, Cate Blanchett as Galadriel, Liv Tyler as Aragorn's love Arwen, and Hugo Weaving as Elrond). It's dark and sinister and scary in places, funny and light in others – and brilliant throughout. Do note that this is not a film for small children (who would have trouble sitting through the movie's three-hour running time anyway), owing to elements such as the frightening-for-grown-ups-too Ringwraiths. ★★★★★

THE LORD OF THE RINGS: THE TWO TOWERS 12 PG-13 U/c

Starring Ian McKellen, Elijah Wood, Viggo Mortensen, Orlando Bloom (2002)

Based, of course, on the second book of JRR Tolkien's classic trilogy about the hobbits, elves and other creatures who populate the land known as Middle Earth, this second film in Peter Jackson's trilogy wastes little time reminding us what happened in the first film (just a brief flashback of wizard Gandalf's demise) and throws us straight into the action.

Hobbits Frodo (Wood) and Sam (Sean Astin) are continuing their quest to destroy the evil ring by heading towards the fiery depths of Mordor, shadowed by the extremely creepy creature Gollum (Andy Serkis). Meanwhile, the other members of the Fellowship have split – hobbits Merry and Pippin (Dominic Monaghan, Billy Boyd) are captured, while elf Legolas (Bloom), warrior Aragorn (Mortensen) and dwarf Gimli (John Rhys-Davies) attempt to track them down.

While more action-packed than *Fellowship*, *The Two Towers* – if you can criticise such a richly detailed epic at all – does in some ways feel like the filling of a sandwich: there is no beginning or conclusion of the plot, just a middle waiting for a finale. Parents should note that it's even darker and creepier than the first film. ★★★★☆

THE LORD OF THE RINGS: THE RETURN OF THE KING 🔟 PG-13 MA 15+

Starring Ian McKellen, Elijah Wood, Viggo Mortensen, Orlando Bloom (2003)

The final, and – if it's possible – scariest instalment of the *Lord of the Rings* trilogy. It's edge-of-the-seat stuff for older kids and adults as hobbits Frodo (Wood) and Sam (Sean Astin) follow the clearly unstable, possibly treacherous Gollum (Andy Serkis) towards the flaming pits of Mordor and the ominous Mount Doom to destroy the Ring, while Gandalf and the other members of the Fellowship prepare to do battle.

And it's bloody stuff when it comes. There's a hideous giant spider that captures Frodo and will scare everyone, not just junior viewers, battles a-plenty and numerous unsavoury characters and creatures to have you hiding behind the sofa. It's not intended for younger viewers, of course, but for those who have been brave enough to sit through parts one and two without their hands over their eyes, this is a stunning, fitting and deservedly Oscar-winning end to a superb series of movies (and if it encourages kids to read the JRR Tolkien books, even better). ★★★★★

MADELINE PG G

Starring Frances McDormand, Nigel Hawthorne (1998)

Lovable redhead Madeline, a young quick-witted orphan forever getting into trouble, faces her toughest task yet when Lord Covington (Hawthorne), the owner of her Paris boarding school, decides to sell without caring about the girls who live there (he's so dastardly he even paints over the wall that marks how each girl has grown over the years).

It's a cute film, based on the character from Ludwig Bemelmans's books, that has Madeline planning an escape to the circus and stumbling across a plot to abduct the son of the neighbouring Spanish ambassador. McDormand is enjoyably stern as the headmistress, Miss Clavel, who often casts a disapproving eye in Madeline's direction, while Hatty Jones (who made her first and only film appearance here) is just as you'd imagine Madeline to be – impish, fun and utterly adorable. ★★★★☆

MATILDA

Starring Danny DeVito, Rhea Perlman, Mara Wilson (1996)

It's a rare family movie that is just as appealing to adults as to the kids it's supposed to be aimed at. *Matilda*, based on Roald Dahl's classic tale, is such a film, thanks in great part to Danny DeVito's spot-on direction and a winning central performance from eight-year-old Mara Wilson in the title role.

Matilda is an incredibly intelligent but lonely little girl in love with books and learning, who is unfortunately cursed with two coarse, dim-witted TV-addicted parents, Harry (DeVito) and Zinnia Wormwood (DeVito's real-life wife Perlman). After much pleading on Matilda's part, they finally let her attend school, but they send her to the sinister Crunchem Hall, run by forbidding, child-hating principal Agatha Trunchbull (Pam Ferris). But with the help of lovable young teacher Miss Honey (Embeth Davidtz), Matilda is soon turning the tables on all the horrible old adults, and uncovering her own special talent, which helps her to turn her dreary life into something much more fun.

The idea of a child being smarter and more cunning than her parents will appeal to junior audiences, while adults will get a kick out of the sassy, grown-up humour and wickedly funny performances from DeVito, Perlman and especially an hilariously over-the-top Pam Ferris. In the director's chair, DeVito keeps the action tight, never allowing the film to be overwhelmed by too many special effects or exaggerated performances. As delicious as Dahl's original work, this is one fantasy that kids and grown-ups still in touch with the naughty child inside them will want to buy into. ★★★★☆

THE MIGHTY 🔺 Ⓜ PG-13

Starring Kieran Culkin, Elden Henson, Sharon Stone, Gillian Anderson (1998)

Thanks to two astonishing performances by child actors Kieran (brother of Macaulay) Culkin and Elden Henson, this tear-jerker rises above the average to become a must-see film for children over ten, and adults, too.

Based on the Rodman Philbrick novel *Freak the Mighty*, the film centres on two loners: Maxwell (Henson), a larger than average and none-too-bright thirteen-year-old living with his grandparents (Harry Dean Stanton and Gena Rowlands), and the fragile, crippled, incredibly intelligent Kevin (Culkin), who moves in next door with his mother (Stone). Both outsiders, the pair strike up a friendship after Kevin is assigned to be Maxwell's reading tutor and introduces him to the knights, swordplay and stories of Arthurian legend. Together, they fight foes both real (school bullies, Maxwell's ex-con lowlife father) and imagined.

You'll be able to guess the ending well before it comes, but with moving turns from Culkin, a glammed-down Stone, Anderson (surprisingly good as a tarty, brittle associate of Maxwell's dad) and especially Henson, you'll remain glued to your seat, man-sized hanky in hand, until the final frame. A small treat. ★★★★☆

NANNY MCPHEE

Starring Emma Thompson, Colin Firth (2005)

Parents tired of super-slick animated movies and family blockbusters that come with their own range of action toys/computer games/breakfast cereals should sit their offspring down to watch this adorably quirky and old-fashioned movie, based on a series of little-known children's books (the *Nurse Matilda* stories by Christianna Brand). Emma Thompson, who wrote the screenplay, stars as Nanny McPhee, the rather ugly and mysterious nanny who turns up on the doorstep of Mr Brown's (Colin Firth) house to bring his seven unruly children into line.

'*Nanny McPhee* has all the elements that I longed for in a story when I was a child – a bit scared, a bit enchanted by romance, a bit funny.' COLIN FIRTH

Of course, there's more to Nanny McPhee than meets the eye and Thompson has terrific fun as the anti-Mary Poppins (imagine Supernanny mixed with Anne Robinson and you'll get an idea where Thompson is coming from), backed by an impressive child cast and British actors such as Celia Imrie, Imelda Staunton, Angela

Lansbury and Kelly Macdonald. Absolutely enchanting for everyone.
★★★★☆

THE NEW ADVENTURES OF PIPPI LONGSTOCKING G

Starring Tami Erin, David Seaman Jr, Eileen Brennan (1988)

Swedish author Astrid Lindgren's character Pippi Långstrump, to give her her Swedish name, has appeared in a handful of Swedish and German movies since 1949, but it wasn't until 1988 that an English-language version was made. It's not brilliant (Pippi seems bratty rather than endearing, and the plot is non-existent) but young fans of the books will enjoy red-haired, pigtailed Pippi's adventures with pals Tommy and Annika, her horse Alfonso and pet monkey Mr Nilsson – it's kiddie heaven as they have food fights, pillow fights and break all the grown-ups' rules. Adults, however, will find Erin's portrayal of precocious Pippi quite grating.

The other English language version of Pippi's adventures is the animated *Pippi Longstocking* from 1997. A Swedish/German/Canadian co-production, it features very simple animation that may seem tiresome to kids brought up on *Shrek* and *Finding Nemo*, but passes the time amiably enough. ★★☆☆☆

NORTH PG PG

Starring Elijah Wood, Bruce Willis, Jason Alexander (1994)

Almost universally slated by critics when it was released, this adaptation of Alan Zweibel's novel isn't good by any means, but it isn't as awful as everyone made it sound either (renowned critic Roger Ebert described it as 'one of the worst movies ever made'). It's the story of young North (Wood), who has had enough of his parents ignoring him. So he takes them to court and the judge rules that North can find new parents, but if he doesn't succeed, he has to return to his real ones within two months. So begins a journey around the world as North 'auditions' prospective parents, including couples from Alaska (Kathy Bates and Graham Greene) and Texas (Dan Aykroyd and Reba McEntire) – while in each place he visits North comes across a mysterious man (played in each incarnation by Bruce Willis) who could possibly be his guardian angel.

The main flaw with the plot is that North's parents haven't done anything that bad to make him want to divorce them, while the main flaw with the film is that it just isn't that funny, for kids or adults. All the comic actors are forced to play caricatures rather than real people, and what should have been a whimsical movie ends up being just a curious one. ★★☆☆☆

OLIVER!

Starring Ron Moody, Mark Lester, Jack Wild (1968)

If you want a serious adaptation of Dickens's novel, check out *Oliver Twist*, below. But if you're looking for something more entertaining, this musical version is a real treat. The story remains the same – young orphan Oliver (Lester) leaves the workhouse and runs away to London where he falls in with a gang of pickpockets who work for the devious Fagin (Moody) – but it is the performances here that are so superb, from Moody's perfect Fagin to Wild's cheeky Artful Dodger and Oliver Reed's sinister Bill Sikes.

And, of course, there are the fantastic Lionel Bart songs – the rollicking 'Food, Glorious Food', 'Consider Yourself', 'You've Got to Pick a Pocket or Two', 'I'd Do Anything' and Nancy's mournful 'As Long As He Needs Me' – that make this such a toe-tapping, sing-a-long classic. It was the winner of five Oscars, including Best Picture (beating *Funny Girl* and *The Lion in Winter*). ★★★★★

OLIVER TWIST

Starring Robert Newton, Alec Guinness, John Howard Davies (1948)

There are numerous versions of Dickens's classic tale – including an animated one from 1974 with the Monkees' Davy Jones doing the voice of the Artful Dodger – but nothing beats director David Lean's (*Lawrence of Arabia*) black and white adventure from 1948. Oliver (Davies) is the orphaned boy in Victorian England who runs away from a workhouse and falls in with a gang of London pickpockets, including the Artful Dodger (Anthony Newley), who are under the supervision of nasty Fagin (Guinness).

On its original release, the film was accused of anti-Semitism owing to Guinness's harsh portrayal of Fagin (and, if nothing else, it will give younger viewers nightmares) and briefly banned in the US, but the actor gives a mesmerising performance that is well worth catching. It's a dark film, though, and adults should note that some of the themes (there's a murder, and the film opens with Oliver's mother's death) aren't suitable for younger eyes. In 2005, Roman Polanski directed an adaptation of the Dickens story, with Ben Kingsley as Fagin, Jamie Foreman as Bill Sikes and Barney Clark as Oliver, which is enjoyable but not particularly memorable. ★★★☆☆

PETER PAN

Voices by Bobby Driscoll, Kathryn Beaumont (1953)

JM Barrie's much-loved tale of the boy who never wants to grow up became a charming Disney animated movie in 1953. It's probably the version everyone remembers best, thanks to the lively animation and timeless tunes like 'The Second Star to the Right', 'You Can Fly!' and 'Never Smile at a Crocodile'.

The story is, of course, about the Darling children – Wendy, John and Michael – who are taken to Neverland by the magical Peter Pan. There's precocious fairy Tinker Bell, of course, and the Lost Boys, as well as bad pirate Captain Hook, who is determined to catch Peter, since he is responsible for Hook losing his hand. (Don't worry about younger viewers – Hook is an utterly comical baddie and not remotely scary.) It's not completely faithful to Barrie's work, but it's a delightful animated adventure nonetheless. ★★★★☆

PETER PAN

Starring Jason Isaacs, Jeremy Sumpter, Rachel Hurd-Wood (2003)

A live-action version of JM Barrie's classic tale, this has impressive sets, costumes and magical moments to rival any *Harry Potter* movie. Definitely one for kids who think the Disney animated *Peter Pan* (reviewed above) is too young for them, this has darkness aplenty as Peter Pan whisks the Darling children off to Neverland, where they come face to face with the dastardly Captain Hook and his bloodthirsty pirates.

Isaacs is enjoyably sinister as Hook and there are lashings of swashbuckling swordfights to thrill kids (boys may not be so keen on the bit when Wendy teaches Peter to kiss – ick). It's not as fun as the cartoon, of course, and Sumpter is a rather awkward Peter (and looks too California-tanned and blond, too), but there's plenty of action and adventure to get your timbers shivering. ★★★☆☆

PETER PAN: RETURN TO NEVERLAND

Voices by Harriet Owen, Blayne Weaver, Corey Burton (2002)

A belated sequel to Disney's animated *Peter Pan* (it only took them half a century to make it!), this joins Peter's pal Wendy, now all grown up, as she tells her own children about Peter Pan and Neverland to give them hope during the London bombings of the Second World War. Her twelve-year-old daughter Jane doesn't believe the stories, until Captain Hook, mistaking her for Wendy, kidnaps her and takes her to Neverland in order to lure Peter out to rescue her.

It's all a rather tired retread of the original, lacking all of the first movie's charm. Very young, undemanding viewers may not mind (and will have no trouble with the film's brief running time), but anyone who has seen *Peter Pan* will just shake their heads in disbelief that there is actually a Pan film worse than *Hook*. ★★☆☆☆

THE PHANTOM TOLLBOOTH

Voices by Mel Blanc, Butch Patrick (1970)

One of those kids' books that was a must-read for over a decade after it was published in 1961 but now is sadly difficult to track down, *The Phantom Tollbooth* is the story of a young boy who finds a tollbooth, drives his toy car through it and finds himself in a world full of adventure and strange characters, as the King of Dictionopolis, who believes in the supremacy of words, and the King of Digitopolis, who believes in – you guessed it – the importance of numbers, declare war. It's up to young Milo and his new friends to bring back the Princesses of Rhyme and Reason to restore order in the world.

Directed by Looney Tunes' Chuck Jones and based on Norton

Juster's book, this features the voice of Mel Blanc for some of the pun-filled characters like Officer Short Shrift and the Demon of Insincerity while Butch Patrick (who played Eddie in the TV series *The Munsters*) supplies the voice of young Milo. Though not as good as the book on which it is based (some bonkers moments are better left to a reader's imagination), this is fun – and educational! – entertainment for the over-fours. ★★★☆☆

POCAHONTAS

Voices by Mel Gibson, Irene Bedard, David Ogden Stiers (1995)

Disney's 33rd animated feature was the first to be based on the adventures of a real historical figure, a twelve-year-old Native American girl who in 1607 saved adventurer John Smith from being put to death by her tribe. In Disney's version, Pocahontas is a fully developed young woman when she meets Smith (Gibson), who arrives in the New World with a greedy governor (Stiers) and his men in search of treasure.

Being a girl who likes adventure, it's not long before Poccy and Smith are having secret assignations while the British and the natives get increasingly annoyed with each other. In between, Mel gets to sing (not bad), the pair visit Grandmother Willow (a tree-dwelling spirit) and the various animals provide some of the most rib-tickling moments of humour. It's unlikely little boys will sit through an adventure that's also a romance (yuck), but grown-ups and little girls will certainly enjoy the colourful animation, the sing-a-long songs and the well-told tale that are all Disney trademarks. So what if Poccy married a different Englishman and lived in England until she died in real life? As is often the case, the movie ending is much better... ★★★★☆

POLLYANNA

Starring Hayley Mills, Jane Wyman, Richard Egan (1960)

Thirtysomethings will probably remember the eighties TV version with Patsy Kensit, but this is the classic adaptation of Eleanor H Porter's novel for little girls (and they'll love it). Cute-as-a-button Hayley Mills stars as the missionary's daughter who seems permanently cheerful, even though she's now an orphan. Sent to live with her dour Aunt Polly (Wyman) in a small town, Pollyanna is determined to bring joy to everyone she meets there, whether they like it or not.

Like the book on which it is based, *Pollyanna* has a very moral heart and some adults (and older kids) may find the heavily Christian sentiment laid on a bit too thick. But little girls who worship all things pink or pig-tailed will love the optimistic and sunny Pollyanna, and if a few viewers learn her 'glad game' (in which she teaches her friends to find something to be glad about in any situation), it wouldn't be a bad thing! ★★★☆☆

THE PRINCE AND THE PAUPER

Starring Oliver Reed, Raquel Welch, Mark Lester (1977)

Of the twenty-plus versions of Mark Twain's classic story (and there's another coming in 2007), including the Barbie version, Mickey Mouse cartoon (1990), the 1937 Errol Flynn movie and a TV one with Nicholas Lyndhurst (1976), the silliest – and most enjoyable – must be the 1977 version, known as *Crossed Swords* when it was released in the US. Directed by *Fantastic Voyage*'s Richard Fleischer, and featuring a star-studded cast including Oliver Reed, Ernest Borgnine, George C Scott and Rex Harrison (not to mention pin-up Raquel Welch and a hilarious Charlton Heston as King Henry), it's a spirited swashbuckler as poor Tom swaps places with Henry VIII's son Edward (both played by Lester) for a prank that gets out of hand.

While the various American accents clash and Lester seems a little old for the dual role of Tom and Edward, this thunders along with glee, and Reed especially is terrific in his role as Miles Hendon. A rollicking adventure if you don't take it seriously, brimming over with lavish costumes and thigh-slapping fun. ★★★☆☆

RABBIT-PROOF FENCE

Starring Everlyn Sampi, Tianna Sansbury, Kenneth Branagh (2002)

A captivating tale of three young Aboriginal girls in the 1930s who were snatched from their families and taken to an institution 1500 miles away. Based on a true story recounted in the book by Doris Pilkington, the film follows the girls as they escape and attempt to walk across the Australian outback to their home.

Surprisingly unsappy but utterly moving, the film features three terrific performances from the girls (all making their acting debuts) as they make their way across the unrelenting countryside using the wire fence that cuts across Western Australia as their guide. The big surprise, though, is Branagh, as AO Neville, the Chief Protector of the Aborigines – the man responsible for taking 'half-caste' Aboriginal children away from their parents to train as domestic servants and labourers (he believed preventing children of mixed marriages from marrying Aborigines would eventually wipe out the Aboriginal race). While Branagh could have played the man as the root of all evil, he instead gives Neville some humanity, so that while we hate him, he comes across as a misguided man rather than a pantomime villain.

Younger children may be upset by the girls' plight, so this achingly sad story is best reserved for the over-elevens, who will no doubt be moved, especially by Sampi's performance as Molly, the most determined of the three. A fascinating look, for kids and adults, at a piece of recent history Australians would probably rather forget. ★★★★☆

THE SECRET GARDEN

Starring Kate Maberly, Heydon Prowse, Maggie Smith (1993)

While it has been filmed before (including a dull 1994 animated version for TV with voices by Honor Blackman and Derek Jacobi, and the 1949 classic with Margaret O'Brien that's sadly not available on DVD), this is the loveliest adaptation of Frances Hodgson Burnett's novel about a young girl in the 1900s, raised in India, who is sent to England when her parents die. Mary (Maberly) goes to live with her brooding uncle, Lord Craven (John Lynch), at his depressing manor house, and once there she befriends his crippled son Colin (Prowse) and Dickon (Andrew Knott), the young brother of one of the housemaids, who helps her restore a garden she has discovered while exploring the grounds – the first step in her dream of creating a happy family.

Fans of the novel may be disappointed that the text has not been followed too closely, but, taken simply as a serious drama for girls, this is very charming, with unaffected performances from the children, a deliciously scolding one from Maggie Smith as the housekeeper and, even in the gloomy bits, lovely English scenery (scenes were filmed at both Eton and Harrow schools, and also at Fountains Abbey and Allerton Park in North Yorkshire). ★★★★☆

SHREK

Voices by Mike Myers, Eddie Murphy, Cameron Diaz (2001)

Just when we all thought Pixar had the monopoly on blockbuster computer animation with mega hits like *Toy Story* and *A Bug's Life*, along came DreamWorks with this funny, irreverent tale of a big green ogre (voiced by Myers, who reportedly re-recorded all his dialogue after being disappointed by his first attempt, adding the ogre's distinctive Scottish brogue for the recording that was used) living in a land populated by fairy-tale characters, who is reluctantly sent on a mission with wise-cracking Donkey (Murphy) to rescue independent gal Princess Fiona (Diaz) from a fire-breathing dragon.

Grown-ups can enjoy this tale, based on the kids' book by William Steig, as a hilarious comedy packed with movie references (including *The Matrix* and *Babe*, and some digs at Disney's theme parks when Donkey and Shrek visit the park-like kingdom of Duloc), and marvel at the luscious animation that took four years to film, while kids are charmed by the duo's adventure, the numerous recognisable fairy-tale creatures and the antics of the grumpy anti-hero who bathes in mud and uses his own earwax for candles. Just brilliant. ★★★★★

SHREK 2

Voices by Mike Myers, Eddie Murphy, Antonio Banderas, Cameron Diaz (2004)

Everyone's favourite big green ogre returns for a sequel to 2001's animated smash (*Shrek 3* and *Shrek 4* are also in the pipeline). It picks up where the first movie left off, with Shrek (Myers) and his new wife, princess-turned-ogre Fiona (Diaz), going off on their honeymoon. On their return to Shrek's swamp, they are greeted by pal Donkey (Murphy) and an invitation for the newlyweds to visit Fiona's parents, the King (John Cleese) and Queen (Julie Andrews) of Far Far Away. Of course, Fiona's parents aren't aware that she has married an ogre, let alone become one herself, so Shrek's visit to his in-laws was never going to go smoothly. But throw in a Prince Charming (Rupert Everett) who believes he should have married Fiona, a meddling fairy godmother (Jennifer Saunders) and an assassin tabby cat named Puss In Boots (Banderas) and it looks like a recipe for marital disaster.

Packed with in-jokes and movie references to keep adults amused – *Spider-Man* and *From Here to Eternity* are alluded to in the first five minutes, while the land of Far Far Away is a terrifically realised facsimile of Beverly Hills, complete with stores such as Versarchery (for Versace) and Baskin Robinhood – they come so thick and fast they almost, but not quite, overpower the plot. Many of the (often very funny) references will probably fly over the heads of junior members of the audience, but there are enough universal jokes, adventures and even songs (Saunders belting out a perfect 'Holding Out for a Hero') to keep them thoroughly enchanted.

Best of all, of course, are the characters. Myers, Diaz and especially Murphy once again deliver terrific vocal performances, but their talents are almost eclipsed by Saunders, who is just perfect as the domineering fairy godmother, and the wonderful Banderas, spoofing his own Zorro and managing to make an animated moggy somehow sexy in the process. Only the ill-advised idea to dub two of the voices for the UK release (Jonathan Ross replacing Larry King, and Kate Thornton dubbing over Joan Rivers, despite the animation concerned looking exactly like Rivers) spoil what is a truly fun and funny family film.
★★★★☆

SIMON BIRCH

Starring Ian Michael Smith, Joseph Mazzello, Ashley Judd (1998)

'Suggested' by John Irving's novel *A Prayer for Owen Meany* (he asked for it to have a different title as he wasn't happy with the script for the film), this drama should come with its own box of tissues as it's definitely a weepie. Young Simon (Smith) believes God has a special plan for him. When he was born, he wasn't expected to live because of his small size, but he has, even though his dwarfism means he is treated as something of a misfit. His best friend is Joe, who doesn't fit in either. Joe's illegitimate, and wants to know the identity of his father, though his mother Rebecca (Judd) refuses to tell him.

There's tragedy aplenty here (although the opening present-day scenes, with Jim Carrey playing a grown-up Joe, do reveal that two characters are now dead, softening the blow when it comes) and the film itself is unashamedly sentimental. Smith is superb (although his sparky character may annoy some viewers) and there's nice support from Oliver Platt as Rebecca's suitor. If you've read the book, this will be a disappointment, as it only touches on parts of the story, but if you're in the mood for a slushy film, this could fit the bill. Because of the two deaths and some upsetting moments, this isn't suitable for very young viewers. ★★★☆☆

SWALLOWS AND AMAZONS

Starring Virginia McKenna, Ronald Fraser (1974)

The only film version of Arthur Ransome's classic children's book – and sadly, only available on DVD in a set with *The Railway Children* – this British film has rather dated but is still worth catching if you or your little ones are fans of the book.

It's simple stuff – in the Lake District in 1929, four children are allowed by their mother (McKenna, luminous as ever) to sail their little boat, the *Swallow*, to a nearby island to set up camp. Unfortunately for them, they soon discover that two girls, who have a boat named the *Amazon*, think that the island is their territory, and a rivalry between the two camps begins. It's all rather sweet and very English, stiff-upper-lipped stuff that's definitely wholesome entertainment for all ages. The kids – played by Simon West, Suzanna Hamilton, Sophie Neville, Stephen Grendon, Kit Seymour and Lesley Bennett – wouldn't win any acting awards (only Hamilton continued an acting career into adulthood) but it's cute nonetheless. ★★☆☆☆

SWISS FAMILY ROBINSON

Starring John Mills, Dorothy McGuire, James McArthur (1960)

Johann Wyss's novel had been filmed before in 1940 but this Disney version is the treat (rumour has it Disney bought the rights to the 1940 film and scooped up all the copies so no one could see it to compare it with their remake – it's not available on video or DVD to this day). John Mills is just lovely as Father Robinson, who is heading with his Swiss family for a new life in New Guinea when their ship is caught in a terrible storm and they end up shipwrecked on a deserted island.

While dad goes about building the most impressive treehouse in the movies (which, as some lucky kids will know, has been recreated at Disney's theme parks), complete with running water and various balconied levels, the kids befriend some of the island's animals and everything moves along nicely until the family discover there are other people on the island... pirates (gasp)! But parents of little ones shouldn't worry, as the final showdown is as slapstick and full of fun as the rest of this movie, and there are no scares to be had. Good old-fashioned frolics in the sun, then. A new Disney version is being made for release in 2007. ★★★★☆

TARKA THE OTTER

Narrated by Peter Ustinov (1979)

The seventies was a terrific time for films of living, breathing animals (as opposed to the animated Disney kind) – there was *Survival* on the telly and movies like *Black Beauty*, *The Black Stallion* and *Tarka the Otter* in the cinemas. Of course, they were made at a time before people fretted too much about how watching an animal in peril may affect a small viewer, so if you are concerned that your tot may be upset by that, this is probably one classic kids' movie that's best left on the shelf (which would be a shame).

For while it is the tale of Tarka the otter's life, from young pup to an adult otter who finds love of his own (aaahhhh), this film, based on the Henry Williamson novel of the same name, does have some sad moments as death haunts the film. Both Tarka's parents die and (plot revelation ahead!) Tarka doesn't make it to the end either, but it's no more traumatising than Simba's dad biting the dust in *The Lion King* or Bambi's mother getting shot. And the beautiful filming of this otter's often humorous adventure through life is well worth watching. ★★★☆☆

TARZAN

Voices by Minnie Driver, Tony Goldwyn (1999)

A slick, entertaining adaptation from Disney's animators of Edgar Rice Burroughs's classic tale of the orphan raised in the jungle by gorillas. Backed by a soundtrack by Phil Collins (which isn't as bad as you might expect), the loincloth-wearing apeman (Goldwyn) meets and falls for a young Englishwoman named Jane (Driver) who is accompanying her father on an expedition.

Humans who can't be trusted, the requisite cuddly little animals and more warm, fuzzy feelings than you can shake a swinging vine at are all perfectly mixed together in the Disney style, which may feel like just another one off an assembly line for cynical adults but will enchant the young tots who dragged them in front of the TV. ★★★☆☆

TO KILL A MOCKINGBIRD u/c

Starring Gregory Peck, Mary Badham, Robert Duvall (1962)

One of the best American novels of all time (written by Harper Lee) was adapted into one of the best American family films ever made. Gregory Peck is just superb and won a well-deserved Oscar as Atticus Finch, the lawyer in 1930s Alabama who defends a black man falsely accused of raping a white girl. As seen through the eyes of Atticus's young daughter Scout (Badham, sister of *WarGames* director John), it's as much about the lessons his children learn about courage and fairness as it is about the case and racism in the South.

Badham is natural and believable (she was nominated for an Oscar), and there is moving support from Philip Alford as her older brother Jem and John Megna as their pal Dill (when Lee wrote the book, she modelled Dill on her childhood friend, Truman Capote). Meanwhile, Robert Duvall, in his first big-screen role, makes a lasting impression as kids' boogeyman Boo Radley, the neighbour who, according to Jem, is kept chained up by his father, 'eats raw squirrels and all the cats he can catch… his teeth are yella and rotten. His eyes are popped. And he drools most of the time.' Yes, there are moments that some children may find scary, and the film does have adult themes, but it's essential, heartfelt viewing for everyone. ★★★★★

TREASURE ISLAND   u/c

Starring Robert Newton, Bobby Driscoll, Basil Sydney (1950)

Wallace Beery, Jack Palance and Orson Welles have all tackled the role of Long John Silver (and don't forget there is also Tim Curry's comic version in *Muppet Treasure Island*), but it was Robert Newton who best captured the infamous pirate in this Disney family movie.

As students of the Robert Louis Stevenson classic already know, young Jim Hawkins (child actor Driscoll, who provided the voice for Disney's animated Peter Pan) joins Squire Trelawney (Walter Fitzgerald) and Dr Livesey (Denis O'Dea) aboard the *Hispaniola* in search of buried treasure in the Caribbean. Also on board, of course, is Long John Silver, the one-legged pirate with nefarious plans of his own.

A must-see for little boys and girls who love pirates, this is fine for all ages (if you don't mind that most of the shipmates swig alcohol throughout) and is packed with action and fun performances. And fact fans should note – while it's supposedly set around the Caribbean, it was actually filmed in sunny Cornwall! ★★★★☆

TREASURE PLANET

Voices by Joseph Gordon-Levitt, Patrick McGoohan, Brian Murray, Emma Thompson (2002)

Poor Robert Louis Stevenson must have spun in his grave faster than a spinning top when this Disney sci-fi animated movie based on his classic novel *Treasure Island* was made in 2002. And, yes, it is as bad as it sounds. Young Jim Hawkins (Gordon-Levitt) is now a restless, broody teen with a holographic map to a treasure planet who flies off into outer space aboard a space galleon to find the loot. There's comedy in the form of Dr Doppler (voiced by David Hyde Pierce) and BEN (Martin Short as a computerised navigator), while other changes include a female (and feline) ship's captain (Thompson) and, horror of horrors, Long John Silver is now John Silver, a cyborg (Murray)!

While the animation is slick and very impressive in places, this is otherwise a right mess – why do the space ships of the future look like galleons and have sails? How come they can stand on the deck when there's no oxygen in space? And, most importantly, what on earth were Disney thinking? ★★☆☆☆

WATERSHIP DOWN

Voices by Richard Briers, John Hurt (1978)

Most famous, of course, for the Art Garfunkel theme song, 'Bright Eyes', this is a quirky animated movie based on Richard Adams's novel.

It's odd in an anti-Disney sort of way – there are no cute songs, the whole tone of the movie is dark and creepy, and the animals here (wild rabbits) are not really fuzzy wuzzy. But then if it was likely that your life was going to be cut short by a car brutally mowing you down, you probably wouldn't feel that sweet and furry either.

If you haven't already realised, this is definitely not a movie for small children, who would be disturbed by some of the imagery, such as the destruction of a burrow and the rabbits that are crushed there. It's the story of a group of rabbits who leave their warren after one of their number, Fiver (Briers), predicts something awful is to happen to their home. The animation adds to the feeling of disquiet you get while watching the film – it looks like watercolour paintings come to life – while the haunting appearance of the black rabbit of death is remembered by many who first saw the film as a child. Both sad and frightening, this remains true to the novel, so is a must for fans of Adams's book. ★★★★☆

WHITE FANG

Starring Klaus Maria Brandauer, Ethan Hawke (1991)

Jack London's classic adventure story about the friendship that develops between a man and a wolf gets the Disney treatment. Filmed against stunning Alaskan scenery, it's the story of teenage Jack (Hawke), who has come to the Yukon of 1898 to prospect his father's claim during the Gold Rush. Teaming up with two prospectors, he heads into the wilds and it's there he first meets the orphaned wolf (with some dog's blood in him) known as White Fang.

While not a great representation of the novel – Jack wasn't a teenager in the book, and the book was more about White Fang than it was about Jack – this is nonetheless an enjoyable wilderness adventure focusing on an interesting slice of American history. Hawke is fine as Jack, but the most acting praise should be given to Jed (who also appeared in *The Journey of Natty Gann*), the dog playing the role of White Fang, as he steals the movie away from all his human co-stars. Fans of Jean-Jacques Annaud's *The Bear* and the adventure *Legends of the Fall* should note that their star, Bart the bear, has a brief role here. ★★★☆☆

WILLY WONKA AND THE CHOCOLATE FACTORY

Starring Gene Wilder, Jack Albertson, Peter Ostrum (1971)

This was the first adaptation of Roald Dahl's *Charlie and the Chocolate Factory* and it remains the best, with Gene Wilder especially memorable as Willy Wonka, the eccentric owner of the local chocolate factory. Following a worldwide competition, young Charlie Bucket (Ostrum) is one of five lucky children in possession of a golden ticket that invites him on a tour of the famous factory with Wonka himself. Taking Grandpa (Albertson) with him, Charlie joins the other (rather obnoxious) children in the adventure of a lifetime, exploring the strange factory and meeting the odd Oompa-Loompas who works there.

A colourful, lively musical with a delicious thread of malice, this features spectacular sets, jokes aplenty and fun performances from the kiddie cast, of whom only one, Julie Dawn Cole (aka Veruca Salt), carried on acting as a grown-up (Peter Ostrum is now a veterinarian in New York State). ★★★★☆

THE WIND IN THE WILLOWS

Starring Steve Coogan, Eric Idle, Terry Jones, Antony Sher (1996)

Very small viewers can be introduced to Toad and his pals through the Thames TV animated series that ran from 1984 and featured voices by David Jason, Michael Hordern and Peter Sallis, or the lovely animated made-for-TV film featuring Alan Bennett, Michael Palin and Rik Mayall (1995). But the best adaptation of Kenneth Grahame's novel for all the family is 1996's barking adventure from former *Monty Python* star Terry Jones that brings Toad Hall and the riverbank to glorious life.

Poor Mole (Coogan) is mourning the loss of his home thanks to vandalism by nasty weasels. Ratty (Idle) suggests a picnic to cheer him up, but they get waylaid by the motorcar-obsessed Toad (Jones), and soon the whole of their idyllic lifestyle is threatened by Chief Weasel (Sher) and his gang. There are no animal costumes or computer trickery to tell the tale (just a bit of clever make-up), but each actor gets under the skin (or fur) of his character brilliantly, and the laughs come thick and fast. It's completely bonkers in a delightfully British sort of way, and a must-see for all ages. The film was released as *Mr Toad's Wild*

Ride in the US, presumably to encourage audiences familiar with the Disneyland theme park ride of the same name. ★★★★☆

THE WITCHES

Starring Anjelica Huston, Mai Zetterling (1990)

Nic Roeg – who made such haunting 'grown-up' films as *Don't Look Now* and *The Man Who Fell to Earth* – seems an unlikely choice for the director of a children's film, but in fact his quirky style is perfect for this movie based on Roald Dahl's book.

Luke (Jasen Fisher, who also played one of the Lost Boys in *Hook*) is taken by his grandmother on holiday to a posh English seaside hotel. Little do they know that a coven of witches is holding its convention there, and the Grand High Witch (a marvellous Huston) has decreed that all the children in England should be turned into mice by giving them special sweets – starting with Luke, who overhears her plan. Can he, now a helpless mouse, escape from the witches, alert grown-ups and change back to a boy?

With clever mouse effects by Jim Henson's Creature Shop, this is thrilling stuff, with more than a hint of the macabre (witches pushing babies in prams off cliffs, that sort of thing), and not suitable for the easily frightened (young or old may find Huston in full witch make-up quite alarming). Roeg stays true to the occasionally malicious tone of Dahl's novel, yet delivers sweetness too, making this a perfect piece of entertainment for older kids and their parents wanting a bit of nasty fun. ★★★★☆

YOUNG SHERLOCK HOLMES

Starring Nicholas Rowe, Alan Cox, Sophie Ward (1985)

Sir Arthur Conan Doyle's infamous detective, Sherlock Holmes, gets a teenage makeover for this adventure executive-produced by Steven Spielberg. While it bears no resemblance to any of Conan Doyle's novels, as an idea for a movie it's kind of cute – Sherlock (Rowe) is at boarding school when he meets young John Watson (Cox) for the first time. Together they investigate a mystery involving a religious cult, Egyptian mummification and murder – the first, of course, of many such crime-solving adventures.

A sleuthing adventure set against a foggy English backdrop, this is part Indiana Jones, part Victorian gothic drama and part tongue-in-cheek comedy, as the duo put their detective skills to the test. Lovers of Conan Doyle's crime novels may be horrified to see their hero given the Spielberg touch (there's more swashbuckling than deduction here, and there are some very un-Victorian special effects), but as a piece of entertainment it's fun throughout. The movie, originally titled *Young Sherlock Holmes and the Pyramid of Fear*, presumably because the filmmakers expected it to spawn a sequel or two, wasn't a great success at the box office, so no sequel was made. Cox has since appeared in episodes of TV's *Casualty* and *Midsomer Murders*, while Rowe has also appeared in *Midsomer Murders*, and series including *Holby City* and *Kavanagh QC*. ★★★☆☆

Cheat Sheet

While the films below aren't aimed at kids and in the main wouldn't be classed as family films either, they're certainly worth checking out if someone in the house is studying the books on which they are based for school exams. Not that they should cheat and not read the actual books, of course...

Shakespeare

As a general rule (and ignoring his musical version of *Love's Labour's Lost*) you can't go too wrong with a Shakespeare adaptation directed by Kenneth Branagh. His *Henry V* (1989) is impressive and epic – though not quite as good as Laurence Olivier's in 1944, while 1993's *Much Ado About Nothing* was a fun romp through the Italian countryside featuring an all-star cast of Emma Thompson, Denzel Washington, Michael Keaton and Keanu Reeves (who isn't that bad, honest). Branagh also made (and starred in) the most meticulous film version of *Hamlet* (1996) you are likely to find at a whopping four hours in length. If that is too much (though it's definitely the best version for students of the text), then 1990's version, with Mel Gibson as the tortured prince and Helena Bonham Carter as Ophelia, does cover the text well, as do Laurence Olivier's 1948 black and white adaptation, which won five Oscars, and a funky modern update with Ethan Hawke, Liev Schreiber and Bill Murray from 2000.

Other Shakespeare movie adaptations that are worth watching include 2004's *The Merchant of Venice*, with Jeremy Irons and Al Pacino, Orson Welles's *Othello* (1952), Baz Luhrmann's stunning transfer of *Romeo and Juliet* (*William Shakespeare's Romeo + Juliet*) to modern-day California, with Leonardo DiCaprio and Claire Danes, and 1967's *The Taming of the Shrew* with Richard Burton and Elizabeth Taylor. Students of *Richard III*, meanwhile, should check out both the 1995 film with Ian McKellen and 1996's *Looking For Richard*, an interesting film directed by Al Pacino that features scenes from the play, rehearsals and sessions in which actors and directors discuss it.

Jane Austen

For detail, and the dishiest (and wettest) Darcy you are likely to find, the best version of Jane Austen's *Pride and Prejudice* is actually the 1995 BBC TV series with Colin Firth. For movie versions, it is hard to choose between the 1940's film with Greer Garson and Laurence Olivier (phew, that man was busy) and the 2005 version, starring a terrific Keira Knightley and a miscast (he's sulky rather than brooding) Matthew Macfadyen. (Avoid the 2004 Bollywood 'remake' *Bride and Prejudice* – it's about as close to the text as *Bridget Jones's Diary*.)

The 1996 adaptation of Austen's *Emma* is pretty good, with Gwyneth Paltrow in the lead role, but you'll be hard-pressed to find a good version of *Mansfield Park*. The 1999 film with Frances O'Connor as heroine Fanny is dull and the only other adaptation was for TV. Thank goodness for Emma Thompson's marvellous 1995 adaptation of *Sense and Sensibility* (for which she won an Oscar for Best Adapted Screenplay), starring Emma, Kate Winslet, Hugh Grant and Alan Rickman, and the little-seen but worth seeking out 1995 film of *Persuasion*, starring Amanda Root and Ciaran Hinds.

The Brontë Sisters

Alas, Anne Brontë's *The Tenant of Wildfell Hall* has only been made for TV. But there have been more than ten adaptations of sister Emily's *Wuthering Heights* and a similar number of versions of Charlotte's *Jane Eyre*. The best ones? Well, it's hard to beat 1939's *Wuthering Heights*, with Merle Oberon as Cathy and Laurence Olivier as Heathcliff. A 1992 adaptation with Ralph Fiennes and Juliette Binoche is surprisingly awful, while the version with Timothy Dalton (1970) is also best left on the shelf. Do the same with Franco Zeffirelli's horrendously miscast *Jane Eyre*, made in 1996 with Charlotte Gainsbourg torturing the English accent as Jane and William Hurt not doing much better as Mr Rochester (while Billie Whitelaw gets the over-acting award as Grace Poole) and go for the 1944 version with Orson Welles (perfectly brooding as Rochester) and Joan Fontaine (all wide-eyed shock as Jane).

Unfortunately Charlotte's *Shirley* has only been filmed once, in

1922, and her novel *Villette* has only been filmed as a BBC TV series, made in 1970. Anne's *Agnes Grey* has never been committed to celluloid.

Oscar Wilde

All of Wilde's plays work best on stage, but there have also been some good film versions. The 1952 adaptation of *The Importance of Being Earnest*, with Edith Evans giving a barnstorming performance as Lady Bracknell, is a scream and offers nice turns from Michael Redgrave, Joan Greenwood and Margaret Rutherford. In 2002, director Oliver Parker tackled the text and it's amiable enough – Rupert Everett and Colin Firth are terrific as Algernon and Jack, and Judi Dench is a good Bracknell, but the two leading ladies (Frances O'Connor and Reese Witherspoon) are a little miscast.

Parker also directed a 1999 version of *An Ideal Husband*, with Rupert Everett again stealing the show, as Lord Goring. Once again, the rest of the cast are a bit odd for their roles (Minnie Driver as Mabel is fine, but Cate Blanchett as Lady Gertrude and Julianne Moore as Mrs Cheveley are a bit too modern), but it is a good adaptation with some grand-looking locations. There is also a little-seen version made the year before, with James Wilby, Sadie Frost and support from socialites Tamara Beckwith and Tara Palmer-Tomkinson, that's best left on the shelf, and Alexander Korda's stylish 1947 interpretation with Michael Wilding and Paulette Goddard.

Students of *Lady Windemere's Fan* will have less success finding a movie adaptation. While English-language films were made of it in 1916, 1925 and 1949 (Otto Preminger's *The Fan*), none are currently available on DVD in the UK, which leaves the dreadful 2004 reworking of the text, *A Good Woman*, with Helen Hunt, Scarlett Johansson and John Standing. Avoid at all costs. *Salome* doesn't fare much better (*Hellraiser* creator Clive Barker made a short film with no dialogue in 1973, Pedro Almodóvar did his own short in 1978, while Ken Russell made the raunchy, bizarre '18' certificate *Salome's Last Dance* in 1988), while *The Picture of Dorian Gray* may have been filmed many times, but none of the versions (many updating the action to modern times) do the novel justice (the best is the 1945 drama with George Sanders, Donna Reed and Angela Lansbury).

Charles Dickens

Dickens's more child-friendly novels, *David Copperfield*, *Oliver Twist* and *A Christmas Carol*, are reviewed in their various versions elsewhere in this book. His more grown-up tomes have been filmed many times, so here is the pick of the best. For *Bleak House*, 2005's BBC drama with Gillian Anderson eclipses all movie versions (the most recent being made in 1922), for *Hard Times*, the BBC scores again (1994), while for *Little Dorrit*, you want the 350-minute adaptation (yes, really) from 1988 that was originally shown in two parts and features sterling performances from Derek Jacobi and Alec Guinness.

The 1946 adaptation of *Great Expectations*, directed by David Lean and starring John Mills as Pip, Jean Simmons as Estella and Finlay Currie as Magwitch, remains the best – avoid the hideous 1998 'update', relocated to New York with Ethan Hawke as a dull, renamed Finn (instead of Pip), Gwyneth Paltrow as Estella, and Robert De Niro, hilarious as the convict. Meanwhile, *A Tale of Two Cities* was nicely adapted in 1958 with Dirk Bogarde in the lead, 1952's *The Pickwick Papers* is a treat (and was nominated for an Academy Award for its costume design) and *Nicholas Nickleby* was given a lavish big-screen treatment in 2002, with Charlie Hunnam as Nicholas, and support from Tom Courtenay, Christopher Plummer and Jim Broadbent.

Animals

• •

This is the biggest section of the book, with good reason. Hundreds of movies have been made, aimed at children and families, that feature cute and cuddly (and often furry) creatures that we can all watch and say 'aaaahhhh' about. Most of the films – but not all – are suitable for every age, especially the animated ones, but parents beware: just because a film features the fuzzy-wuzzy antics of an adorable mutt/cat/bear/seal/deer/pony, etc, that doesn't mean you and your little ones won't be reaching for the tissues by the end of the movie. Many of the films featured here have scenes of animals in peril, and, as anyone who has seen *Bambi*, *Finding Nemo* or *The Yearling* (to name just a few) knows, film-makers have no qualms about killing off a main animal character, even in kids' films. (Those that have upsetting moments are mentioned in the individual reviews so you can have Kleenex at the ready.)

For other films featuring animals, check out the Adaptations section that features movies based on well-known books, while mythical creatures can be found in the Fairy Tales, Fantasies and Legends chapter.

101 DALMATIANS

Starring Glenn Close, Jeff Daniels, Joely Richardson (1996)

A live-action update of Disney's classic animated tale. Glenn Close is deliriously over the top as ultimate screen villainess Cruella De Vil, the rich bitch who wants to turn lots of adorable little spotted Dalmatian puppies into her latest fur coat.

Joely Richardson and Jeff Daniels (in a role reportedly first offered to Hugh Grant) are more bland as the couple trying to stop her, but there is some amusement to be had from the slapstick events along the way. Those sentimental for the animated original may miss the cartoon doggy expressions since live dogs are used here (and, unlike their animated counterparts, they had to be tempted to 'act' – in one scene actors who were meant to be licked by the canines had to have steak juice rubbed on their skin), but the puppies are very cute to watch and there's fun support from Hugh Laurie, Joan Plowright and Tim McInnerny. ★★★☆☆

102 DALMATIANS

Starring Glenn Close, Gérard Depardieu, Ioan Gruffudd, Alice Evans (2000)

After the success of the live-action *101 Dalmatians*, and especially Glenn Close's memorable performances as villainess Cruella De Vil, it wasn't a surprise when she and the adorable puppies returned for a sequel four years later. After being released from prison, it seems Cruella is a changed woman, but it's not long before she's after the puppies belonging to her parole officer Chloe (Evans) and animal shelter owner Kevin (Gruffud).

From then on, it's pretty much a reworking of the first film, with Depardieu going over the top as fashion designer Monsieur Le Pelt, *Blackadder*'s Tim McInnerny providing the laughs as Cruella's servant, and Gruffudd and Evans's characters falling in love while trying to save the dogs (the couple also found love in real life). Very predictable stuff, but the dogs are cute. ★★☆☆☆

THE ADVENTURES OF GREYFRIARS BOBBY

u/c u/c

Starring Oliver Golding, James Cosmo, Gina McKee (2005)

Greyfriars Bobby was a real dog, who loved his owner so much that he held a vigil, sitting by his master's Edinburgh grave for over fourteen years after he died. And, er, that's it. Not much to make a movie out of, is it? And that's the problem – while the story has already spawned a book by Eleanor Atkinson and a Disney movie in 1961 – there's very little plot to keep even the most ardent dog lovers interested.

Set in 1858, we see Bobby the terrier accompanying policeman John Gray (Thomas Lockyer) on his beat – until the day he is killed. So

Bobby sits by his master's grave, and even when he is moved twenty miles away by Gray's widow, he charges across the fields to get back to the cemetery. There are a few Dickensian plot quirks in the second half, and some odd characters come and go (including comic Ardal O'Hanlon as a tramp and Christopher Lee as the man who comes to Bobby's aid when he is threatened with being put down). Dull stuff, so seek out the cuter 1961 Disney version, *Greyfriars Bobby: The True Story of a Dog*, instead. ★★☆☆☆

AIR BUD ▲ G ▲

Starring Michael Jeter, Kevin Zegers (1997)

You may not have heard of *Air Bud*, but the movie has spawned an impressive five sequels (*Air Bud: Golden Receiver*, *Air Bud: World Pup*, *Air Bud: Seventh Inning Fetch*, *Air Bud: Spikes Back* and 2006's *Air Buddies*). Yes, in case you haven't figured it out yet, a dog named Buddy (and, in later films, his pups) is the hero in all these films and his skill is in the sports arena. While the later movies have Bud playing American football, soccer, baseball and volleyball, the first film has the golden retriever showing off his skill on the basketball court.

And skilled he is. When a lonely kid named Josh (Zegers) befriends him, the two practise dunking, dribbling and scoring together, eventually joining the school basketball team (with Buddy as mascot and player). Unfortunately, Buddy's original owner decides he wants the mutt back, but since this is a Disney movie, you know it will all end okay, with a little humour thrown in. Sadly the dog who played Buddy in the first film died of cancer shortly after the film was released. ★★★☆☆

ALASKA ▲ PG PG

Starring Thora Birch, Vincent Kartheiser, Dirk Benedict, Charlton Heston (1996)

Kids brave the elements to save their missing dad in this adventure story. When pilot Jake Barnes's (*The A-Team*'s Benedict) small plane crashes, leaving him stuck on a cliff with no radio and a wounded leg, his two kids, Sean and Jessie (Kartheiser and Birch), decide to find him themselves after the rescue teams give up. Along the way they befriend

Cubby, a gorgeous baby polar bear, and also have to shield him from the evil poacher (a hammy Heston) after the cub for his fur.

Directed by Fraser Heston (son of Charlton), this has a bit of a hokey plot (the kids don't get along, but after some bickering on their trek you know it's all going to end in a big group hug), but the stunning scenery (actually British Columbia) more than makes up for it. Best of all is the performance of Agee, the bear who plays Cubby and steals every scene from the more experienced human actors. Parents should note that young viewers may be very upset by a scene in which Cubby is caged and one of the horrible poachers waves the head of his dead mother in front of him. ★★★☆☆

ALL DOGS GO TO HEAVEN

Voices by Burt Reynolds, Dom DeLuise, Judith Barsi (1989)

An inventive little animated movie from Don Bluth (*The Secret of NIMH*), this is a cautionary tale about a casino-owning dog named Charlie (Reynolds) who is bumped off by one of his business associates, named Carface (Vic Tayback). Charlie wakes up in heaven (because, as the title tells us, all dogs go there, even greedy ones), but conspires to get back down to earth so he can settle the score.

Yes, it's a canine *Sopranos*, with a cute human orphan thrown in who can talk to animals and has an uncanny knack for predicting winners at the track (a help for Charlie's scheme). It's got bright animation, fun characters, enjoyable (but not too scary) bad guys and some musical numbers, too. A passable sequel, *All Dogs Go to Heaven 2*, followed in 1996, with Charlie Sheen filling in for Reynolds as the voice of Charlie. ★★★☆☆

AN AMERICAN TAIL

Voices by Phillip Glasser, Dom DeLuise, Christopher Plummer (1986)

A cute mousey tale that's very popular with young viewers. It's the story of a group of immigrants to America – a family of Russian mice (the Mousekewitzes, of course) who set sail for America in 1885, a land where they believe the streets are paved with cheese. However, young Fievel (Glasser) is separated from the rest of the family during a storm on the boat, and when he washes up in New York he is rescued by

French pigeon Henri (Plummer), who is overseeing the construction of the Statue of Liberty in the harbour, and who decides to help Fievel find his family.

A story of one little mouse's courage, this has quite a depressing middle as Fievel (named after producer Steven Spielberg's grandfather) searches for his family and encounters lots of nasty characters (including a cat masquerading as a rat), while his family believe he perished in the storm. Kids don't seem to mind, though, as this spawned a sequel – 1991's *An American Tail 2: Fievel Goes West*, in which the family head to western America (featuring James Stewart's final movie performance, providing the voice of sheriff Wylie Burp) – and two further video/DVD movies plus a spin-off series, *Fievel's American Tails*. ★★★☆☆

ANDRE ![U] ![PG] ![G]

Starring Tina Majorino, Keith Carradine, Joshua Jackson (1994)

Based on a true story, this is the tale of a cuddly seal named Andre, who is adopted by Maine harbour master Harry (Carradine) and his animal-loving family (they already have chickens, ducks, goats and frogs). Little Toni (Majorino) especially takes to the seal, but there's trouble ahead as a local fisherman reports the family to the authorities (apparently you're not supposed to keep a wild animal as a pet).

Kids will love the cute seal (actually played by a sea lion called Tory because seals are harder to train) as he has bubble baths, balances balls on his nose, blows raspberries, claps his flippers and even changes the TV channel to an episode of *Lassie*. Parents will notice there's not much else to the movie except Andre's tricks, though, so this one is probably best left to junior members of the audience (there are a few moments of seal and kiddie peril, but nothing too scary). ★★★☆☆

ANTZ ![PG] ![PG] ![PG]

Voices by Woody Allen, Sharon Stone (1998)

Z-4195 (Allen) is a worker ant, tired of being just one in a billion, who falls for the colony's Princess Bala (Stone), even though the bug caste system means he has no chance with her. Enlisting the help of his

Lassie

The most famous dog in the world, Lassie the collie first appeared in the 1943 movie *Lassie Come Home* (based on the Eric Knight novel) and – despite being a female character – was played by a male dog named Pal, who went on to appear in four more movies and made a cameo appearance in the 1954 *Lassie* TV series that followed.

Lassie Come Home remains the classic Lassie movie – it's a tear-jerker for all the family to sob through as young Joe's (Roddy McDowall) family has to sell Lassie to a wealthy duke, and the duke's granddaughter (Elizabeth Taylor) helps the dog escape from the mean kennelmaster so she can be reunited with Joe. And you'll need more tissues for the family during 1945's *Son of Lassie* (grown-up Joe, played by Peter Lawford, and Laddie, son of Lassie, are trapped during the Second World War). *Courage of Lassie*, from 1946 and with Elizabeth Taylor as a different character who adopts the dog, who is helping the US war effort in the Philippines, is surprisingly nasty for a family film (poor Lassie, now rechristened Bill, is hit by a truck, and shot more than once), but things get easier in 1948's *Hills of Home* (also known as *Master of Lassie*, and set back in the peaceful Scottish countryside) and 1949's *Challenge to Lassie*, which has a similar plot to 2005's *The Adventures of Greyfriars Bobby*.

There have been more recent additions to the Lassie legend. As well as various TV movies, the long-running series and the forgettable *The Magic of Lassie* (1978), there's also 1994's weepie *Lassie* and 2005's *Lassie*, directed by Charles Sturridge (*FairyTale: A True Story*), which features a well-known cast (Peter O'Toole, John Lynch, Nicholas Lyndhurst, Robert Hardy, Edward Fox, Samantha Morton and *The Station Agent*'s Peter Dinklage) in a tale similar to the 1943 movie that started it all.

soldier ant pal Weaver (Sylvester Stallone), Zee ends up in battle and becomes a thorn in the side of General Mandible (Gene Hackman), an ant who has nefarious plans for the colony.

DreamWorks's animated adventure is superb to look at and features some great vocal characterisations from the famous cast (which also includes Anne Bancroft, Danny Glover, Jennifer Lopez and Christopher Walken), but don't expect your little ones to be as enchanted as you may be. The gruesome bug battle scenes make Starship Troopers look like Teletubbies, so would scare the life out of small kids, and Zee's neuroses are clearly aimed at filmgoers old enough to know who Woody Allen is and get the joke. Make sure the under-10s are in bed and enjoy it as a witty and fun cartoon for grown-ups. ★★★★☆

THE ARISTOCATS

Voices by Phil Harris, Eva Gabor, Scatman Crothers (1970)

A feline alternative to *One Hundred and One Dalmatians*, this Disney animated movie is cute, though not perhaps one of the studio's best. The animation's a bit scrappy, but kids will enjoy the tale of Duchess (Gabor) and her three kittens, Marie, Toulouse and Berlioz, who are torn from their pampered life in Paris by mean butler Edgar (the cats are to inherit the luxury home of their mistress, but he has other ideas) and dumped in the countryside. With the help of streetwise puss J Thomas O'Malley (Harris), however, they may just find their way home and put a stop to Edgar's schemes.

It's all a little similar to the more luscious *Lady and the Tramp*, but the vocal performances here are fun (Crothers is best as 'Scat Cat', the jazz-playing feline), the story is short and sweet, the kittens are utterly adorable, and there is a memorable motorcycle chase to keep everyone amused. Meow. ★★★☆☆

BABE

Voices by Christine Cavanaugh, Miriam Margolyes, Hugo Weaving (1995)

A short children's novel by British author Dick King-Smith was turned into one of the loveliest children's films ever, thanks to writer/producer George Miller (a man better known for writing and directing the *Mad*

Max movies) and director Chris Noonan. As well as having an adorable story at its heart, what makes this movie so special is that the animals 'speak' thanks to computer trickery and animatronic doubles (the film won an Oscar for its visual effects).

It is, of course, the story of an orphaned pig named Babe, who is taken in by Farmer Hoggett (a wonderful James Cromwell). (Those of a sensitive nature should note that the circumstances that bring Babe to his farm may bring on a few tears.) Mrs Hoggett (Magda Szubanski) isn't too impressed by the new addition, but Farmer Hoggett warms to the little cutie (as voiced by Cavanaugh), especially when Babe – who shares a barn with various animals, including the sheepdogs – shows an aptitude for herding the sheep. Should Hoggett enter Babe the 'sheep pig' in a sheep-herding competition, risking ridicule from the other farmers?

Even the most animal-phobic person will melt at Babe's adventures (actually forty-eight piglets were used during filming as they grow so fast), many of which are very funny, and his pals, including the duck who thinks he's a rooster and gets Babe into much trouble. With the various 'chapters' of the film introduced by a chorus of singing mice, this is cuter than a room full of fluffy puppies and purring kittens and is a must for all ages. A sequel, *Babe: Pig in the City* (1998), is much darker (Babe has to fend for himself in the mean old big city, populated by backstabbing animals and fierce dogs) and not suitable for easily scared children. ★★★★★

BALTO 🎬 G 🎬

Voices by Kevin Bacon, Bob Hoskins, Bridget Fonda (1995)

An animated version of the true story of a half-husky, half-wolf sled dog named Balto (Bacon) that, with a dog team, brought a diphtheria serum 600 miles across snowy wilderness to the remote town of Nome in Alaska in 1925 (a trek that inspired the Iditarod dog sled race).

It's sentimental, of course, as Balto is depicted as a half-breed doggy social outcast who proves to the other dogs what he's made of (including girlie dog Jenna, voiced by Fonda), but there is some humour, as provided by Hoskins (as Balto's pal Boris, a Russian snow goose, and polar bears Muk and Luck – both voiced by Phil Collins – who think Balto is their uncle). With a rather obvious plot and unimpressive animation, it's not a great animated movie, but it's a cute shaggy dog story for kids. (Note that, for some odd reason, there is a commemorative statue for the brave dogs – not in Nome, but in Central Park, New York.) ★★★☆☆

BAMBI

Voices by Hardie Albright, Stan Alexander, Donnie Dunagan (1942)

A surprising number of Disney animated movies feature the traumatic death of a parent or an orphaned child (*The Lion King*, *Finding Nemo*, *The Jungle Book*, *Oliver & Company*, etc) but *Bambi* has the most agonising moment of all, which has distressed children (and adults) for over sixty years. Grown men have been known to weep as young deer Bambi's mother is shot by hunters, and it is extremely upsetting (even though you don't see anything – the sound of the gun is chilling and the expression on Bambi's face heart-breaking), but well worth the entire box of tissues you will need, as the film is truly a delight.

> '*Bambi* was the most frightening film for me as a child. The idea that they had shot Bambi's mother would keep me awake at night. I was truly affected by the horror of it all.'
> MICHAEL WINNER

The animation is lovely, especially when a stumbling Bambi slides across an icy lake, and there are laughs from Bambi's pals Thumper the bunny and the skunk named Flower. The film follows a year in the life of the fawn as he speaks his first word ('bird') and learns about life in the forest. It's utterly charming, exciting (the escape from the forest fire) and moving (not bad for a film only nine minutes longer than an hour) – just make sure you or your little one don't watch it alone, as you'll both need a cuddle afterwards. ★★★★★

BASIL THE GREAT MOUSE DETECTIVE

Voices by Vincent Price, Barrie Ingham, Val Bettin (1986)

Based on Eve Titus's children's novel, *Basil of Baker Street*, this is a fun adventure about a mouse named Basil (Ingham) who is a legendary, Sherlock Holmes-style detective, complete with deerstalker hat and magnifying glass (the 'real' Sherlock does pop up, too, with Basil Rathbone's voice, thanks to a recording taken from one of Rathbone's movie performances as the detective). With the aid of his assistant, Dr Dawson (Bettin), Basil investigates the kidnapping of a toymaker and discovers that his nemesis, the rat Professor Ratigan (the marvellous Vincent Price), is behind it and is planning something far more sinister.

A funny, entertaining introduction for younger viewers to sleuthing adventures, this is a fun twist on the Sherlock Holmes stories penned by Arthur Conan Doyle ('It's elementary, my dear Dawson,' comments Basil) that will amuse grown-ups as much as the kids it is aimed at. A treat. ★★★★☆

THE BEAR

Starring Bart the Bear, Youk the Bear, Tcheky Karyo (1988)

Director Jean-Jacques Annaud – who also made another beautiful animal movie, *Two Brothers* (2004), about two tiger cubs that's worth seeking out – was the man behind the camera for this stunning nature drama (also known by its French title, *L'Ours*).

The Kodiak bear of the title, played by Bart the Bear (who also starred in *The Edge*, *Legends of the Fall* and *White Fang*), protects a young orphaned cub (Youk) from hunters. There's virtually no dialogue (and a very small human cast) as the pair evade the men, but this is riveting throughout (parents of younger children should note that Bart does get lucky with another bear at one point!) as the young female cub and the older male bond and try to survive. Beautifully filmed, this may bore (or frighten) younger viewers, but will fascinate older kids and adults. ★★★★☆

BECAUSE OF WINN-DIXIE

Starring AnnaSophia Robb, Jeff Daniels, Cicely Tyson (2005)

Based on the children's novel by Kate DiCamillo, and directed by Wayne Wang (better known for grown-up fare such as *The Joy Luck Club* and *The Center of the World*), this is the fluffy story of a ten-year-old girl named Opal (Robb), who has just moved to a new town (Naomi, Florida) with her preacher dad (Daniels). One day at the grocery store she spots a stray dog, adopts him and names him after the shop (Winn-Dixie), and the pair are soon bringing warmth and cheer to the townspeople, from the lonely librarian (Eva Marie Saint) to the singing pet shop employee (played by musician Dave Matthews).

It's a well-meaning movie about growing up, as Opal learns about life and stuff from local old woman Gloria (Tyson) and spreads joy to the depressed locals (absolutely everyone seems to have a reason to be depressed, making Naomi the town you'd least like to visit). But for a film that tackles war, alcoholism (Opal's absent mother), death and divorce, and has a big fluffy dog at its centre, it's surprisingly dull and unlikely to charm anyone but the most ardent pooch lover. ★★☆☆☆

BEETHOVEN

Starring Charles Grodin, Bonnie Hunt (1992)

A fluffy dog story that's as innocent as the Disney family comedies of the sixties, this has lots of laughs as dad George (Grodin) reluctantly allows his kids to keep the lost puppy they have found, only for it to grow to be a 200-pound, slobbering St Bernard. There's a villain – former *Herbie* star Dean Jones in a rare bad-guy role – a veterinarian who wants Beethoven to be part of his animal experiments, but really it's all about the dog, played by a real mutt, a guy in a dog suit and an animatronic puppet.

Watch out for Oliver Platt and Stanley Tucci, hilarious as two inept dognappers, and *The X Files*' David Duchovny in a supporting role. The film was such a hit with families, it spawned four sequels (*Beethoven's 2nd*, in which he becomes a dad, *Beethoven's 3rd*, etc) and an animated TV series. ★★★☆☆

BLACK BEAUTY

Starring Sean Bean, David Thewlis (1994)

Anna Sewell's classic Victorian novel about a horse has been filmed numerous times, including a missable 1946 version, a 1978 animated TV series and a 1971 movie with Mark Lester and Patrick Mower. The most recent is a British 1994 movie, in which Beauty himself, as voiced by Alan Cumming, relates his story as he experiences life with different owners, some harsh and some kind, like the London cabbie (Thewlis) he goes to work for.

Beautifully filmed, with the most gorgeous horse you have ever seen, this has some nasty moments that may upset younger viewers, but is well worth a look if you're a fan of the novel, or horses in general. There's even romance as Beauty falls in love with a mare named Ginger. Aaah. ★★★☆☆

THE BLACK STALLION

Starring Mickey Rooney, Teri Garr, Kelly Reno (1979)

A lovely, almost mythical tale about a boy and his horse, this begins with young Alec (Reno, an experienced rider and son of cattle ranchers) surviving a shipwreck – along with a horse who was being transported on the boat. Alone together on a deserted island, the graceful stallion and the boy bond, and when they are rescued and returned to civilisation, they become jockey and racehorse thanks to the determination of them both and the coaching of trainer Henry Dailey (Rooney, in a role that garnered him an Oscar nomination).

An absolutely cracking family film – how many movies boast a shipwreck *and* edge-of-the-seat racing scenes? – this features one of the most beautiful horses you're likely to see on film, as played by Arabian stallion Cass Ole (who had to have mane extensions as his was usually cropped, while white marks on his legs were dyed with black hair dye). An enjoyable sequel, *The Black Stallion Returns* (1983) followed Alec as he tried to track down his horse when it is kidnapped by Arabs and taken to Morocco. ★★★★☆

BORN FREE

Starring Virginia McKenna, Bill Travers (1966)

Joy Adamson's famous book, based on the adventures she and her husband George had while raising Elsa the lion cub in 1950s Kenya, was made into this classic movie starring real-life husband and wife McKenna and Travers. From the opening swirling moments of John Barry's Oscar-winning score (and especially when you hear the theme song 'Born Free' itself), you'll need the tissues for this lovingly filmed tale that follows Joy and George as they raise three orphaned lion cubs (two are then sent to a zoo), and Joy falls in love with one of them, Elsa, and keeps her on the reserve until she realises the lioness is too big to be kept and has to be trained to survive back out in the wild.

It's really like a nature documentary with some story thrown in, but it's charming nonetheless, and sweet and innocent, too – one perfect for younger children interested in the animals of Africa (do note that they may be upset by the notion of the cubs being without their parents – both were shot). Unfortunately, in real life, both George and Joy Adamson were murdered in separate incidents, while Elsa (who had her own cubs and survived in the wild for a time) died of a blood disease in 1961. She is buried in Meru National Park in Kenya. ★★★☆☆

A BUG'S LIFE

Voices by Kevin Spacey, Julia-Louis Dreyfus, David Hyde Pierce (1998)

Disney/Pixar, who made *Toy Story*, followed that success with this computer-animated creature feature. Like *Antz*, *A Bug's Life* follows the adventures of one lowly ant, in this case the clumsy Flik (voiced by Dave Foley). Each year, his ant colony collects food for the bigger and meaner grasshoppers, but when Flik accidentally destroys the offering, he's sent off into the wilderness to try and recruit an army of tough bugs to help the ants' crusade against the grasshoppers. Of course, he manages to get this wrong as well, and inadvertently recruits a troupe of circus-performing insects instead.

Aimed firmly at a family audience, but with a few star names (Kevin Spacey, *Frasier*'s David Hyde Pierce, Denis Leary) doing voice-overs to entertain the grown-ups, this is a beautifully animated and entertaining adventure. While not quite as funny as *Toy Story*, the end credits feature some fab spoof out-takes that are guaranteed to make you laugh. ★★★★☆

CASEY'S SHADOW   u/c

Starring Walter Matthau, Alexis Smith (1978)

Lloyd Bourdelle (Matthau) used to be a successful horse trainer, but now every horse he trains ends up a loser. That is, of course, until a new colt – named Casey's Shadow after the youngest of his three sons, who befriends the horse – comes along and looks like he might actually be a successful race horse. Soon, rich people are offering the poor Bourdelles money to part with their potential winner, but Lloyd is determined to enter the horse in a prestigious race, even if the poor creature is injured.

The problem with this horsey adventure is that the lead human characters just aren't very likeable. Matthau's Lloyd is a boozing grump while youngest son Casey (Michael Hershewe) is just irritating – in fact, the only one who's remotely nice is poor Casey's Shadow himself. One for equine fans only. ★★☆☆☆

THE CAT FROM OUTER SPACE

Starring Ken Berry, Sandy Duncan, Roddy McDowall (1978)

Four years before *ET*, a rather more furry alien got stuck on earth – an extraterrestrial cat named Jake who can communicate with humans thanks to telepathy and a rather clever collar. He really wants to rendezvous with his kitty pals before the government gets him, so he hooks up with a scientist (Berry) and two other doctors (McLean Stevenson and Duncan), in the hope they can help him return to his feline friends.

Deliciously silly stuff – things get extremely daft when Jake announces he needs $120,000 worth of gold to get his spaceship in orbit again, so he and the humans go gambling, making use of Jake's telepathy – it's harmless Disney fun for kids too young for *Close Encounters of the Third Kind* (which was released the same year). ★★★☆☆

CATS & DOGS

Starring Jeff Goldblum, **voices by** Tobey Maguire, Alec Baldwin, Susan Sarandon, Sean Hayes (2001)

As most pet owners are already aware, the world is secretly being run by our feline and canine friends. Cats and dogs are in fact locked in a struggle for world domination, and sweet little beagle Lou (Maguire) becomes the dogs' latest recruit when he is adopted by scientist

Professor Brody (Goldblum) and his family. You see, Brody is working on a vaccine that will forever stop humans being allergic to dogs, and the cats want to get their hands on it and destroy it, so it's not long before sneaky Siamese kitties and other furry hitmen are despatched at the behest of the evil puss, Mr Tinkles (voiced by *Will and Grace*'s Hayes).

A mix of live action, animatronics and animation to make the animals appear to be talking, it's a must-see for junior and adult pet owners, but those with an allergy to all things furry may be bored by the slim plot and annoyed by the sometimes ineffective merging of animation and live-action footage. If you own the DVD, it's worth checking out the extras, including Mr Tinkles's auditions for various movie roles, which are funnier than anything in the actual film. ★★★☆☆

CATS DON'T DANCE

Voices by Scott Bakula, Jasmine Guy, Natalie Cole (1997)

Mark Dindal, who also directed *Chicken Little*, is the director of this animated musical about a cat named Danny (Bakula) who wants to make it big in Hollywood but discovers that cats only get supporting roles in films to humans like spoiled little girl star Darla Dimple.

It's actually a spoof of thirties Hollywood (a caricature of MGM's legendary Louis B Mayer even pops up and Gene Kelly was credited as a choreography consultant) that will fly over the heads of young viewers, but they'll enjoy scenes of Danny with his new Hollywood pals, Woolie the elephant (John Rhys-Davies) and feline actress Sawyer (voiced by Guy, but with Cole singing), and some cute songs and jokes along the way. ★★☆☆☆

CHICKEN LITTLE

Voices by Zach Braff, Joan Cusack (2006)

Chicken Little, as parents who have read the short story aloud to their tots will know, was a bit like the Boy Who Cried Wolf – except Chicken predicted the sky was falling. That's the basis for this amiable if forgettable family animated adventure – only here Chicken Little (as voiced by *Scrubs* star Braff) is a glasses-wearing geeky bird with ruffled feathers who's a disappointment to his sports hero dad even before he tells the entire town of Oakley Oaks that a chunk of sky has landed on his head. Of course, Chicken Little can't prove it, but when another piece drops down, his nerdy pals are there to back him up and it soon becomes clear it's not actually sky falling at all, but the first sign of an alien invasion.

Hmmmm. With nods to Steven Spielberg's *War of the Worlds* (scenes that may scare smaller kids if they haven't nodded off during the slow first half), a character in love with disco (Little's porky pal Runt), and a few pokes at Hollywood (Little's story is made into a blockbuster movie), this has a few moments that will make grown-ups smile but may be lost on kids. But they're likely to be persuaded by some bright animation and the movie's perky little star, who's possibly the cutest chick in animation since Tweety Pie. (When the movie was released in the UK, there was a fast-food tie-in with McDonald's – one can only hope you didn't get a free Little figure with every McChicken sandwich, as that's just too disturbing...) ★★★☆☆

CHICKEN RUN

Voices by Mel Gibson, Julia Sawalha (2000)

Nick Park and Aardman Animations – the brains behind *Wallace and Gromit* and TV's *Creature Comforts* – delivered a divinely silly yet also sharply witty tale for their first full-length animated movie. Packed with smart jokes and a nod to classic wartime POW movies like *The Great Escape* for adults, and slapstick humour and brilliant 'claymation' for the kids, it's the story of a group of hens, led by the feisty Ginger (Sawalha), who plan their escape from captivity before the evil Mrs Tweedy (voiced by Miranda Richardson) can fatten them up and put them in her soon-to-be-marketed chicken pies.

The hens' attempts at escape have always been hampered by their lack of flying ability, so when a cocky rooster named Rocky (Gibson) literally lands in their midst, Ginger is convinced he can help them finally fly the coop. Packed with terrific set pieces – check out Rocky and Ginger's adventure in the pie-making machine, and then watch *Star Wars: Attack of the Clones* for what looks like a homage to it featuring Anakin and Padmé! – and an all-star voice cast (including Imelda Staunton, Timothy Spall and Jane Horrocks), this is sheer perfection for everyone. ★★★★★

DIGBY THE BIGGEST DOG IN THE WORLD

Starring Jim Dale, Spike Milligan (1973)

A shaggy British comedy from former *Goon Show* director Joseph McGrath, this will be nostalgic stuff for grown-ups who remember the British TV comedies of the seventies – as well as Spike Milligan, the cast also includes *Carry On* actress Angela Douglas, *Benny Hill Show* actor Bob Todd and Welsh raconteur Victor Spinetti.

Jim Dale is the bumbling lab assistant who steals some growth-enhancing powder (hoping to improve his roses) that ends up being eaten by Digby the dog, who grows to gigantic size. It's all pretty slapstick stuff as the dog rampages around (and kids may not be impressed by the seventies effects) but it's fun, too. For younger viewers it's an enjoyably silly slice of entertainment, for older viewers it's a classic slice of British movie-making! ★★☆☆☆

DINOSAUR

Voices by DB Sweeney, Alfre Woodard, Julianna Margulies, Joan Plowright (2000)

With a plot spookily similar to the earlier *The Land Before Time*, this animated movie from Disney was rumoured to have cost a whopping $120 million to make, partly due to the expensive techniques used to make it look incredibly impressive, with live-action backgrounds and computer animation. Unfortunately less cash was, it seems, spent on the forgettable story. Aladar the dinosaur has been brought up by a colony of lemurs, but when a meteor shower destroys their home, he and his pals have to wander the land looking for a new place to live. Along the way, they meet other dinosaurs (some friendly and some hungry), and Aladar grows into something of a saviour to all of them.

The animation here is amazing – no cute cuddly creatures, these dinos owe more to *Jurassic Park* than Barney and come complete with detailed scales – but because it is so realistic, it's pretty scary when the meteor shower comes down or anything threatening happens (there are some very nasty meat-eating creatures for starters). There's also something of a message that will fly over the heads of younger viewers – Aladar's group includes a couple of doddery old 'saurs to prove all life is sacred, and the meek and plodding are just as good as the fit and stomping creatures – which makes you wonder quite who the film-makers were aiming this at. Nonetheless, it is visually stunning and a must for prehistory fans (eight and over). ★★★☆☆

DOCTOR DOLITTLE

Starring Rex Harrison, Samantha Eggar, Anthony Newley, Richard Attenborough (1967)

A fawn accidentally drank paint on the set and had to have his stomach pumped, squirrels chomped the scenery causing expensive repairs, a parrot mimicked the director and yelled 'Cut!' halfway through a scene, and a young Sir Ranulph Fiennes (then a member of the SAS) blew up a concrete dam built for the film that offended him, leading to his discharge from the Special Forces. And that's just what happened behind the scenes of this classic animal musical!

The adventures actually committed to film are just as fun. Based on the books by Hugh Lofting, it's the story of a doctor (Harrison) in the mid-19th century who can talk to animals. His house, in Puddleby-on-the-Marsh, is filled with them, and he has mastered over 200 animal languages, including that of a new addition – a two-headed llama called a pushmi-pullyu. And now Dr Dolittle wants to go to sea and find another strange creature, the giant pink sea snail. A box-office disaster at the time, this has since become a classic family movie, thanks to Harrison's wacky performance, and songs such as 'If I Could Talk to the Animals' and 'I've Never Seen Anything Like It'. It has dated somewhat, but there's something endearing about this cute sing-a-long movie nonetheless. ★★★★☆

DOCTOR DOLITTLE

Starring Eddie Murphy, Ossie Davis, Oliver Platt (1998)

A (non-musical) update of the 1967 classic, this has comic Eddie Murphy starring as Dr John Dolittle, who finds he can suddenly understand what animals are saying. Unfortunately, this means lots of animals are coming to him for medical advice, while his family and business partners think he's gone crazy.

Fans of the Hugh Lofting books won't recognise many similarities to them in this modern reworking of the story, and parents looking for a piece of wholesome entertainment should note that these animals don't only have a late-20th century attitude, they have the occasionally raunchy language to match. But it's very funny in places, thanks to a witty script and stars including Albert Brooks, Ellen DeGeneres, Paul Reubens and Chris Rock providing the animal voices, and it looks impressive when the animals talk, thanks to some clever computer wizardry. A sequel, *Dr Dolittle 2*, in which the doc has to save a circus bear, isn't quite as funny but is worth a look if you like the first movie. ★★★☆☆

DREAMER: INSPIRED BY A TRUE STORY

Starring Kurt Russell, Dakota Fanning, Kris Kristofferson (2005)

A sort-of *Seabiscuit* drama for girls too young to have discovered boys or cynicism, this is the old-fashioned tale of a cute little girl (Fanning) and her horse. It's actually an injured thoroughbred named Soñador (which means 'dreamer' in Spanish) that her horse trainer dad (Russell) saves from being put down. Despite the family being on the verge of bankruptcy, Dad helps return the horse to fitness and even entertains the notion of entering the filly against all odds in the tough Breeders' Cup. Do you think she can win?

A sweet if rather predictable family drama that will appeal most to little girls who love ponies and all things equine. ★★★☆☆

DUMBO

Voices by Edward Brophy, Herman Bing (1941)

A classic animated movie from Disney, this tugs at the heartstrings as much now as it did over sixty years ago when it was made. Based on a little-known book by Helen Aberson, it's the only Disney animated film in which the lead character, Dumbo himself, doesn't have a word of dialogue. But he doesn't need to say anything. From the moment the stork brings a

'I have always adored *Dumbo* because it makes me laugh and cry.'
ANGELINA JOLIE

baby elephant to Mrs Jumbo, his big eyes say everything that needs to be said.

Along with *Bambi*, this is one of the loveliest Disney animal movies, which will have viewers of all ages reaching for boxes of tissues as the little elephant sneezes, and his huge ears make their first appearance. He's teased by the other circus animals, and dubbed 'Dumbo', but his only friend, a mouse named Timothy (Brophy), is determined to see Dumbo live up to his true potential. There's lots of humour, of course, but also incredibly moving moments between Dumbo and his mother (and that bizarre pink elephant hallucination, too). Wonderful stuff, this has more drama and fun than many movies twice its length (it's only sixty-four minutes long). ★★★★★

DUNSTON CHECKS IN

Starring Jason Alexander, Faye Dunaway, Rupert Everett (1996)

A daft family farce, this has *Seinfeld*'s Jason Alexander as a widower with two kids who is also the manager of a swanky hotel. His bitch of a boss (Dunaway) wants him to work when he should be on vacation with his family, because a hotel inspector is rumoured to be visiting, and things are further complicated by difficult guest Lord Rutledge (Everett, devilishly villainous), who, unbeknownst to everyone, is actually a con artist with an orang-utan pet that is trained to rob hotel guests.

Parents may think this sounds awful, but it's actually an entertaining zany comedy, in which everyone overacts as if they are in panto, but do so with infectious glee. It's pretty imaginative and never sentimental, packed with slapstick and silly performances, including a nice turn from Paul Reubens (aka Pee-wee Herman), a bonkers pet detective. ★★★☆☆

EIGHT BELOW

Starring Paul Walker, Bruce Greenwood (2006)

Loosely based on a true story – and a 1983 Japanese film called *Nankyoku Monogatari* (aka *Antarctica*) – this moving story of a pack of brave husky dogs was a surprise box-office hit.

Jerry Shepard's (Walker) sled team of eight dogs transport scientist

Davis McClaren (Greenwood) across the icy Antarctic wastes, but when a storm comes in and the humans have to be airlifted out, the dogs are left behind because there's no room for them on board. The plan is for the plane to return once everyone has been dropped off safely, but the severe weather conditions make that impossible. So the eight dogs are left stranded, likely to die of hunger and exposure, but while Jerry tries to organise a rescue mission, they begin to fend for themselves in an attempt to survive. Dog fans will blub throughout at the gorgeous animals (six huskies and two malamutes) as the days tick by (their time in the snowy wilderness counted by subtitles across the screen), and while Walker is a little wishy-washy in the lead, the doggy performances and the amazing scenery (Norway, Canada and Greenland) more than make up for it. ★★★★☆

FAR FROM HOME: THE ADVENTURES OF YELLOW DOG ⒰ PG ⒢

Starring Mimi Rogers, Bruce Davison, Jesse Bradford (1995)

Nice-looking but ultimately dull tale of a boy named Angus and his dog. Bradford is nice enough as the kid who adopts a stray labrador and names him Yellow, then finds himself and the mutt stranded on a deserted shore when the boat they were in capsizes in a storm. While his distraught parents (Rogers and Davison) pray he will be found and the coastguard are looking for him, Angus and Yellow brave the elements, the wild animals and the rugged British Columbia terrain together.

It looks breathtakingly lovely and the dog is adorable, but with minimal dialogue and story, this feels much longer than it really is (just eighty minutes). Be warned if you do watch – parents will want to book a holiday to Canada to embrace the stunning scenery while kids will demand a dog after seeing this incredibly cute and valiant one. ★★★☆☆

FINDING NEMO ⒰ G ⒢

Voices by Albert Brooks, Ellen DeGeneres (2003)

Pixar, the company who made *Toy Story* and *Monsters, Inc*, delivered another slice of luscious computer animation with this cute family adventure set in the ocean depths. After watching his wife and all their baby eggs (except one) swallowed up by a big sea creature (in a scene that rivals Bambi's mother's death in terms of weepiness; it may be too much for little ones), clownfish Marlin (Brooks) is understandably protective of the one baby that survived, Nemo (Alexander Gould). When the inquisitive Nemo is snatched by scuba divers, however, Marlin has to conquer his nervousness of the big blue sea in an attempt to rescue his son, with the help of a memory-impaired fish, Dory (DeGeneres), and a team of turtles who sound like surfer dudes.

It's another adorable tale from Disney that's enchanting for children, especially during the scenes in which plucky Nemo finds himself scooped out of the ocean and dropped in a dentist's fish tank. And while not as sharp in humour as *Toy Story*, grown-ups will get quite a few laughs from the vocal performances of DeGeneres and Brooks, Willem Dafoe, Geoffrey Rush and Barry Humphries (who gets some of the best lines as a shark who confesses his cravings at Fish Eaters Anonymous). A fishy classic. ★★★★★

FLIPPER

Starring Chuck Connors, Luke Halpin (1963)

Cinema's most famous dolphin first flapped his flippers in this sweet family drama. It's simple stuff – young Sandy (Halpin) lives with his family (dad's a fisherman) in the Florida Keys and spends his days after school diving off the coast. On one such day he finds a dolphin wounded by a harpoon, so with the help of his mum he nurses it back to health and calls it Flipper. Unfortunately, Dad (Connors) then deems it time to release Flipper back into the ocean, but don't worry, a boy and his dolphin aren't parted for long, and when trouble brews, Flipper is soon back to rescue Sandy.

A spin-off TV series followed, in which Flipper, like Lassie, seemed to rescue a different person in peril every week. There is also a remake from 1996 with Elijah Wood as Sandy and Aussie comedian Paul Hogan as his uncle. Filmed in the Bahamas, it looks gorgeous but has a slightly ridiculous plot involving a bad guy dumping hazardous waste in the ocean. ★★★☆☆

FLY AWAY HOME

Starring Anna Paquin, Jeff Daniels (1996)

A real weepie. After her mother is killed in a car crash, young Amy (Paquin) is reunited with the eccentric dad (Daniels) she barely knows. Unhappy in her new situation, Amy withdraws from everyone until one day she finds a nest of goose eggs that have been abandoned, so she raises the chicks when they hatch. The problem is, the geese need to fly south for the winter but have no one to show them how it is done, so Amy convinces her dad to help her – with the help of some light aircraft.

Inspired by Bill Lishman's autobiography (a man who experimented to see if Canada geese could be taught migration routes by humans in microlight aircraft), this could have been a pile of sentimental slush, but instead it is surprisingly restrained, and all the better for it. Paquin and Daniels make a believable dad and daughter learning about each other, but the best moments are those featuring the birds in flight, moments that are often truly spectacular. ★★★★☆

THE FOX AND THE HOUND

Voices by Mickey Rooney, Kurt Russell, Keith Mitchell, Corey Feldman (1981)

Widely considered to be one of Disney's most lacklustre animated movies, this marked the last collaboration between the original Disney animators and the younger animators who would go on to make ground-breaking movies for the studio in the nineties, like *Beauty and the Beast* and *The Lion King*.

It's the story of – as the title hints – a young fox cub named Tod and a puppy named Copper. They become friends, not knowing that when they are older, Copper will be a trained hunting dog and (gasp) Tod will be his prey. Despite that serious plot (which, rest assured, has a happy ending – it is Disney, after all), there are some very twee moments as the pair are growing up and frolicking about, and a sleep-inducing soundtrack of songs. Not one of the studio's best, but a diversion, perhaps, for younger viewers who have seen all the good Disney animated movies already. ★★☆☆☆

FREDDIE AS F.R.O.7 u/c

Voices by Jenny Agutter, Ben Kingsley, Brian Blessed (1992)

One of the clunkiest movie titles ever, *Freddie As F.R.O.7* (or *Freddie the Frog* as it was known in the US) is the story of a French, man-sized secret agent frog who works for the British government. It's similar (but not as fun) as the UK TV series *Danger Mouse*, as Freddie (Kingsley) is sent to England to help us Brits combat bad guys who are causing monuments such as the Tower of London, Buckingham Palace and Stonehenge to vanish. With the help of agents Daffers (Agutter), Scotty (John Sessions) and Loch Ness monster Nessie, he investigates and discovers that the dastardly mind behind this plot is the same person who turned him from a prince into a frog years before.

It's all a bit complicated for young viewers, and the animation isn't sparkling enough to draw their attention either. Kingsley does a great job as Freddie, however (while his son Edmund provides the voice of Freddie when he was young), and this is almost worth catching for his humorous vocal turn. (Alternatively, your money may be better spent buying *Danger Mouse* on DVD.) ★★☆☆☆

FREE WILLY

Starring Jason James Richter, Michael Madsen (1993)

The adorable story of a boy and his killer whale (yes, really), this made a star out of an orca whale named Keiko. In fact, a movie could be made out of his life – after starring in the film, Keiko was later found living in horrible conditions at a Mexican aquarium and money was raised to save him. In 1998, he was airlifted to Iceland (where he was born) and trained to survive in the wild. But Keiko missed human contact and in 2002 appeared off the coast of Norway. (He sadly died of pneumonia the following year.)

In *Free Willy*, he acts the humans off the screen as the whale befriended by a troubled young boy. Willy lives at the local aquatic park and is neglected, so it is up to young Jesse (Richter) to save the whale and set him free. It's very cute stuff, which grown-ups will find predictable but kids will love, with nice performances from Lori Petty as Willy's trainer and Michael Madsen as Jesse's foster dad (plus Michael Ironside, always reliable as the bad guy). The film was followed by two amiable sequels, 1995's *Free Willy 2: The Adventure Home* and 1997's *Free Willy 3: The Rescue*. ★★★★☆

GOOD BOY! 🅤 PG Ⓖ

Starring Molly Shannon, Liam Aiken (2003)

A cute little doggy comedy for younger viewers. After much nagging to his parents, young Owen (Aiken) convinces them to let him have a dog. The pooch they get is a little terrier named Hubble, but he's not your average mutt. His real name is Canid3942 and he's from Sirius (the dog star, of course), sent to earth to see how his doggie counterparts here are ruling over their human slaves. Oops. Soon Owen discovers he can understand his new dog, and Hubble explains that unless earth's dogs pull themselves together and take over the world, they'll all be sent back to Sirius. So Owen and some neighbourhood dogs have to help Hubble rectify the situation before the arrival on earth of the impressive-sounding Greater Dane (voiced by Vanessa Redgrave), who will decide all the dogs' fates.

This has an impressive cast providing the dogs' voices (as well as Matthew Broderick as Hubble, there's Carl Reiner, comic actress Delta Burke and Brittany Murphy), but the humour is clearly aimed at kids (grown-ups will groan at some of the jokes) and probably won't be cool enough to impress the over-tens. ★★★☆☆

HELP I'M A FISH 🅤 Ⓖ Ⓖ

Voices by Alan Rickman, Terry Jones (2000)

A Danish animated adventure that was re-dubbed into English. Three kids stumble across the secret lab of Professor MacKrill (Jones), and when one of them drinks some potion she finds there (duh!) she turns into a starfish. The only way her two pals can rescue her is if they become fish themselves, so they swig some liquid along with the professor and are soon swimming around. But there's danger in the briny in the form of pilot fish Joe (Rickman), who has got his gills/hands/flippers on the antidote and has discovered it gives him brains and the power of speech, so he wants to capture the fishy kids and professor to force them to make more of it.

Kids will no doubt ignore the underlying global warming message (the professor created the potion so humans could survive the rising ocean levels), but they'll enjoy Rickman's megalomaniac fish and his shark sidekick. The underwater animation is nice, but children and parents used to the Technicolor glories of *Finding Nemo* will be disappointed at the images here. ★★★☆☆

HOME ON THE RANGE

Voices by GW Bailey, Roseanne Barr, Steve Buscemi, Judi Dench (2004)

Disney goes Western in this cute tale – apparently the last conventional cartoon feature the company are planning to do in this age of computer animation – of three cows who go on an adventure to find outlaw Alameda Slim (Randy Quaid) and collect the reward on his head in order to save their farm from debt collectors.

The vocal cast reads like a who's who of Oscar winners and nominees (Dench, Quaid, Cuba Gooding Jr, Jennifer Tilly), but the story itself is just average, the jokes obvious and things only really perk up during a yodelling musical number involving dancing steers. It's likeable, inoffensive stuff, and perhaps worth showing to little ones with an interest in Westerns (but who are too young for the movies themselves), but kids weaned on slick fare like *Shrek* and *Finding Nemo* may be unimpressed. ★★☆☆☆

HOMEWARD BOUND: THE INCREDIBLE JOURNEY

Voices by Michael J Fox, Sally Field, Don Ameche (1993)

In 1963, Disney made the classic *The Incredible Journey*, the story of three pets who lose their owners while on vacation and have to find their way home across 200 miles of the mountains and forests of the Canadian Rockies, with a narrator 'explaining' their thoughts. Astonishingly, the much-loved film isn't available on DVD at all, but there was a 1993 remake that almost makes up for it.

The story is the roughly the same – old dog Shadow, young mutt Chance and cat Sassy are forced to get along on their perilous journey after their owners move across the country and they are left behind. The big difference here is that each animal's thoughts are given a voice, courtesy of the well-known vocal cast (unsurprisingly, Ameche is Shadow, Fox is Chance and Field is Sassy). It's packed with beautiful scenery (the movie was filmed mainly in Oregon), some witty 'dialogue' (on seeing a porcupine for the first time, Chance comments that he thinks it is 'probably a squirrel having a really bad hair day') and terrific performances, both from the live animals and the actors voicing them. Just lovely. (The film was followed by an inoffensive sequel, *Homeward Bound II: Lost in San Francisco*, in 1996.) ★★★★☆

ICE AGE

Voices by Ray Romano, John Leguizamo, Denis Leary, Jack Black (2002)

A cute animated buddy movie from Chris Wedge, who also directed *Robots*. The Ice Age is coming and animals are busy scurrying around in preparation for what will be a very wintry time indeed. A little human baby has been separated from his dad in the rush, and it's up to woolly mammoth Manny (Romano), a sloth named Sid (Leguizamo) and a sabre-toothed tiger named Diego (Leary) to put aside their differences and band together to take the adorable little baby to safety.

From the opening credits, this is a hoot (as squirrel Scrat tries – unsuccessfully and rather disastrously – to bury his prize acorn), with zippy dialogue, great vocal performances and quirky-looking characters. There's danger, too, as tigers follow the ragtag group's every move, hoping to grab and kill the child and eat the animals, plus a bit of sentimentality towards the end, and it all adds up to loads of fun – a sort of road movie for all ages with added frosty goodness. A so-so 2006 sequel, *Ice Age 2: The Meltdown*, follows Diego, Manny and Sid as the ice starts to melt and they have to warn everyone of the impending danger. ★★★★☆

INTERNATIONAL VELVET

Starring Tatum O'Neal, Christopher Plummer (1978)

A belated sequel to 1944's *National Velvet*, which was the story of how Velvet Brown entered her beloved horse in the Grand National. Now

Velvet is all grown up (as played by Nanette Newman, wife of the movie's director, Bryan Forbes) and has a niece named Sarah (O'Neal) who wants to be an Olympic horsewoman with the help of trainer Captain Johnson (Anthony Hopkins).

The plot here is pretty weak, but there are a few classy British actors (as well as Hopkins, there's Peter Barkworth, Stephanie Cole and a handful of recognisable character actors) to spur things along until the climactic end. Watch out for Newman and Forbes's daughter Emma Forbes (now a TV presenter) in a small role. One for horsey fans only. ★★☆☆☆

THE JUNGLE BOOK

Voices by Phil Harris, Louis Prima, George Sanders (1967)

If the favourite Disney animated film for little girls is *Snow White and the Seven Dwarfs* or *Cinderella*, the favourite for boys has to be this fun adventure based on Rudyard Kipling's story. It wasn't the first adaptation – there was a live-action movie in 1942 starring Sabu – but this is the one against which all other adaptations will always be measured.

The animation isn't that striking, but it's the vocal performances and the songs ('Bare Necessities', 'I Wanna Be Like You') that give this movie such a large helping of charm. It's the story, of course, of young Mowgli (Bruce Reitherman), who is raised in the jungle by wolves who decide to send him to a local 'man tribe' when they hear the villainous tiger Shere Khan (Sanders) is on the prowl. It's on the journey that he meets Baloo the bear (Harris) and orang-utan King Louie (Prima). This was the last animated movie overseen by Walt Disney, who died during production in 1966. ★★★★☆

THE JUNGLE BOOK 2

Voices by John Goodman, Haley Joel Osment, Mae Whitman (2003)

Thirty-six years after *The Jungle Book* was released, along came this missable sequel. It picks up some time after boy Mowgli returned to life in a human village, but he's missing his old pals, so when Baloo the bear arrives he heads back into the jungle, unaware that nasty tiger Shere Khan is on the prowl.

It's almost a remake, rather than a sequel, as old characters crop up and a few new ones are added (including Phil Collins voicing Lucky the buzzard), but nothing much happens. Goodman makes a good substitute for Phil Harris as the voice of Baloo, and the film-makers must agree, as they have him singing 'The Bare Necessities' not once, but at least three times. It's all inoffensive stuff, perhaps, but pretty dull, too. ★★☆☆☆

KES

Starring David Bradley, Freddie Fletcher (1969)

A powerful movie from director Ken Loach (best known for gritty grown-up movies like *Land and Freedom* and *Bread and Roses*), this is based on the Barry Hines novel *A Kestrel for a Knave*.

It's Loach's most moving film, the story of a lonely, abused boy named Billy (Bradley) who lives in the Yorkshire mining town of Barnsley. One day he spots a kestrel's nest in the woods, steals a young kestrel and begins to train the bird in scenes that Loach captures beautifully, revealing how Billy gradually sees that there is more to life than his working-class surroundings. It's very downbeat and grimy stuff – while Brian Glover's mean PE teacher is just hideous. It's only for older kids (twelve-plus), but they will be moved by this fascinating film. ★★★★☆

'I've been very influenced by *Kes*, which could have been my childhood in Sheffield. It said everything about how I felt as a boy there then.' SEAN BEAN

LADY AND THE TRAMP

Voices by Peggy Lee, Barbara Luddy, Larry Roberts (1955)

Like many of the early Disney feature-length cartoons, this doggy animated classic has stood the test of time, and also has enough deft humour to keep adults as entertained as their junior companions.

For those with rusty memories, this is the one about the pampered spaniel, Lady, who ends up on the mean streets with vagrant hound Tramp after she mistakenly believes her owners don't want her any more. While the shared spaghetti-eating scene between the pair still ranks as one of the cutest romantic scenes in movie history (human and non-human), the most entertaining moments are actually sidebars to the main story – the manic tree-chomping beaver, the arrival of those malevolent Siamese cats and, of course, Peggy Lee (as Tramp's sexy pal) being as seductive as an animated dog can be singing 'He's a Tramp'. Simply gorgeous. ★★★★★

THE LAND BEFORE TIME

Voices by Gabriel Damon, Candace Hutson (1988)

An adorable prehistoric adventure about an orphan dinosaur (what is it with animators and orphans?), this movie has spawned a phenomenal ten video/DVD sequels. Executive-produced by Steven Spielberg and George Lucas, it follows the adventures of cute brontosaurus Littlefoot (Damon), who is making his way with some other cuddly dinos to the mythical Great Valley, home to the lush vegetation they all need to survive.

It's sweet, almost sleepy fare, aimed at the youngest of audiences, although some perilous scenes in the middle as the group come across predators and earthquakes may be a bit scary for them. There are some very cute moments, too, like when a young pterodactyl learns to fly, that should enchant everyone. ★★★☆☆

THE LAST FLIGHT OF NOAH'S ARK

Starring Elliott Gould, Genevieve Bujold, Ricky Schroder (1980)

Many years before he was a tough cop on *NYPD Blue*, Rick Schroder was a cute, blond-haired child actor (anyone remember his starring role in the TV sitcom *Silver Spoons*?). Here, he's cheek-squeezingly adorable as one of two young orphans who stow away on a creaky plane that missionary Miss Lafleur (Bujold) has hired to transport a cargo of animals to a remote island. The pilot, Noah (Gould), has reluctantly agreed to fly her there because he is avoiding a couple of nasty bookies, but when they fly off course and are forced to land in the middle of nowhere, all of them – plus two Japanese soldiers who have been stranded there since the Second World War and think the war is still on – have to band together to turn the damaged plane into a boat for them and the animals to sail away in.

Unfortunately this isn't as funny as it sounds, and it's pretty predictable, too. Very young viewers may find the two kids and the animals cute, but parents should be warned there are some worrisome stereotypes in the depiction of the two Japanese soldiers. Nice Hawaiian scenery, though. ★★☆☆☆

THE LION KING

Voices by Matthew Broderick, James Earl Jones, Jeremy Irons (1994)

One of the most successful animated movies ever made (and it has since been turned into an equally successful stage musical), Disney's *The Lion King* combines all the classic touches you expect from Walt's studio (great songs, adorable characters, a truly scary bad guy) with beautiful, slick computer and hand-drawn animation.

Simba is the young lion cub who sees his father die (a very upsetting scene, no matter what age you are – have a whole box of hankies to hand) and is then exiled by the new 'king' of the pride, his nasty uncle Scar (voiced in a suitably creepy manner by Irons). Luckily Simba is befriended by Pumbaa the warthog and Timon the meerkat, and with them he learns some street smarts before returning to his family to claim his rightful place. Whoopi Goldberg, Nathan Lane and Rowan Atkinson are among the other stars lending their vocal talents to this terrific adventure, while Elton John and Tim Rice provided the memorable songs, including 'Circle of Life', 'Can You Feel the Love Tonight?' and 'Hakuna Matata'. A couple of video/DVD sequels have followed, and also a TV series, *Timon and Pumbaa*. ★★★★★

MADAGASCAR

Voices by Ben Stiller, Chris Rock, David Schwimmer, Jada Pinkett Smith (2005)

Another animated adventure from DreamWorks, the studio behind *Shrek*, this is the fun story of a group of spoiled animals – egotistical Alex the Lion (Stiller), Marty the Zebra (Rock), Melman the nervous giraffe (Schwimmer) and Gloria the hippo (Smith) – from Central Park Zoo in Manhattan who accidentally end up in the wild, stranded on the island of Madagascar without their home comforts.

The real comic stars of the movie are actually a group of penguins who are planning their own escape from the zoo and 'mission' to the frozen arctic wastes via a container ship, and there's also some humorous vocal support from Sacha Baron Cohen (aka Ali G) as Julien, one of the exotic creatures the animals meet in Madagascar. While it all slows a bit towards the middle (very young viewers may get a little bored), this is an enjoyable, if not particularly fresh, animated adventure. Trivia fans should note that, while there are penguins at the real Central Park Zoo in New York, the zoo doesn't have any hippos, lions, giraffes or zebras in residence. ★★★☆☆

MARCH OF THE PENGUINS

Narrated by Morgan Freeman (2005)

The surprise hit of 2005, *March of the Penguins* could be described as part love story, part tragic drama, part tale of survival against the odds. It's actually a documentary (and an Oscar-winning one at that), about the extraordinary journey emperor penguins take each year during their breeding ritual in one of the harshest places on earth, Antarctica. The penguins waddle great distances from the ocean to their breeding ground on the ice, find a mate who they remain faithful to for the year, and then attempt to breed and protect their young through blizzards and with the threat of starvation ever present.

Beautifully filmed, this is an astonishing look at the penguins' yearly march that is moving, funny and unmissable. (Note that small children may find scenes of some of the penguins and their babies dying very upsetting.) ★★★★★

MIGHTY JOE YOUNG

Starring Bill Paxton, Charlize Theron (1998)

A remake of the 1949 adventure, this is basically a fun junior version of the more grown-up *King Kong*, starring a 15ft gorilla. Theron stars as Jill, a woman raised in Africa whose mother (Charlize-lookalike Linda Purl) was murdered by poachers when she tried to protect the gorillas she loved. A baby gorilla whom the young Jill named Joe was also orphaned in the attack, and years later the fearsome ball of hair is still putty in the hands of his human pal. However, their idyllic existence can't last after Joe is discovered by both greedy poachers and zoologist Gregg (Paxton), who convinces Jill to move the beast to a Californian preserve where he'll be safe (except we know he won't be, don't we, boys and girls?).

It's terrific family fare (apart from a few nasty bits not suitable for really young viewers, like the aforementioned attack), with nice performances from the good-looking cast and, of course, a moving and hilarious one from Joe himself (courtesy of the impressive trickery of ILM and Rick Baker's creature effects). Impossibly cute. ★★★★☆

MILO AND OTIS

Narrated by Dudley Moore (1986)

A Japanese movie – its proper title is *Koneko Monogatari* – about the adventures of a cat (Milo) and his doggie pal (Otis), this follows the pair as they grow up together on a farm. One day they are separated, and the two begin perilous journeys to find each other again, across mountains, fields and snowy landscapes.

Beautifully filmed over four years by author and zoologist Masanori Hata, this is an adorable buddy movie featuring an entirely animal cast (apparently over thirty animals doubled for the leading pair), which is brightened up by Moore's zippy narration, based on a script written by Mark Saltzman (who previously wrote for *Sesame Street*). A simple tale that's a must for smaller viewers. ★★★★☆

MONKEY TROUBLE

Starring Finster, Thora Birch, Harvey Keitel, Mimi Rogers (1994)

Fans of *Reservoir Dogs* will be stunned to see Mr White himself, Harvey Keitel, in this kiddie comedy (he apparently agreed to do it for his young daughter). And he does look a tad uncomfortable as the small-time gypsy thief who has a monkey named Dodger (Finster, who really does get top billing over Keitel), trained to pick the pockets of people walking by. Things get complicated when the Mob want to borrow the creature for their own ends, and instead it runs away and is taken in by little Eva (Birch), who gets a shock when it brings her the treasures of everyone in the neighbourhood.

Finster, who also appeared in *Cutthroat Island*, steals the show, and Birch makes for a cute kiddie lead. There's nice support from Mimi Rogers and Christopher McDonald as Eva's mum and stepdad, but anyone over the age of twelve will find the high jinks boring, while grown-ups will be distracted by Keitel's disconcerting and at times bizarre performance. ★★☆☆☆

MOUSE HUNT

Starring Nathan Lane, Lee Evans (1997)

Gore Verbinski, who went on to make the *Pirates of the Caribbean* movies, directed this comic romp featuring hilarious performances from Nathan Lane and Lee Evans. They are Ernie and Lars Smuntz, two idiotic brothers who inherit a crumbling old mansion, only to discover there's a mouse inside who just won't leave. A scary feline, Catzilla, doesn't catch it, neither does exterminator Caeser (Christopher Walken in a truly side-achingly funny cameo). As Eddie himself says about the mouse: 'He's Hitler with a tail. He's *The Omen* with whiskers!'

It's *Home Alone* with extra cheese (and tons more laughs) as the slapstick comedy comes thick and fast while the bumbling brothers destroy half the house in their attempts to rid the place of the pesky critter (played by a real mouse, mixed with computer-generated effects and animatronic ones, plus, apparently, a rat stunt double). Terrific, and proof that you don't need a complicated plot to make a great family movie. ★★★★☆

MY DOG SKIP

Starring Frankie Muniz, Diane Lane, Luke Wilson, Kevin Bacon (2000)

Based on the real-life memoir by Willie Morris about growing up in Mississippi in the 1940s, this is a syrupy but nonetheless enjoyable tale of a lonely young boy Willie (Muniz) who is given a dog by his mother (Lane) ('I was an only child. He was an only dog.'). Boy and dog bond, especially because Dad (Bacon), who lost his leg in the Spanish Civil War, is pretty unreachable. In fact, Willie's only human confidant is grown-up Dink (Wilson), a neighbour who soon goes off to war himself.

It's melodramatic, to be sure, but while it occasionally views the past through rose-tinted glasses, it also shows the rough stuff, too – anyone who has ever lost a pet will agonise along with Willie when Skip runs away and he goes searching for him, while very young eyes should be shielded when a deer is shot in front of Willie. A nostalgic treat, but be warned, a weepie, too. ★★★☆☆

MY FRIEND FLICKA

Starring Roddy McDowall, Preston Foster (1943)

A Western tale for younger viewers, this remains a classic thanks to some breathtaking scenery (mainly filmed in Utah) and a sweet central performance from a young Roddy McDowall.

He's the son of a rancher who decides to train a colt named Flicka, much to his father's disapproval, who believes Flicka may not be mentally well (Flicka's mother was a rather temperamental mare, it seems). Of course, dad doesn't count on a boy's love for his horse, and eventually the stubborn colt becomes a great four-footed friend. A sincere little film based on the Mary O'Hara novel, this was followed by 1945's *Thunderhead – Son of Flicka* (which also starred McDowall), 1948's *Green Grass of Wyoming* (with a new cast) and a 1956 TV series. ★★★☆☆

NATIONAL VELVET

Starring Mickey Rooney, Elizabeth Taylor (1944)

The classic little-girl-and-her-horse movie, which made Elizabeth Taylor a star as Velvet (in a role, incidentally, that former MP Shirley Williams auditioned for). She's the girl who wants to enter her horse, Pie, in the Grand National, with the help of young trainer Mi (Rooney). Soon Velvet is cutting her hair to pass herself off as a male jockey, ready to ride that famous race at Aintree.

Nominated for five Oscars, and winner of two (Best Editing and Best Supporting Actress for Anne Revere as Velvet's mum), this is a slice of old England (even if it was made by Americans and filmed in California!). One for every girl, young or old, who has dreamed of having a horse of her very own. ★★★★☆

'The film I saw as a child that really inspired me was *National Velvet*, with all the drama and romance and style and excitement. It has every emotion and great horses.'
EMMA WATSON (aka *Harry Potter*'s Hermione)

OLD YELLER

Starring Dorothy McGuire, Tommy Kirk (1957)

Fans of *Friends* may remember that this is the movie Phoebe's mother turned off before the end so Phoebe would think it had a happy ending. It's a Disney classic, based on Fred Gipson's novel, but it's not for the faint-hearted – strong men have been known to melt into heaps of blubbering mush by the movie's end.

Set in 1860s Texas, it's the story of a boy named Travis (Kirk, who's wonderful) who lives on the family ranch with his mother (McGuire) and brother while their father goes off on a cattle drive. When a yellow dog wanders onto the ranch, Travis adopts him and has a series of adventures with the mutt he names Old Yeller. It's a very old-fashioned story about a boy and his dog that has been imitated many times. But this remains the best, even if the ending (don't read any further if you don't already know) is the most upsetting family movie moment ever – even worse than the death of Bambi's mum. ★★★★☆

OLIVER & COMPANY

Voices by Joey Lawrence, Billy Joel, Dom DeLuise (1988)

If you think all the various adaptations (even the musical *Oliver!*) of Charles Dickens's *Oliver Twist* are too bleak for your tot, then you haven't seen this Disney animated twist of the tale, featuring cats and dogs. 'Inspired by' rather than based on the classic novel (only four original characters remain – Fagin, Oliver, Sikes and the Artful Dodger), it's the story of a little homeless kitten named Oliver (Lawrence) roaming the mean streets of New York, who is taken in by Dodger (Joel, who surprisingly only gets to sing one song), a mutt who is a member of a gang of dogs who steal for thoroughly nasty human Fagin (DeLuise). But when Oliver is taken in by a rich little girl named Jenny, Fagin and Sikes (an even worse chap, to whom Fagin owes money, voiced by Robert Loggia) decide to grab Oliver back so Jenny will come looking for him and they'll be able to kidnap her for a large ransom.

The first Disney animated movie to extensively use computer-generated imagery, this doesn't look as impressive as their later work (*Beauty and the Beast* etc) but is cute and colourful enough to satisfy younger viewers (although the message from the dogs that it's okay to steal so long as it's for a good reason may disturb some grown-ups). ★★★☆☆

ONE HUNDRED AND ONE DALMATIANS

Voices by Rod Taylor, Betty Lou Gerson (1961)

Kids are more likely to have seen the live-action remake (and its sequel) but this Disney animated version of Dodie Smith's book remains the best, partly due to the superb depiction of that ultimate villainess, Cruella De Vil. She's the dastardly woman who steals the lovely Dalmatian puppies (the offspring of Pongo and Perdita), hoping to make a fur coat out of them. As seen through the dogs' eyes (Pongo begins the tale with the story of how he met Perdita in a London park and they contrived to get their owners together), it's a terrific adventure as the doggy couple discover their fifteen pups have been thrown in with eighty-four others, ready for Cruella's cruel plan.

While this isn't as much of a classic as, say, *Snow White and the Seven Dwarfs*, there's plenty of fun to be had. Kids may not be impressed by the animation – it's flat, and some of the backgrounds are muted, like a TV cartoon – but they'll enjoy the canine adventures and yell at the screen every time evil Cruella appears (she's more of a pantomime dame than a truly scary character). ★★★★☆

OVER THE HEDGE

Voices by Bruce Willis, Garry Shandling (2006)

Following a slew of animated animal capers in 2005 and early 2006 – *Ice Age 2*, *The Wild*, *Madagascar*, *Curious George*, *Chicken Little* – was this summer 2006 offering featuring a vocal cast bound to impress grown-up comedy fans. Sharing the mic alongside Bruce Willis (as the voice of mischievous racoon RJ) are such notable names as Garry Shandling (from *The Larry Sanders Show*), Steve Carrell (*The 40-Year-Old Virgin* and star of the US version of *The Office*), comedienne Wanda Sykes, Thomas Haden Church (Sideways), *The West Wing's*

Allison Janney, *American Pie*'s Eugene Levy, Nick Nolte and William Shatner. Phew.

The story is this: con artist RJ comes across a community of animals who live in fear of humans. With his coaxing, however, the group decide to venture over the hedge into a newly built suburban housing development to forage for food, but when you've got a nervous turtle, a frisky skunk and a family of prickly porcupines as compadres, things are bound to go wrong. It's pretty inoffensive fare with some zippy laughs, as based on the US comic strip of the same name, that will amuse kids and adults but won't split any sides. ★★★☆☆

RACING STRIPES

Voices by Frankie Muniz, Dustin Hoffman (2005)

A sweet live-action, partially animated adventure featuring the voices of Dustin Hoffman, Whoopi Goldberg, *Malcolm in the Middle*'s Frankie Muniz and *Dawson's Creek*'s Joshua Jackson. Made by some of the technical team who brought us that lovable pig who wanted to be a sheepdog, *Babe*, this is a similarly themed tale of a lonely animal wanting to belong. Accidentally abandoned by his circus owners, Stripes the baby zebra (voiced by Muniz) is left alone in the middle of a country road. Single dad farmer and former horse trainer Nolan Walsh (Bruce Greenwood) finds the cute critter and takes him home, raising the zebra with the help of his teenage daughter Channing (Hayden Panettiere). Stripes doesn't realise he's a zebra though, and instead dreams of becoming a champion racehorse like the thoroughbreds he sees racing on the track near the Nolan farm. Will the other farm animals, including goat Franny (Goldberg) and pony Tucker (Hoffman) help Stripes realise his dream? And more to the point, which fool will decide it's okay to enter and ride a zebra in a fast-moving horse race?

While not as heart-warming as *Babe* – Stripes comes across as a bit stubborn and selfish, especially when he is tricking Channing to ride him for the first time – this has some good vocal talent on board and some nice gags delivered by the talking animals (although some parents may not be impressed by the appearance of two animated flies who love squelching around in manure and talking nasty). Greenwood and Wendy Malick (as the racecourse owner) both have fun with their roles as the nicer-than-nice dad and his horrible neighbour, but in the end it's the cute, cuddly animals who steal the show and will no doubt enchant the under-tens. ★★★☆☆

THE RESCUERS

Voices by Bob Newhart, Eva Gabor, Geraldine Page (1977)

Young orphan Penny is being held captive by the nasty Miss Medusa and her henchman Snoops, but she manages to send a message in a bottle asking for help. And help comes in the form of Miss Bianca (Gabor) and Bernard (Newhart), two mice who work for the Rescue Aid Society of mice that's located in the UN building in New York.

It's not a classic Disney film, perhaps, and the animation is a bit scrappy, but this has some cute characters like Orville the albatross to keep kids amused. A sequel (Disney's first animated-movie sequel to be released at cinemas), *The Rescuers Down Under*, followed in 1990 and was actually an improvement on the original – this time, Bianca and Bernard (both Newhart and Gabor returning to give their vocals) have to save an Australian boy and a golden eagle from a nasty poacher (George C Scott) with the help of another albatross, Wilbur (geddit – Wilbur and Orville... the Wright Brothers?), as voiced by John Candy. ★★☆☆☆

RING OF BRIGHT WATER

Starring Bill Travers, Virginia McKenna (1969)

The married stars of classic animal movie *Born Free* reunited on screen for this movie based on the Gavin Maxwell book. Directed by Jack Couffer, who was a cinematographer for Disney animal movies and documentaries like *The Legend of Lobo* and *Secrets of Life* as well as the director of *Born Free* sequel *Living Free*, it's the story of a lovable otter named Mij. Graham (Travers) discovers the little furry friend in a London pet shop, and after Mij has created havoc in his city home, Graham decides the only solution is to move them both to the Scottish coast. Cue lots of otter frolicking in the water, while Graham does some frolicking of his own, falling for town doctor Mary (McKenna).

Grown-ups will want to move to Scotland after watching this gorgeous-looking film, all bubbling brooks and icy sea, while kids will no doubt want an otter of their very own. Like *Born Free*, this is something of a hybrid – part drama, part nature movie – that works really well and benefits from some truly funny moments courtesy of that mischievous otter. ★★★★☆

ROCK-A-DOODLE   u/c

Voices by Glen Campbell, Sandy Duncan (1991)

A disappointing animated movie from ex-Disney animator Don Bluth. It's a sort of chicken homage to Elvis Presley (if such a thing were needed), as rooster Chanticleer (voiced by country singer Campbell of 'Rhinestone Cowboy' fame), falls foul (sorry) of his barnyard pals when he forgets to crow in the morning to make the sun rise, and they realise it rises without him anyway. So Chanticleer heads off to the city, but when it begins to rain and rain some more on the farm (and there's no sign of the sun), some of the animals go off in search of the rambling rooster.

When they get to the city, they discover Chanticleer has become a music phenomenon known as the King, complete with greedy manager, a girlfriend named Goldie and bodyguards. There are some moments of fun in the group's adventures, but the central character comes across as unlikeable rather than cute, and kids are unlikely to be amused (or to get the Elvis allusions). ★★☆☆☆

RUDYARD KIPLING'S THE JUNGLE BOOK

Starring Jason Scott Lee, Cary Elwes, John Cleese (1994)

Anyone expecting a cute and cuddly live-action version of Rudyard Kipling's book along the lines of the animated classic will be in for a bit of a shock when they behold the rippling bare torso of Jason Scott Lee as Mowgli in this adventure. As you've probably gathered, Mowgli is all grown up now, having been reared by wolves and taught the necessities of life by Baloo the bear, and now he learns about girls when he spots a pretty Englishwoman (Lena Headey) strolling through the jungle on safari. He goes with her to the city, she teaches him manners and why it's not polite to growl at people, but her nasty soldier boyfriend (Elwes) is lurking in the background, hoping that Mowgli will lead him to a treasure lost in the jungle.

A luscious interpretation of Kipling's work, this isn't much more faithful than the 1967 cartoon, but it boasts exotic locations, adventure and an impressive mix of animatronic and real animals. Lee is more Tarzan than man-cub, perhaps, but it's an enjoyable adventure that owes much to *Raiders of the Lost Ark* in its climactic scenes (which are a bit intense for young viewers) as Mowgli dodges traps, quicksand and other dangers to save the girl. A stylish but plotless prequel of sorts, *The Second Jungle Book: Mowgli and Baloo*, was released in 1997 but isn't worth searching for. ★★★★☆

THE SECRET OF NIMH

Voices by Derek Jacobi, Elizabeth Hartman, Dom DeLuise (1982)

According to Hollywood gossip, director Don Bluth and fellow animators John Pomeroy and Gary Goldman left their jobs at Disney to make this movie (which the bigwigs at Disney had deemed too dark to be a success). It's certainly not the most commercial animated movie, as based on the Robert C O'Brien book. It's the story of a widow mouse, Mrs Brisby, who seeks the help of a group of rats when her home and children are under threat from a tractor ploughing the field where they live. The rats, it seems, are all escapees from NIMH (National Institute of Mental Health), so are super-intelligent and have built their own underground lair.

Small children may find the plot too complicated and the animation too gloomy (and it's sort of creepy, too), but for everyone else it is a very interesting and beautiful-to-look-at film, with more depth than your average feature-length cartoon. Alas, for Bluth and pals, it wasn't a box-office success, but it is well worth seeking out for a look-over twenty years on. ★★★☆☆

SEE SPOT RUN

Starring David Arquette, Michael Clarke Duncan (2001)

Incredibly dumb doggy comedy that thinks it can coast by on cheap laughs. There's lots of pratfalling for David Arquette as the dopey postal worker who comes into possession of a bull mastiff dog while he is babysitting a cute six-year-old boy (Angus T Jones, now known for the comedy series *Two and a Half Men*), unaware the pooch works for the FBI and is on the run from a mobster (Paul Sorvino) whose drugs he has sniffed out.

It's all an excuse for slapstick stuff (Arquette falling from a drain-pipe and landing in dog poo, that sort of thing) that kids may giggle at while parents may frown at the vulgarity of it all (basically, if you have a problem with fart jokes, you're really going to hate this movie).
★☆☆☆☆

THE SHAGGY DOG

Starring Tim Allen, Kristin Davis, Robert Downey Jr (2006)

A remake of 1959's *The Shaggy Dog*, which starred Fred MacMurray (and which was followed by the 1976 sequel *The Shaggy DA*). Assistant DA Dave Douglas (Allen) spends too much time at work and not enough at home with his wife and two kids. His latest case – about a teacher who may have attacked a scientific lab doing possible animal tests – takes a strange turn when his daughter Carly (Zena Grey) brings home an adorable sheepdog that's escaped from the lab. Little do they know that this is a special dog, stolen from Tibet and rumoured to be a few centuries old, but Dave certainly knows something is up after the dog bites him and he finds himself turning into a canine.

While Tim Allen (when playing human) looks a bit, well, orange (he must have overdone the fake tan), he gives a funny performance as the man who starts yapping and scratching in the middle of court and leaves a parent/teacher meeting when he spies a cat up a tree he just has to chase. Older viewers will figure out the entire story within minutes – Dave, of course, is going to learn much by being a dog in his own household, and will become a better man if he stops scratching his privates and learns to walk upright again – but there are enough laughs to keep all ages amused, some nice special effects (the lab has been creating hybrids, so there's a snake with a fluffy tail that barks etc) and a deliciously comic turn from Downey Jr as the bad guy.
★★★☆☆

SHARK TALE

Voices by Will Smith, Jack Black, Renée Zellweger (2004)

A computer-animated adventure from the same studio, DreamWorks, that made *Shrek*, this is a slick undersea adventure but one that is unlikely to inspire the chuckles of the *Shrek* movies or the warm fuzziness of the film it's most similar to, *Finding Nemo*.

The watery animated design here certainly isn't as gorgeous as *Nemo*, nor is the story as accessible to all ages. It's the tale of a young fish named Oscar (Smith), who wants to be rich and famous and gets his opportunity when a shark who has terrorised the local fish dies in an accident and everyone assumes Oscar actually killed him. Soon Oscar – the 'sharkslayer' – is a big celebrity, complete with swanky underwater penthouse apartment, but it's just a matter of time before his lie is uncovered. That is, until he befriends a timid, vegetarian shark named Lenny (Black) who just may be able to help him keep up the charade.

Adults will enjoy the movie references, from *Jaws* to *Jerry Maguire*, and especially the vocal talent on board, which includes Angelina Jolie as a vampish fish, Zellweger as Oscar's oldest friend, Martin Scorsese as his boss and Robert De Niro as the Mafioso-style leader of the sharks (and Lenny's dad). But will kids understand the numerous Mob movie references that touch on everything from *The Godfather* to *The Sopranos* (a couple of *Sopranos* cast members also lend their voices to minor shark characters)? It's unlikely, but Scorsese's turn as a simpering blowfish will provide some junior laughs even if children have no idea who is doing the voice (or realise that the animators have done a nice job of making the character look like the famous bushy-browed director). Ultimately, this isn't a bad animated family adventure, but it's not a desperately original one either. ★★★☆☆

SPIRIT: STALLION OF THE CIMARRON

Voices by Matt Damon, James Cromwell (2002)

A stunning-to-look-at piece of animation, this is a beautiful film but one in which so much attention has been paid to the details, that kids may be bored by the lack of actual adventure (or dialogue, for that matter – Spirit doesn't talk, we just hear his thoughts via the film's narration). Set in the Old West, it is the story of a stallion (thoughts voiced by Matt Damon) who wants to run free and is helped by a Lakota brave named Little Creek (Daniel Studi) to escape from mean humans.

There's even an equine love story – Spirit falls for mare Rain – but this is mainly worth catching for the animated scenery that's so carefully rendered it looks real. One for older kids, perhaps, and parents should be warned – songs are provided by Bryan Adams. ★★★☆☆

STUART LITTLE

Starring Jonathan Lipnicki, **the voice of** Michael J Fox (1999)

M Night Shyamalan, writer/director of *The Sixth Sense* and *The Village*, co-wrote the screenplay to this adorable mousey movie, based on the E B White book. Mr and Mrs Little (Hugh Laurie and Geena Davis) decide to adopt a baby boy so their son George (Lipnicki) can have a brother. Instead, they come home from the orphanage with Stuart (Fox), a mouse (computer-animated but furrily realistic) who's cute and sweet, but there's one family member who's not impressed – the family cat Snowbell (voiced by Nathan Lane), who plots to get rid of him with the help of mean alley cat Smokey (voiced by Chazz Palminteri).

There isn't much else to the story, but it's told beautifully, thanks to nice performances from the humans (Laurie, Davis and Lipnicki) and funny vocal ones from Fox, Steve Zahn as the dopey Monty the Mouth, and the wonderful Lane, who gets all the best lines. It looks fantastic too, and has a great mix of wit and adventure, with a nice dollop of sentimentality about the importance of family. ★★★★☆

STUART LITTLE 2

Starring Jonathan Lipnicki, **the voice of** Michael J Fox (2002)

A follow-up to the hit *Stuart Little*, this has all the cast (human and otherwise) returning, plus a few additions – the Littles have a new family member, baby Martha, so Stuart the mouse (voiced by Fox) is feeling left out, especially as big brother George (Lipnicki) has a new school pal, too. So when an injured bird named Margalo (voiced by Melanie Griffith) lands in his toy car, Stuart decides she's his new best friend. Unfortunately for Stuart, she's then snatched by the evil Falcon (menacingly spoken by James Woods), so the little mouse, with reluctant cat pal Snowbell (voiced by Nathan Lane) in tow, heads off to rescue her.

A hugely enjoyable family film that's as good – if not better – than the original, this is a colourful adventure, packed with jokes, action and fun and, of course, a show-stopping performance once again from Lane ('Oh, oh! Hairball! Major hairball! And yet we continue to lick ourselves. Unbelievable!'). ★★★★☆

THAT DARN CAT! 🇺 G PG

Starring Hayley Mills, Dean Jones (1965)

One of Disney's family comedies from the sixties, featuring two of its most popular stars. Patti's (Mills) cat, DC, comes home with a wristwatch around his neck that she thinks belongs to a bank worker (Grayson Hall) who has been taken hostage by two robbers. So Patti alerts the FBI, who arrive in the form of dishy Agent Kelso (Jones). His plan is to monitor DC's nightly roamings, in the hope the cat will return to the kidnappers' lair, but it won't be easy, since Kelso is allergic to cats.

It's an old-fashioned, cute comedy that has heaps of slapstick, wit and fun, as well as a pacy plot. There's nice support from Neville Brand and Frank Gorshin (who went on to play the Riddler in the *Batman* TV series) as the robbers, Roddy McDowall, and Elsa Lanchester and William Demarest as the bickering couple next door. Trivia fans should note that, because the film was based on a book written by former FBI agent Gordon Gordon and his wife, the FBI kept a close eye on proceedings during the movie's production, presumably to make sure no FBI secrets were revealed and the Bureau was portrayed in a good light. A 1997 remake, with Christina Ricci, Doug E Doug and Dean Jones, is a faster-paced but dumber alternative to the original. ★★★★☆

VALIANT

Voices by Ewan McGregor, Ricky Gervais (2005)

Ewan McGregor seems to have spent most of 2004 in a recording studio, first delivering the voice of Rodney Copperbottom in *Robots*, and then voicing the hero of this British animated feature. Here, thankfully, he drops the faux-American accent to play a plucky British pigeon who joins the Royal Homing Pigeon Service during the Second World War. This wing (pardon the pun) of the British military actually existed in a sense, as homing pigeons were used to transport messages between the Allied Forces and some were even awarded medals for their dedication to duty.

It's a very British story of bravery and stiff upper beaks as Valiant and his chubby pal Bugsy (voiced by Ricky Gervais) endure six tough weeks of training before they are despatched on their first mission to France. There are bad guys, too, in the form of deadly falcons (one voiced deliciously by Tim Curry), and while adults will get tons of fun from spotting the famous voices (including John Cleese, Jim Broadbent, Olivia Williams, Hugh Laurie and Rik Mayall), younger viewers will be enchanted by the fun story and slick animation – and they may even learn a bit of British history, too. ★★★★☆

THE WILD

Voices by Kiefer Sutherland, James Belushi, Eddie Izzard (2006)

The plot of *Madagascar* is mixed with *Finding Nemo* as dad lion Samson (Sutherland) has to leave the safety of New York Zoo when his son (Greg Cipes) is accidentally shipped to Africa. Of course, Samson has a few sidekicks to help him navigate the mean streets of Manhattan and the even meaner wilds of the jungle, and these come in the wisecracking form of a koala named Nigel (Izzard), Benny the squirrel (Belushi), giraffe Bridget (Janeane Garofalo) and Larry the snake (Richard Kind).

It's all perfectly watchable entertainment for the family, even if the humour is a bit dumb for older viewers (though grown-ups will snigger at William Shatner's delicious vocal performance as the movie's animal bad guy). And while it is very similar to *Madagascar*, *The Wild*'s makers can't be accused of copying as this film was well into production when *Madagascar* was released in 2005. ★★★☆☆

THE YEARLING

Starring Gregory Peck, Jane Wyman (1946)

A true animal weepie, this apparently upset star Jane Wyman's daughter so much when she saw it that she refused to talk to her mother for a fortnight. So get the hankies ready for this lovely tale of a boy named Jody (Claude Jarman Jr, who won a special Oscar for his acting debut) growing up after the American Civil War. His warm father (Peck) lets him adopt a young fawn and keep it as a pet, but his strict mother (Wyman) is less than impressed when, as a yearling, the animal tramples and eats their crops. Oh dear.

A sad story of loss based on Marjorie Kinnan Rawlings's book, this isn't for children who are very easily upset, as it really tugs at the heartstrings all the way through. But it's also incredibly sweet, and well worth the whole box of tissues you'll need to get through it. Originally released as a two-hour movie, a shorter edition was released in the fifties, and also shown on TV. It's not as good, so make sure you watch the longer version for the full (sob) story. ★★★★☆

Fairy Tales, Fantasies and Legends

....

Once upon a time... there was a princess, and a dashing hero. And perhaps a quest. Or a fire-breathing dragon, evil queen or wicked wizard. With fairy tales and legends, the only limit is our imagination – and, on screen, that means we get to sit back and go on a magical journey to exotic-sounding worlds, filled with enchanted forests and populated by mythical creatures, from genies to vampires (cuddly ones, of course) and witches to fairies.

Disney's animators, of course, have done a brilliant job over the years bringing classic stories like *Cinderella*, *Pinocchio* and *The Little Mermaid* to life, and thrilling children of all ages (and adults) with their colourful adventures (parents should note, though, that just because it says Disney on the DVD box doesn't mean it's not scary. Many grown-ups are still traumatised by childhood memories of the wicked witch in *Snow White and the Seven Dwarfs*, for example).

Featured here are those classics, along with many other animated and live-action fantastical movies for kids, perfect for a little girl who wants to imagine she's a princess or a boy who dreams one day he will have the strength of Hercules or the brawn of Sinbad. And for more magical movies (including the *Harry Potter* films), check out the chapter Adaptations.

THE 5000 FINGERS OF DR T   u/c

Starring Peter Lind Hayes, Mary Healy (1953)

An utterly bonkers musical based on a Dr Seuss story (he also wrote original songs for the film), this is the perfect choice if your little one hates his music lessons. For that is the problem that young Bart has – he detests piano lessons with Dr Terwilliker (Hans Conried). But matters get much worse when Bart (Tommy Rettig) falls asleep at the piano and finds himself at the mercy of Dr T, who has set up a school for boys where they have to tinkle the keys all day, every day – if they try to escape, the boys find their way is blocked by an electric fence. And if that wasn't bad enough, Bart's mother has fallen under Dr T's spell and is going to marry him!

With sets so bright you need sunglasses, this film is in no way subtle. It's loud, brash, barmy and not to everyone's taste, but many kids will love the impressive dancing on the drums, the 500-seat piano the boys are forced to play (using the 5000 fingers of the title, of course), and the sheer surrealness of it all. And they'll never moan about those music lessons again, that's for sure. ★★★☆☆

ALADDIN

Voices by Robin Williams, Scott Weinger, Linda Larkin (1992)

Imprisoned in a magic lamp for 10,000 years, the Genie (Williams) is thrilled when young street urchin Aladdin (Weinger) rubs his lamp and sets him free. He grants the boy three wishes – which may come in handy since there's a pretty Sultan's daughter named Jasmine on the loose and an evil adviser to the Sultan (Jafar, voiced by Jonathan Freeman) who schemes to marry her. Throw in a magic carpet that is beautifully animated, a monkey named Abu and the conniving parrot Iago (Gilbert Gottfried) and you have a rip-roaring Arabian Nights adventure.

Of course, the star of the show is comedian Williams, who gives the Genie his personality and storms through the film as if he was performing stand-up. He's zany, funny, breathlessly energetic and just brilliant, even if some of his jokes don't stand the test of time (his impersonations include Arsenio Hall, who wasn't that well known outside the US in 1992 when the film was released, let alone now). There are some fun songs, too, and the sappy ballad 'A Whole New World', sung when Aladdin and Jasmine enjoy a romantic magic carpet ride. The film was followed by two straight-to-video/DVD sequels, *The Return of Jafar* and *Aladdin and the King of Thieves*. ★★★★☆

THE AMAZING MR BLUNDEN

Starring Laurence Naismith, Lynne Frederick (1972)

An enjoyably spooky story for children based on the Antonia Barber novel *The Ghosts*. In 1918 impoverished widow and mother Mrs Allen is visited by the solicitor Mr Blunden (Naismith), who offers her a job as a housekeeper at a run-down country estate. But when her children, Jamie and Lucy (Frederick, five years before she became Peter Sellers's last wife), go exploring through the house and gardens, they discover all is not as it seems. They encounter the ghosts of young Sara and Georgie Latimer, who have travelled forward in time from 1818 to seek their help. It seems their guardians wanted to kill them and it will happen tomorrow (well, tomorrow back in 1818, if you follow) if Jamie and Lucy don't travel back in time to help.

Surprisingly dark for a children's film, this spends quite some time dwelling on death, which may upset smaller viewers. And as Sara and Georgie tell their story, we see their lives in flashback, and it's warts and all – as one recounts how a woman was a ballerina we see the real truth, that she worked in a bawdy dance hall. But if you view this as a pantomime (easily done, as Diana Dors's turn as the Latimers' guardian is over-the-top villainess), it has lots to recommend it to viewers over the age of eight. ★★★★☆

BEAUTY AND THE BEAST

Voices by Robby Benson, Paige O'Hara (1991)

If you're worried your little girl has been watching too many fairy tales in which the leading lady is a damsel in distress waiting to be rescued, then this is the film for you – the closest thing to a feminist movie that Disney animators have made. It's terrific, too – a luscious film packed with beautiful computer-generated backdrops – as modern heroine Belle (O'Hara) strides purposefully through her French village wishing there was more adventure in her life. And of course there soon is, when her father is captured by the Beast (Benson) and Belle volunteers to take dad's place, imprisoned in the shaggy-haired, gruff Beast's castle with only a talking teapot (Mrs Potts, voiced by Angela Lansbury), candelabra, clock and cute little teacup (Chip) for company. That is, unless she can melt the heart of her grumpy host...

Brimming over with fun tunes ('Be Our Guest', 'Gaston') and with a delightful love story at its heart, this is much more than a kids' animated movie, it's a classic for everyone. A straight-to-video sequel, *Beauty and the Beast: The Enchanted Christmas*, was made in 1997 with many of the original vocal cast returning. ★★★★★

BEDKNOBS AND BROOMSTICKS

Starring Angela Lansbury, David Tomlinson (1971)

A fun mix of live action and animation and music clearly aimed at fans of *Mary Poppins* (both films were directed by Robert Stevenson) and based on the books by Mary Norton, who also wrote *The Borrowers*. It's deliciously British stuff (Bruce Forsyth co-stars!), set in England during the Second World War. Three children are evacuated from London and sent to stay with Eglantine Price (Lansbury), an apprentice witch. They are soon taken on a magical adventure (on a flying bed) to find a special spell book, on the way encountering Eglantine's dishonest magical teacher (Tomlinson), a land of talking animals and evil Nazis.

While the live action/animated sequences occasionally look a bit creaky, this has some terrific moments, such as the soccer match between cartoon animals and the first flight of the magical bed. Do note there are two versions of the film – it was cut by half an hour when originally released, but a full-length (139 min) edition was brought out to celebrate the movie's 25th anniversary. ★★★☆☆

THE BLACK CAULDRON

Voices by Grant Bardsley, Susan Sheridan (1985)

Considered one of Disney's darkest animated movies when it was released, *The Black Cauldron* is notable for the presence of a young Tim Burton (the director of *Batman* and *Charlie and the Chocolate Factory*), who worked on the film as a conceptual artist. It's the story of a young boy, Taran (Bardsley), who is charged with protecting a psychic pig (yes, really) named Hen Wen who knows the location of the mystical Black Cauldron. An evil lord named the Horned King (John Hurt) wants it and will do anything to get it, so Taran and his band of friends have to face all manner of creatures to make sure that the Cauldron doesn't fall into the bad guy's hands.

The story of one boy's quest, this has some bleak moments in the tradition of early Disney animated movies (Bambi's mother dying, the scarier bits of *Pinocchio* and *Snow White*) that may not be appropriate for really young viewers. But slightly older kids will be fascinated by the storytelling (as based on the first two books of Lloyd Alexander's *The Chronicles of Prydain*), while adults will enjoy discovering one of Disney's lesser-known animated movies. ★★★☆☆

CINDERELLA

Voices by Ilene Woods, Verna Felton (1950)

The ultimate little girl fantasy, *Cinderella* was given the Disney animated treatment back in 1950 and is just as lovely over half a century later. Cinderella (Woods) lives with her heartless stepmother and equally nasty stepsisters, Anastasia and Drizella. They're both intending to throw themselves at Prince Charming (voiced by fifties sci-fi star William Phipps) at an upcoming ball, but it is Cinders (thanks to a trusty fairy godmother (Felton), a pumpkin that turns into a coach and a bit of 'Bibbidi-bobbidi-boo') who wins his heart but then has to dash home by midnight, leaving her glass slipper behind.

Walt Disney added cute animals to the original 17th-century story and they're a sweet addition, including the birds who help Cinderella dress and the cat, Lucifer, who is after them, and there are lots of memorable songs throughout too, like 'A Dream is a Wish Your Heart Makes' and, of course, 'Cinderella'. Unlike *Snow White* or *Pinocchio*, there aren't any creepy moments that could bother little viewers – in fact it's just completely yummy. (A belated sequel, *Cinderella II: Dreams Come True*, was made for DVD in 2002. In fact, it's three short films linked together by the fairy godmother's wishes, which should appeal to little girls.) ★★★★★

CLASH OF THE TITANS   PG PG

Starring Harry Hamlin, Laurence Olivier (1981)

Yes, this is an incredibly kitsch adventure from 1981, but that doesn't make it any less enjoyable. It's based on the Greek myth of god Zeus (Olivier), who has a human son, Perseus (Hamlin, more wooden than a dining table and chairs). Perseus has fallen in love with Andromeda

(Judi Bowker), but there's a curse, an offended goddess Thetis (Maggie Smith) and many trials and tribulations to deal with before he can cast aside his sword, sandals and toga and settle down with her.

It's daft stuff that is especially loved by little boys as Perseus battles the evil Medusa (with her head of snakes), captures winged horse Pegasus and faces the Kraken monster, all depicted using stop-motion special effects by Ray Harryhausen. They are creaky in terms of 21st-century computer-generated wizardry, and the story takes some liberties with Greek mythology (a mechanical owl who guides Perseus was made up just for the film), but it's cracking stuff, and adults can enjoy spotting the who's who of British actors (Olivier, Smith, Claire Bloom, Sian Phillips, Tim Piggott-Smith) who play the legendary characters with tongues firmly planted in cheeks. ★★★☆☆

DARBY O'GILL AND THE LITTLE PEOPLE

Starring Albert Sharpe, Sean Connery (1959)

Anyone who thinks that Sean Connery is the coolest man on the planet (and, let's face it, as Bond he was) should check out his decidedly uncool performance (he sings!) in this delightful family film. Brimming with so many Irish clichés you'll feel you've bathed in Guinness, it was actually a pet project of Walt Disney's following a visit to the Emerald Isle in 1948 during which he declared he was going to make a movie about Little People. (And a decade later, with this, he did.)

Ageing Darby (Sharpe) is about to be replaced by strapping young Michael (Connery) as the caretaker of a big estate, but when he falls down a well, Darby ends up in the kingdom of leprechauns and the diminutive little fellows grant him three wishes that could help him provide for himself and his daughter. This is a load of old-fashioned blarney, of course, but beautifully filmed (on location in Ireland) and cleverly made (to make the leprechauns look little in comparison to Darby, the film-makers used 'forced perspective' – putting the leprechaun actors far in the background to make them appear smaller). Connery is a treat as the romantic lead and, Hollywood legend has it, Cubby Broccoli's wife saw him in this role and told her husband he was the most handsome man she had ever seen, leading to Connery's casting in the Broccoli-produced *Dr No*. ★★★★☆

THE DARK CRYSTAL

Voices by Jim Henson, Frank Oz (1982)

Muppet creators Henson and Oz made their first non-Muppet movie here, a dark fantasy epic that should appeal to fans of *The Lord of the Rings*. Scary (and they really are) flying creatures, the Skeksis, rule the land. But there has been a prophecy that a small creature, a Gelfling, could end their rule, so the Skeksis have killed them all. Or so they think. A young Gelfling orphan, raised in secret by mystics, embarks on a quest to find part of the crystal that gives the Skeksis their power so order can be restored to the universe.

Stunning to look at, this is one of the most impressive uses of puppetry on film, and deserved to be a bigger hit than it was when it was released in 1982. There were, perhaps, two reasons it wasn't a success – it was released the same year as the phenomenally successful *ET*, and also there are violent and disturbing moments that make the film inappropriate for smaller children. Nonetheless, for older viewers who like sorcery and fantasy lands, this is definitely worth a look. ★★★☆☆

DRAGONHEART

Starring Dennis Quaid, David Thewlis (1996)

Bowen (Quaid) is a disenchanted knight who roams the countryside aimlessly until he teams up with the last of the great dragons, Draco (voiced by Sean Connery). The pair con locals by performing a fake dragon-slaying act on villages, until their consciences get the better of them and they realise there is a greater foe – King Einon (Thewlis), whose life Draco once saved but who now rules the kingdom harshly.

A fun old-fashioned yarn about knights, honour and adventure, this is a terrific romp for everyone involved – Quaid is deliciously gruff, while Connery's mannerisms are expertly captured in the face of the 18ft-high dragon. The film features nice supporting performances from Jason Isaacs and Pete Postlethwaite (as a monk with a penchant for bad acting) and a menacing one from Thewlis as the evil king (perhaps too menacing for very young viewers). It's not tremendously sophisticated, but there are laughs and adventure to be had (and keep the tissues handy for a weepy moment near the end). ★★★☆☆

DRAGONHEART: A NEW BEGINNING

Starring Chris Masterson, Robby Benson (2000)

A straight-to-DVD sequel to *Dragonheart*, without Dennis Quaid, Sean Connery or, well, virtually anyone involved in the original. Stable boy Geoff (*Malcolm in the Middle*'s Masterson) dreams of being a knight, so when he finds the last living dragon, Drake (voiced by Benson), it looks like his dream may come true. However, there's an evil lord who wants Drake's magic, and only Geoff and two Chinese warriors, Kwan and Lian, can protect him.

This follow-up to the enjoyable first movie is more little-kid friendly, but anyone older will be put off by the cheap special effects (the dragon looks like a cartoon) and lack of charisma of the stars. There's none of the banter there was between Quaid and Connery in the original, while the 'evil' Lord Osric (Harry Van Gorkum) is about as scary as cold custard. Only some martial-arts scenes perk the movie up at all. ★☆☆☆☆

DRAGONSLAYER

Starring Peter MacNicol, Ralph Richardson (1981)

Because this movie was made by Disney, parents expected it to be a warm and fuzzy adventure when it was first released in 1981. It's more of a sword-and-sorcery affair that should appeal to Dungeons and Dragons fans but probably isn't suitable for the under-tens (the dragon's pretty nasty).

The King of Urland has kept peace in his land by making a deal with a dragon – the dragon leaves his kingdom alone in return for the occasional virgin sacrifice (another reason why you may not want younger children to watch this!). Wizard Ulrich (Richardson) may be the only one to stop the ritual, but he is killed, so his inexperienced apprentice Galen (MacNicol) decides it is up to him to destroy the dragon alone.

Filmed in what seems to be a landscape made up entirely of mud, this is less 'pretty' than many mythical screen adventures, but what it lacks in glamour it makes up for in edge-of-the-seat moments when the dragon is finally revealed, flames firing from its angry mouth. ★★★☆☆

DUNGEONS AND DRAGONS

Starring Jeremy Irons, Justin Whalin (2000)

Widely regarded as one of the worst films of 2000 (you have been warned), this fantasy adventure is based on the popular role-playing board game of the same name. Which seems a bit of a dumb movie-making decision – surely all the kids into D&D are going to be too busy playing the game at home to bother going out to see a movie version? To make matters worse, it was something of a labour of love for director Courtney Solomon, who bought the movie rights to the game when he was nineteen and then spent more than a decade raising funds and support to get it made. Only to hear that everyone wishes he hadn't bothered.

The story is set in the land of Izmer, where sixteen-year-old Savina (Thora Birch) has inherited the throne. She's overthrown by nasty Profion (Irons), though, and only a magical rod that can control red dragons will save her. For some reason she puts her faith in two bumbling thieves (Whalin and Marlon Wayans), who have to retrieve it before Profion finds it. And that's about it, once you throw in some clichés, politics, dull dialogue, duller action, a bonkers performance from Irons that's silly rather than scary and a wetter-than-an-April-shower one from Whalin (better known as Jimmy in the TV series *Lois & Clark: The New Adventures of Superman*). ★☆☆☆

THE EMPEROR'S NEW GROOVE

Voices by David Spade, John Goodman (2000)

One of Disney's lesser successes – and the first Disney animated movie to feature a pregnant woman, fact fans – this was actually intended to be a big-budget, epic animated musical with a score by Sting called *Kingdom of the Sun*. When a portion that had been completed was shown to audiences, it wasn't well received though, so the animators literally went back to the drawing board and changed the film to this lighter comedy (some of Sting's music remains on the soundtrack).

Comedian David Spade provides the voice of Kuzco, a spoiled young emperor who is turned into a llama by sorceress Yzma (Eartha Kitt). Abandoned in the jungle, Kuzco the llama is befriended by llama-herder Pacha (Goodman), whom Kuzco, when he was human, was going to evict from his home with his family (it's Pacha's missus who is with child) so he could build a bigger swimming pool. It's all far more slapstick and silly than you expect from a Disney animated movie, mainly thanks to a fun character called Kronk (voiced by Patrick Warburton of *Seinfeld* fame) and some nicely timed gags that should amuse both young and older viewers. ★★★☆☆

ESCAPE TO WITCH MOUNTAIN

Starring Eddie Albert, Ray Milland (1975)

A live-action success for Disney, this has all the key ingredients for a children's adventure – orphans in peril, an evil man and his hench-man, mystery, magical powers and the gruff old guy with a heart of gold. As the title suggests, young Tony and Tia are escaping said bad guy (a millionaire who wants to exploit their psychic powers) and heading towards a mountain that may hold the secret to who they really are.

Based on the Alexander Key novel, it's an enjoyable (rather than tense) adventure that romps along thanks to some not-bad-for-the-seventies special effects and nice performances from Kim Richards and Ike Eisenmann as the kids, and a grown-up cast that includes Milland (as the rich evil guy), Donald Pleasence (his henchman) and Albert. A pretty awful sequel, *Return from Witch Mountain*, followed in 1978 with the kids returning alongside Bette Davis (yes, really) and Christopher Lee. And Ike Eisenmann made (and starred in) a short film called *The Blair Witch Mountain Project* in 2002, a spoof of *The Blair Witch Project* in which a reporter attempts to find Tia and Tony. ★★★☆☆

EVER AFTER

Starring Drew Barrymore, Anjelica Huston, Dougray Scott (1998)

A sort-of modern reworking of the Cinderella legend that's set in 16th-century France, but boasts a thoroughly modern spunky heroine (Barrymore's Danielle) who hits her prince (Scott) in the head with an apple and reads Thomas More's *Utopia* in her spare time.

While there's no fairy godmother (the role of matchmaker is taken by Patrick Godfrey's Leonardo da Vinci) or wand-waving magic, this is still an enchanting tale for kids that looks absolutely luscious and has a nice grown-up sense of humour (much of it in Huston's performance as Danielle's bitch of a stepmother) that makes it as much of a hit with adults as the young girls it was aimed at. ★★★★☆

FAIRYTALE: A TRUE STORY

Starring Harvey Keitel, Peter O'Toole (1997)

An utterly adorable tale, loosely based on the true story of two little girls at the beginning of the 20th century who caused controversy when they produced photos they said proved the existence of fairies. Here, during the First World War, young Frances (Elizabeth Earl), whose father is missing in action, goes to live with her cousin Elsie (Florence Hoath) and the pair discover fairies in the garden and photograph them to show Frances's parents. Their evidence leads them to London, where they are championed by none other than Harry Houdini (Keitel) and Sir Arthur Conan Doyle (O'Toole).

A film about belief and faith rather than twinkly winged creatures, this is truly moving and sweet for children and adults, and is jam-packed with terrific actors, including Paul McGann, Bob Peck, Peter Mullan, Bill Nighy and, in an uncredited performance, Mel Gibson. A must-see (with tissues in hand, of course). ★★★★☆

FANTASIA

Narrated by Deems Taylor (1940)

Made in 1940, *Fantasia* remains one of Disney's most ambitious animated movies. It's actually a series of interpretations of pieces of classical music, some surreal, some fantastical. 'The Sorcerer's Apprentice' is perhaps the best known, as Mickey Mouse borrows a magic hat and animates a broom to carry water for him, only to have things get out of control when the broom won't stop. There's also 'The Nutcracker Suite', featuring dancing fairies and animals, 'Dance of the Hours', featuring the trippy dancing hippos, and 'Toccata and Fugue in D Minor', in which an orchestra's instruments come to life, among others.

Anyone who was a teenager during the sixties and seventies may remember this movie's reputation as one best enjoyed, shall we say, under the influence of illegal substances. It is certainly bizarre, and probably not the first choice for most children who, while they may

find the animation interesting, will probably be bored by the lack of story. That said, it's a fascinating look at what Disney animators could do, and might be a way of introducing kids to classical music without having to sit in a draughty concert hall. And if they like this, there is also a sequel, *Fantasia 2000*, which includes animation set to Gershwin's 'Rhapsody in Blue' and Elgar's 'Pomp and Circumstance'.
★★★★☆

FERNGULLY: THE LAST RAINFOREST

Voices by Tim Curry, Samantha Mathis, Christian Slater (1992)

An eco-friendly animated adventure doesn't sound very enjoyable, but actually it's pretty sweet, especially as the environmental message isn't bludgeoned into the viewer's consciousness at every available opportunity.

Zak's (Jonathan Ward) job is to mow down vegetation, but he soon learns what he is doing is wrong when a cutesy fairy named Crysta (Mathis) shrinks him to her size and shows him what damage he and his big human hands have been doing. Unfortunately, it isn't just humans who are causing trouble, so Zak, Crysta and a bat named Batty (voiced by Robin Williams) also have to do battle with the evil spirit Hexxus (Curry), who is quite happy for the fairies' home of FernGully to be demolished.

It's quite entertaining stuff, with good vocal performances from the cast (Curry and Williams especially) and lush animation that should keep kids entertained while they unwittingly absorb the eco-message. A video sequel, *FernGully 2: The Magical Rescue*, followed in 1997, but with none of the original voice cast and only half as much charm.
★★★☆☆

THE GOLDEN VOYAGE OF SINBAD

Starring John Phillip Law, Caroline Munro (1974)

A follow-up (more than a decade later) to *The 7th Voyage of Sinbad*, this was, so the movie posters said, filmed in Dynarama – basically a fancy word for Ray Harryhausen's terrific stop-motion special effects ('stop motion' being the trick where film-makers shoot a single frame as if they are using a still camera, and then another and another, altering the position of the creature a little between each shot to make it look as if it is moving). The bad guy this time is sorcerer Koura (Tom Baker, in a pre-*Dr Who* performance), who is after the same amulet that Sinbad is looking for.

Kids will enjoy the creatures and battles – especially a terrific scene in which the six-armed statue of Kali comes to life and engages Sinbad in a sword fight – though knuckle-chewing moments with the griffin and a one-eyed centaur mean this is most suitable for the over-nines. Watch out for Bond girl Caroline Munro and a young Martin Shaw (of TV's *The Professionals*) in the mainly British cast. ★★☆☆☆

GRIMM BROTHERS' SNOW WHITE (AKA SNOW WHITE: A TALE OF TERROR) 15 R u/c

Starring Sigourney Weaver, Sam Neill, Monica Keena (1997)

The classic fairy tale of Snow White and her seven vertically challenged pals gets a decidedly un-Disney reworking in this grown-up drama that's not for the under-twelves. Gone are the cutesy dwarfs – replaced by a group of disfigured outsiders who risk their lives mining for the gold they need to survive – and instead of an evil queen who's wicked just for the sake of it, we have a beautiful woman (Weaver), twisted and bitter following a gruesome miscarriage, who finds refuge in black magic when she believes her husband (Neill) loves his daughter Lilli (Keena) more than her.

While the 15th-century Black Forest setting is all dense, dark trees and atmospheric flickering candles, this never quite gets beyond slightly creepy, despite a deliciously seething performance from Sigourney Weaver. Director Michael Cohn may have been trying for a *Company of Wolves*-style bloody fairy tale to have grown-ups hiding behind their seats, but instead he's made a nicely acted, beautifully photographed but ultimately small-screen version of a well-loved tale, best suited to a rainy night in front of the telly. ★★★☆☆

HANS CHRISTIAN ANDERSEN

Starring Danny Kaye, Farley Granger (1952)

A film that admits straight away it's not really the biography of fairy-tale writer Hans Christian Andersen (Kaye), this is actually an entertaining but completely fictional family musical that showcases some of his best-known stories. A must for little girls (it features a Little Mermaid ballet that's just adorable and a love story with Hans and a ballerina that may put little boys off), it's packed with songs that should enchant little ones and spark memories in grown-ups.

Hans is a cobbler with a gift for spinning a yarn who makes it big in Copenhagen but then is scuppered when he falls in love with an unattainable dancer. But forget the subplot, it's his stories that are enjoyable here, such as Thumbelina and the Ugly Duckling, and their songs, especially 'Inchworm', a short little chant about numbers which parents should tape and play back to any kids who are learning their mathematical tables. ★★★★☆

HERCULES

Voices by Tate Donovan, Danny DeVito, James Woods (1997)

The classic Greek myth of super-strong Hercules gets the Disney animated treatment, and while it's not among the studio's best, it's nonetheless a fun adventure. Hercules (Donovan) is the son of god Zeus (Rip Torn). He's born immortal but sent to live on earth as a human and to battle terrible monsters like the Hydra, the Cyclops and the Titans.

For adults, the most interesting elements here are the characters, based on the drawings of Gerald Scarfe, and the digs at merchandising – when Hercules becomes a hero, Herculade, air-Hercs and a Hercules doll ('you know you're a real hero when you get your own action figure') go on sale. Kids, meanwhile, will enjoy the movie's humour and the scary-but-not-too-scary bits, such as the arrival of Hades, the god of the Underworld (as voiced by Woods), whose flaming hair changes colour depending on how mad he is, and the monsters who use fire and ice to destroy the earth. It's cheerful nonsense (the Greek legend isn't adhered to too closely, for starters), packed with fun and songs performed by the muses, a soulful group of gals who perform like animated Supremes. A TV series followed, and a feature, *Hercules: Zero to Hero*, which is actually three episodes put together. ★★★☆☆

HOCUS POCUS

Starring Bette Midler, Sarah Jessica Parker, Kathy Najimy (1993)

It's not often you come across a Disney family film in which the main characters suck the life out of children. But that's what witches Winifred (Midler), Sarah (Parker) and Mary (Najimy) did in 1693 that caused them to be sentenced to death by the people of Salem. And now, three centuries later, young Max has found and lit the black candle that brings them back to life. Oops.

Of course, while this is surprisingly dark for a Disney movie, many kids will like it for just that. As Max and his pals try to find a way to stop the witches, Midler, Parker and Najimy have a ball, flying around on vacuum cleaners, cackling at all and sundry and spouting fun dialogue (Midler: 'You know, I've always wanted a child. And now I think I'll have one... on toast!'). There's not much else to the plot, although grown-ups should note that if they haven't discussed the birds and the bees with their kids yet, it may come up after watching this, since it turns out the reason Max was able to revive the witches from the dead is that the black candle required a virgin to light it for the magic to work. ★★★☆☆

HOODWINKED

Voices by Anne Hathaway, Glenn Close, Jim Belushi (2005)

Ever wondered what really happened in the story of Little Red Riding Hood? Well, this computer-animated adventure attempts to put a modern twist on the fairytale (à la Shrek). It begins as police storm a cabin in the woods and arrest spunky teen Red (Hathaway), a wolf (Patrick Warburton), Granny (Close) and a confused, axe-wielding Woodsman (Belushi). It seems a bandit has been stealing recipes from the people and creatures of the forest, and one of these four could be the culprit.

So we learn about the events that led the four to the cabin from each one's perspective. This starts off fun, as Red's adventure involves a bonkers singing goat, an exploding cable car and a rollercoaster adventure on a mountain, but by the time we see what the wolf, woodsman and Granny have been up to (although there are some laughs as she's a grey-haired old dear addicted to extreme sports) it's all worn a little thin. There are some good jokes, some predictable ones, a few unnecessary musical moments, and a general air of cheekiness that will amuse even if there is nothing much new on display to impress. ★★★☆☆

HOWL'S MOVING CASTLE

Voices by Chieko Baisho, Takuya Kimura (2004)

Another beautiful animated feature from Hayao Miyazaki, who made the Oscar-winning and quite marvellous *Spirited Away*.

Young Sophie is transformed by a jealous witch into an old hag, so she flees town and heads for the wizard Howl's castle. Once there, she is drawn into a bizarre world, caught between two kingdoms at war and the enigmatic Howl himself, who seems to be fighting for both sides. Based on the novel by Welsh author Diana Wynne Jones, this isn't as magical as Miyazaki's previous film, but nonetheless is fascinating as you try to puzzle your way through the movie's surreal landscapes and head-scratching plot twists. One for both adults and children, who often understand more of what's going on so can explain it to the grown-ups. (Note that the film is available with English subtitles or in a dubbed version featuring the voices of Lauren Bacall, Billy Crystal and Christian Bale.) ★★★★☆

THE INDIAN IN THE CUPBOARD

Starring Hal Scardino, Litefoot (1995)

Young Omri (Scardino) gets more than he bargained for on his ninth birthday – one gift, a small cupboard, turns out to be magic, and when Omri places a small plastic toy Indian inside, it comes alive. Unfortunately, when Omri's pal Patrick discovers the secret, he pops a cowboy doll (David Keith) in the cupboard, which probably isn't the best idea.

The idea of toys or games coming to life is always an interesting one

– be it in the noisy, special-effects-heavy *Jumanji* or the slightly subtler *Small Soldiers*. Here it is delivered in a quiet and perhaps even creepy way (it's upsetting to see the tiny Indian, obviously frightened by his transformation and the giant-sized boy in front of him), which may not enthral younger children, while older ones may find the ultimate message of being good to others a bit preachy. A shame, because the film has its heart in the right place and features two great performances from Keith and Litefoot (a former rap artist) as the mini-men. ★★★☆☆

INTO THE WEST

Starring Gabriel Byrne, Ellen Barkin (1992)

An Irish family adventure written by Jim Sheridan, this starts off as fairly gritty stuff (not surprisingly, as Sheridan is better known for grim fare like *My Left Foot* and *In the Name of the Father*) and ends up as an utterly enchanting fable. Two young brothers, Ossie and Tito, live in grim Dublin slums with their dad, Papa Reilly (Byrne). He was once a traveller (gypsy), but following the death of his wife he has decided to stay in the same place and drown his sorrows. The kids, meanwhile, are shown a beautiful white horse by their grandpa, and when the police take it away, they decide to steal back the creature – which they believe is magical and born of the sea.

Directed by Mike Newell (*Four Weddings and a Funeral*), this is a lyrical tale that never gets bogged down in sentimentality, as the boys come to terms with their mother's death. Byrne is terrific as the boys' dad, and Ellen Barkin (Byrne's wife at the time) gives a good performance as the gypsy who helps him on his quest to track down his on-the-run kids. Just lovely. ★★★★☆

JASON AND THE ARGONAUTS

Starring Todd Armstrong, Honor Blackman (1963)

Made back in 1963, this *Boy's Own* fantasy adventure is best remembered for the effects by stop-motion genius Ray Harryhausen, who also worked on *Clash of the Titans* and *The 7th Voyage of Sinbad*. According to Greek mythology, Jason (Armstrong) cannot claim the throne of Thessaly until he returns with the magical Golden Fleece.

So off he sails with the brave Argonauts to do battle with whoever crosses their path on their way to retrieve it.

Very young viewers would probably be scared by creatures such as the seven-headed Hydra, but young boys who love sword-and-sandal epics will thrill at the army of skeletons Jason has to battle and adults will be pretty impressed as well – it still looks great today and remains Harryhausen's most impressive special effect from all his films. ★★★★☆

LABYRINTH

Starring David Bowie, Jennifer Connelly (1986)

Jim Henson, of *The Muppets* and *Sesame Street* fame, directed this fantastical adventure. Sarah (Connelly) is a sixteen-year-old girl, annoyed that she has to look after her younger brother Toby. So she wishes goblins would come and take the baby away… and they actually do. Realising she has to rescue him, Sarah has to bargain with the evil goblin king Jareth (Bowie) – if she can navigate his puzzle-filled labyrinth within thirteen hours, he will give Toby back.

Filled with impressive creatures, this is a jaw-dropping movie to look at, as Henson's puppets roam the fairy-tale landscapes (Connelly and Bowie are the only 'humans' in the film). There's plenty of adventure (although a masked ball scene slows things down a bit) and scary moments (smaller kids – and mums! – may find the whole idea of a kidnapped baby upsetting to begin with), while adults are more likely to be frightened by Bowie's naff accompanying soundtrack (including 'Underground' and 'As the World Falls Down'). ★★★☆☆

THE LAST UNICORN

Voices by Jeff Bridges, Mia Farrow, Christopher Lee, Alan Arkin (1982)

Based on the novel by Peter Beagle, this is the story of a unicorn (Farrow) who believes she may be the last of her kind. She sets out in search of any other unicorns, and while she has the help of apprentice magician Schmendrick (Arkin) and Prince Lir (Bridges), she also has an enemy – the vicious Red Bull (which may provoke sniggers from viewers familiar with the canned drink of the same name), who was conjured up by grumpy King Haggard (Lee) to rid the kingdom of unicorns.

It's a lovely, melancholy story, but the film isn't as enchanting as it should be, thanks to lacklustre animation and some very naff songs. Little viewers probably won't mind, but older ones should probably wait for the new, live-action version of the story (in which Lee and Farrow appear, Lee reprising his original role), which is due for release in 2007. ★★☆☆☆

LEGEND

Starring Tom Cruise, Mia Sara, Tim Curry (1985)

This definitely isn't for kids of every age (if you think *The Lord of the Rings* is too grown-up for your children, then so is this), but young teens and adults who enjoy mythical adventures should check it out, especially as it is directed by visual genius Ridley Scott (*Gladiator*, *Blade Runner*). It's a strange film that suffers from the miscasting of a young bucktoothed Tom Cruise in the lead as Jack, a young hero living on earth at a time long ago when unicorns roamed the land. An evil prince named Darkness (Curry) wants to blot out the sun for ever, which he can do if he kills the last unicorns with the help of Jack's virginal but corruptible love, Princess Lili (Sara).

Beautiful to look at as Tom and Mia frolic in luscious green forests while fairies, trolls and elves pass by, the film gets blacker as Darkness takes his hold and is altogether pretty creepy when Curry appears in full make-up and horns. Often criticised as being an exercise in style over substance – and it *is* stunning to look at – this is nonetheless an interesting fable, nicely played by Curry and Sara, even if Cruise is awkward throughout. ★★★☆☆

LILO & STITCH

Voices by Daveigh Chase, Chris Sanders (2002)

A fun animated comedy fantasy adventure from Disney that was a deserved hit among younger viewers (the under-tens will love this the most – parents may find the characters a bit irritating). It's the story of the friendship between cute little Hawaiian Lilo (Chase) and naughty alien Stitch (Sanders), but it also manages to touch on serious issues such as the threat of Lilo being taken into care and the message that everyone (including ETs, it seems) is created equal.

Of course, little viewers probably won't notice all that and instead will just be enchanted by the duo's fun adventures, the lush animation and Stitch's cheeky behaviour. A straight-to-DVD sequel, *Stitch! The Movie* (2003), and a TV spin-off series followed and are a must for fans. ★★★★☆

THE LITTLE MERMAID

Voices by Jodi Benson, Christopher Daniel Barnes (1989)

After more than two decades of lacklustre animated movies, Disney was back on form in 1989 with this magical film based on the much-loved Hans Christian Andersen fairy tale. Mermaid Ariel (Benson), the daughter of King Triton, secretly wants to be human. She falls for the dashing Prince Eric (Barnes) after she rescues him from a shipwreck and, in order to experience life on land, agrees to give her voice to the nasty sea witch Ursula, in exchange for a pair of human legs. There's a catch, of course – she can be human for three days, but if she does not receive the kiss of true love from Eric in that time, Ariel will be Ursula's slave for ever.

While this sounds like a sappy love story only little girls would love, it's actually surprisingly fun, thanks to slapstick moments throughout and a cast of quirky supporting characters, including Sebastian the crab and Flounder the fish. The music's terrific too, and it won't just be smaller viewers humming along to 'Kiss the Girl' or the calypso 'Under the Sea' by the end. (There is a passable straight-to-video sequel, *The Little Mermaid II: Return to the Sea* (2000), which features the adventures of Ariel's daughter.) ★★★☆☆

THE LITTLE VAMPIRE

Starring Jonathan Lipnicki, Richard E Grant (2000)

That cute little munchkin from *Jerry Maguire* and *Stuart Little*, Jonathan Lipnicki, is Tony, the Californian poppet who can't quite settle in his new Scottish home until a young vampire boy flies in through his window and befriends him. It seems the fanged Rudolph (Rollo Weeks) and his family are being hunted by the nasty Rookery (Jim Carter), but if they can get their hands on a special stone (with Tony's help, of course), they can be turned back into mortals.

Based on a series of German children's books, this is fun stuff for kids over the age of eight (younger ones may not like watching vampires drink, even if it is from cows), who will love all the 'horror' aspects (though it isn't scary) like coffins, stakes, the aforementioned bovine blood-drinking and other such ghoulishness. Lipnicki is a cutie, and there's terrific support from Alice Krige and Richard E Grant as Rudolph's parents. ★★★★☆

LOCH NESS 🔺 PG 🔺

Starring Ted Danson, Joely Richardson (1996)

Actually made for US television (and at the time, with a budget of $12 million, it was one of the most expensive TV movies ever made), this has zoologist Dr Dempsey (Danson) attempting to prove that the Loch Ness monster really does exist. He becomes involved with local innkeeper Laura (Richardson), and begins to believe there really may be a creature nestling in the Scottish loch, and that the secrets of Nessie's existence are actually being protected by locals.

With effects from Jim Henson's Creature Shop (the team behind the Muppets, *Labyrinth* and other fantastical movies) you'd expect this to be terrific. Unfortunately, far too much time is spent on Laura and Dempsey's budding romance, and not enough on what's lurking under the water (and when you do get to see something, it's only fleetingly). Kids will be bored while adults will want to gag at the sheer niceness of it all. ★★☆☆☆

MULAN 🔺 G 🔺

Voices by Eddie Murphy, Ming-Na Wen, Pat Morita (1998)

An unusual choice for Disney's animators, *Mulan* is based on the popular Chinese legend of a young girl (voiced by *ER*'s Ming-Na Wen) who assumes male identity so she can run off and join the Chinese army and fight for her country against the evil Huns.

Of course, this being Disney, there has to be a cuddly creature in there somewhere, and here it's in the form of Mushu, a mini-dragon voiced by Murphy (practising his voiceover skills a few years before his movie-stealing performance as Donkey in *Shrek*). Unfortunately, even his wisecracks can't brighten up what is otherwise a lacklustre and predictable tale that is virtually devoid of the trademark Disney tunes that could have perked things up a bit. Technically terrific, but kids aren't likely to be amused. ★★☆☆☆

THE NEVERENDING STORY

Starring Barret Oliver, Noah Hathaway (1984)

This movie's proper title is *Die Unendliche Geschichte*, as it's based on Bavarian author Michael Ende's novel, partly filmed in Germany and directed by Wolfgang (*Troy*, *In the Line of Fire*) Petersen (his first English-language movie). It looks glossy and American though (and features a Giorgio Moroder theme song, sung by eighties British pop star Limahl), and boasts some impressive special effects, sure to impress the young kids it is aimed at.

Chased by bullies, ten-year-old Bastian (Oliver) hides in a second-hand bookshop where the owner shows him an old book that he describes as dangerous – once you enter the book's fantasy world you can't escape. Of course, Bastian takes no notice, 'borrows' the book and starts to read it in the school attic, only to discover he has soon become a part of the land (Fantasia) and the adventures of Atreyu (Hathaway), a boy charged with saving Fantasia from destruction.

While parents may be slightly concerned that the movie's protagonist plays truant and steals in the first half-hour, overall this is a well-meaning, spirited adventure packed with giant turtles, wolves, snails and the big floppy-eared Luckdragon that kids will enjoy. ★★★☆☆

THE NEVERENDING STORY II: THE NEXT CHAPTER

Starring Jonathan Brandis, Kenny Morrison (1990)

While the original *NeverEnding Story* only covered about half of the Michael Ende book on which is was based, this sequel doesn't pick up the rest of the book's story but instead is a completely new adventure concerning some of the same characters. Young Bastian (Brandis) returns to the storybook world of Fantasia, finding it in an even worse state than it was before, so he joins forces with Atreyu (Morrison) to find the Childlike Empress (Alexandra Johnes). Unfortunately, our

Fairy Tales, Fantasies and Legends

young hero falls under the spell of the evil Xayide (Clarissa Burt) along the way, and his actions could actually be making things worse.

Filled with splashy special effects (including some beetle-like giant creatures that could disturb younger viewers – or anyone with a dislike for creepy-crawlies, for that matter), this looks impressive but doesn't have the interesting storyline of the first movie (in this one Bastian just drops into the book, whereas in Part I there was the more menacing feeling he was being drawn in and merged with it). A further sequel, *The NeverEnding Story III*, was made in 1994 but even fans of the series thought it was dreadful and it is only notable now for an early performance from *School of Rock* star Jack Black. ★★☆☆☆

THE PAGEMASTER

Starring Macaulay Culkin, Christopher Lloyd (1994)

Young Richard (Culkin) is a little boy frightened of everything, having calculated the possibility of having an accident for just about every childish activity you can think of. One day a storm breaks and he ends up seeking shelter in a strange library, and a bump to his head takes him into an animated world of books. The Pagemaster (Lloyd) can help him to escape, but first he has to experience adventures in literature in which he meets such characters as Long John Silver and Dr Jekyll.

A mixture of live action and animation, this scores points for being a movie that encourages kids to pick up a book once in a while. It's packed with recognisable voices as Richard goes on his literary journey, from Patrick Stewart (as Adventure) to Whoopi Goldberg (Fantasy) and Leonard Nimoy (Dr Jekyll and Mr Hyde). But it's also a bit dreary, thanks to some uninspired, dull animation, so while there's a good message (books are fun!), many viewers may not stay awake long enough to notice it. ★★☆☆☆

PETE'S DRAGON

Starring Helen Reddy, Mickey Rooney, Shelley Winters (1977)

Live action and animation are combined for this 1977 musical tale of a cuddly green dragon named Elliott (voiced by Charlie Callas) and a young boy who befriends him, Pete (Sean Marshall). Very young children may find the story a little scary – Pete has to escape from a nasty family to whom he's been sold into slavery and a travelling medicine man (Jim Dale) wants to capture Elliott and put him on display – but there is fun stuff, too, especially when Elliott makes himself invisible and causes chaos in the town.

It has dated somewhat – and most kids familiar with *Who Framed Roger Rabbit* and other live-action and animated adventures will have seen the blend done better – but younger viewers may at least think the dragon is cute. ★★☆☆☆

PINOCCHIO

Voices by Mel Blanc, Dickie Jones (1940)

A Disney animated classic from 1940, this one's a true weepie. Old man Geppetto makes a wooden puppet boy, but Pinocchio wants to be a real boy. The Blue Fairy grants his wish, and appoints Jiminy Cricket to be his conscience. But when Geppetto sends Pinocchio off to school, he is seduced away by two villains who sell him to a travelling circus. Could things get any worse? Oh yes, as Pinocchio is kidnapped and taken to an island where bad little boys are turned into donkeys, while Geppetto puts his own life in danger searching for his beloved little boy.

Beautifully animated, this has some really scary bits (even the waves shrink back in horror as Monstro the Whale swims towards us, and Pinocchio's adventures on Pleasure Island may upset some viewers) but lovely ones, too, like Jiminy Cricket's high-wire balancing act and the song 'When You Wish Upon a Star'. Wonderful. ★★★★★

THE PRINCESS BRIDE

Starring Cary Elwes, Robin Wright (1987)

A classic fairy tale with a modern spin, this wonderful film from *When Harry Met Sally* director Rob Reiner is a must-see for all ages. A young boy (*The Wonder Years'* Fred Savage) lies ill in bed, so his grandfather (Peter Falk) decides to read him a story of giants, an evil prince, a beautiful princess and a dashing hero.

The story begins with young Westley (Elwes) who falls in love with the lovely Buttercup (Wright). But their path to true love is a rocky one

– first she believes Westley has died, then she is kidnapped by a gang led by the calculating Vizzini (Wallace Shawn). The mysterious Dread Pirate Roberts tries to rescue her – could he be Westley in disguise? And can Westley stop the dastardly Prince Humperdinck (Chris Sarandon) from marrying his one true love?

Set in a strange land populated with memorable characters like revenge-seeking swordsman Inigo Montoya (the superb Mandy Patinkin), the stubborn magician Miracle Max (Billy Crystal) and well-meaning, amazingly strong giant Fezzik (André the Giant), this is a terrific adventure for kids but has heaps of delicious humour for older audiences. In fact, there are not words to describe how utterly brilliant this film is. Buy it, even if you don't have kids. It's wonderful. ★★★★★

PRINCESS MONONOKE

Voices by Yoji Matsuda, Yuriko Ishida (1997)

Before the acclaimed *Spirited Away*, Japanese director Hayao Miyazaki made this animated fantasy that is available in both a subtitled and dubbed version (with the voices of Minnie Driver, Claire Danes, Gillian Anderson and Billy Bob Thornton). Set in medieval Japan, it's the story of a young warrior, Ashitaka, who searches for a cure for the gods' evil wrath while being caught in a conflict that is destroying nature around him.

A beautiful example of mainly hand-drawn Japanese anime (much done by Hayao Miyazaki himself), this is often complicated stuff that won't appeal to younger viewers but should intrigue teens (and grown-ups) and is a must-see for fans of original, clever animation. ★★★★☆

THE RETURN OF JAFAR

Voices by Jonathan Freeman, Gilbert Gottfried (1994)

A straight-to-video sequel to the hugely successful Disney animated movie *Aladdin*, this features many of the original cast providing voices, except Robin Williams, who didn't return as the Genie due to some contractual disagreements with Disney (here, his voice is provided by Dan Castellaneta of *The Simpsons* fame). The evil Jafar (Freeman) has been imprisoned in a lamp, which is discovered by thief Abis Mal (Jason Alexander). Once freed, Jafar has genie's powers and determines to use them in revenge against Aladdin, sending his parrot Iago (Gottfried) to convince Aladdin he is a reformed bird so he can infiltrate the palace.

While the film does lack Williams's vocal presence, this is a decent sequel to *Aladdin*, aimed more at younger viewers who liked the first film rather than adults who found it funny. There is also a second follow-up, *Aladdin and the King of Thieves* (1995), in which Robin Williams did supply the voice of the Genie (he'd made up with Disney by then). ★★★☆☆

THE ROAD TO EL DORADO

Voices by Kenneth Branagh, Kevin Kline (2000)

Elton John and Tim Rice provided the music for this underrated animated adventure from DreamWorks (who had previously made *Antz*). It's the 16th-century-set story of two Spaniards (Kline and Branagh) who find El Dorado, the legendary city of gold, and are bizarrely mistaken for gods by the residents. Keen to run off with the loot, they nonetheless stay awhile pretending they really are deities, facing the wrath of nasty High Priest Tzekel-Kan (Armand Assante) along the way.

The animation's slick, the music punchy and, best of all, the vocal performances – especially Assante, Kline and Rosie Perez (as Chel) – are spot-on. While it slows in the middle, it's often funny, with lots of junior action and adventure to enjoy. ★★★☆☆

ROBIN HOOD

Voices by Brian Bedford, Peter Ustinov, Terry-Thomas (1973)

As a rule of thumb, if a Disney animated movie was made between 1970 and 1989 (when girlie favourite *The Little Mermaid* was released), chances are it isn't very good. And 1973's Robin Hood proves the rule – the animation is dated, the humour only mildly amusing... and the animals aren't even that cute!

That's unfortunate, since this Disney musical movie is entirely populated with animals playing the roles of Robin Hood, his Merry Men, Maid Marian and the Sheriff of Nottingham. Robin is a sly fox (literally), helping the poor with his band of merry men from deep in

Sherwood Forest, robbing the nasty Sheriff of Nottingham when he gets the chance. There are a couple of fun chases and some sprightly slapstick moments, but all in all this is forgettable stuff that's far less entertaining than other retellings of the Robin Hood story, such as 1938's *The Adventures of Robin Hood*, with a swashbuckling Errol Flynn, and 1991's daftly enjoyable *Robin Hood: Prince of Thieves* with Kevin Costner. ★★☆☆☆

ROBIN HOOD: PRINCE OF THIEVES

Starring Kevin Costner, Mary Elizabeth Mastrantonio (1991)

The Bryan Adams theme song 'Everything I Do...' still haunts most adults (and not in a good way) and more than a decade later Costner is no more convincing as Robin, but this is still a fun – if somewhat ludicrous – family romp through Sherwood Forest.

Robin of Locksley (Costner) returns to England from the Crusades with trusty Moor Azeem (Morgan Freeman) and heads off to his home in Nottingham (bizarrely going via Hadrian's Wall, so this isn't a great choice if you're teaching your kids British geography). Unfortunately, a new nasty sheriff (Alan Rickman, stealing every scene) has taken over, forcing our hero to become an outlaw and – after some amusing male posturing – team up with a merry band that includes Will Scarlett (Christian Slater), Friar Tuck (Michael McShane) and Little John (Nick Brimble). There's romance too, of course, between Robin and Marian (Mastrantonio, looking as out of place in Ye Olde England as Costner), but this is best enjoyed by adults and kids as a rip-roaring adventure, with Rickman providing more chuckles than scares as the pantomime-style ('...And call off Christmas!') villain. ★★★☆☆

THE SECRET OF ROAN INISH

Starring Jeni Courtney, Susan Lynch (1994)

A lovely Irish family drama, this was in fact made by independent American director John Sayles (*Lone Star*). Based on Rosalie Fry's novel *The Secret of Ron Mor Skerry*, it's the story of ten-year-old Fiona (Courtney), who is sent to live with her grandparents following the death of her mother. They live on the Irish coast near Roan Inish, an island her family has been linked with for generations, and Fiona soon hears the magical stories of selkies (seals that can become human) and of her own little brother Jamie, who was swept out to sea in his cradle.

Beautifully filmed, this is perhaps too slow for very young viewers but is a must-see for older (eight and over) children and adults looking for an intelligent, adorable little film that's just as much about family and tradition as it is about fairy-tale sea creatures. ★★★★☆

THE 7TH VOYAGE OF SINBAD

Starring Kerwin Matthews, Kathryn Grant (1958)

Considered by many to be the best film to feature Ray Harryhausen's ground-breaking stop-motion special effects, this is a rip-roaring adventure from 1958 that's just as fun now, almost half a century later.

Sinbad (Matthews) and his crew battle a dragon and a cyclops (who deliciously rotates a few annoying sailors on a spit – a scene which will more likely delight kids than scare them) and save a princess who has been shrunk to just a few inches tall, but the best bit by far is our hero's fight with a skeleton. The dialogue is a bit ropey (and adults will spot the major plot twist a few miles away) but the effects are terrific, and if your kids like this one they should also see Harryhausen's work on *Sinbad and the Eye of the Tiger*, *Jason and the Argonauts* and, if they're a bit older, *The Beast from 20,000 Fathoms*, *It Came from Beneath the Sea* and *Mysterious Island*. (Dads, meanwhile, would probably prefer Harryhausen's dinosaur epic *One Million Years BC*, mainly for a young Raquel Welch in a leather bikini.) ★★★★☆

A SIMPLE WISH

Starring Martin Short, Kathleen Turner, Mara Wilson (1997)

Adorable little Anabel (Wilson) dreams of a fairy godmother who will give her struggling actor father (Robert Pastorelli) a lead role in a Broadway play. However, instead of granting Anabel her wish, clumsy fairy godfather Murray (Short) accidentally turns her dad into a statue, and things get even worse when evil ex-fairy Claudia (Turner) and her sidekick Boots (Amanda Plummer) capture all the other fairy godmothers' wands, leaving Murray with no one to turn to for help.

For little kids this is a sweet film that boasts some neat special effects and Martin Short's deft comic touch. However, for anyone male past puberty, the main attraction must be a striking-looking Kathleen Turner, whose deliciously evil performance is surely too sexy for most seven-year-olds to handle. ★★★☆☆

SINBAD AND THE EYE OF THE TIGER

Starring Patrick Wayne, Jane Seymour (1977)

A couple of decades after *The 7th Voyage of Sinbad*, this high-seas adventure once again features special effects by maestro Ray Harryhausen. The plot isn't exactly Shakespeare – Sinbad (Wayne) wants to marry Farah (Seymour) but must first help her brother who has been turned into a baboon (yes, really) by the evil Zenobia (Margaret Whiting). There's a living statue, a sabre-toothed tiger and some skeletons to fight (parents take note, this is more violent than the earlier Sinbad films), as well as some big nasty insects, but even some neat effects can't hide the fact that this just isn't as good as the older Sinbad movies.

Grown-ups will enjoy spotting ex-*Dr Who* Patrick Troughton as Melanthius, and noting that Wayne is actually the son of legendary actor John (but sadly didn't inherit more than an ounce of dad's talent). ★★☆☆☆

SINBAD: LEGEND OF THE SEVEN SEAS

Voices by Brad Pitt, Catherine Zeta Jones, Michelle Pfeiffer (2003)

Oh dear. This dull adventure is proof, if it were needed, that an impressive vocal cast does not a good animated movie make. Brad Pitt lends his voice to Sinbad – here a thoroughly unlikeable, rather snarky and brash character (not great qualities for a movie hero) – who sails off to steal the Book of Life, only to find it is in his best friend Proteus's (Joseph Fiennes) possession. When a monster attacks his ship (the only slightly scary bit), Sinbad is saved from drowning by the Goddess of Chaos, Eris (Pfeiffer), and she demands he steals the book for her. A few tedious plot twists later and Sinbad is on a journey to retrieve it, with Proteus's fiancée Marina (Zeta Jones) on board, willing him to return it to save her fiancé's life.

What should be an epic adventure ends up being a predictable and tedious one, made worse by the fact that Sinbad is a selfish sort who seems to have no qualms making googly eyes at his friend's (who is under the threat of execution until Sinbad returns) girlfriend. Yes, some of the animation is great – the seas look terrific and some of the creatures, too – but who cares if the story and characters are annoying? ★★☆☆☆

SLEEPING BEAUTY

Voices by Mary Costa, Bill Shirley (1959)

Rumoured to be Walt Disney's favourite of all his animated movies, this is, of course, based on the classic fairy tale that inspired Tchaikovsky's ballet score (which is used to beautiful effect in the film). Nasty Maleficent predicts to the king that his infant daughter Aurora will prick her finger on a spinning wheel before her sixteenth birthday and fall into a deep sleep. Despite everyone's best intentions, the inevitable happens, and it is up to the hunky Prince Philip to kiss Princess Aurora awake with love's first kiss, and vanquish Maleficent once and for all.

Adults will be impressed by the beautiful animation (some of the backgrounds are based on medieval paintings) while kids – especially little girls – will love the romantic story. That's not to say that young boys won't be entertained – they'll like Maleficent, who is a mean old sorceress who can change into a fire-breathing dragon in a manner both enjoyable and a little bit frightening, and they'll have some laughs at the three fairies (Merryweather, Flora and Fauna) who raise Aurora (renaming her Briar Rose) away from the palace, hoping to save her from her fate. Simply gorgeous. ★★★★★

THE SLIPPER AND THE ROSE

Starring Gemma Craven, Richard Chamberlain (1976)

A twist on the classic Cinderella tale told from Prince Charming's point of view, this old-fashioned musical is so very English it should be watched while eating scones with clotted cream and jam. Edward

(Chamberlain), the prince of tiny fictitious country Euphrania, is to be married off on the instructions of his father, the King (Michael Hordern). A bride-finding ball is arranged, and it is there Edward meets and falls in love with Cinderella (Craven), but instead of everything ending happily ever after, the King intervenes and insists Edward marries a more suitable woman to cement a political alliance.

Although it has dated massively, little girls will probably enjoy this dreamily filmed tale that brims over with floaty costumes, soft focus, romantic shots of Craven and Chamberlain, picturesque Austrian scenery and lavish song-and-dance numbers such as 'What Has Love Got to Do With Getting Married', and 'Protocoligorically Correct'. Adults will find it all a bit naff but can spend their time spotting the who's who of old-fashioned British stars who appear, including Annette Crosbie (as the fairy godmother), Kenneth More (Lord Chamberlain) and Edith Evans (the sarcastic Dowager Queen). ★★★☆☆

SNOW WHITE AND THE SEVEN DWARFS

Voices by Adriana Caselotti, Lucille La Verne (1937)

'I was about six years old when I saw *Snow White*. I loved being frightened at that age, so when the stepmother turned into the wicked witch I thought it was just wonderful. When I look at it now, I can see how frightening it is – you probably wouldn't be able to do that now in a family film – especially the woodsman being paid to go after Snow White with a big knife!' NICK PARK, CREATOR OF WALLACE AND GROMIT

It was made way back in 1937, but *Snow White and the Seven Dwarfs* remains one of Disney's best ever animated movies (and it was actually its first – dubbed 'Disney's folly' in Hollywood at the time by people who thought it wouldn't be a success). It is, of course, based on the Grimm Brothers story of the beautiful young girl Snow White. When a wicked queen asks her enchanted mirror who is the fairest of them all (and expects the answer to be herself) she discovers it is instead the ruby-lipped, raven-haired Snow White, so she commands a woodsman to take the young girl into the woods and kill her. He can't do it, and instead Snow White flees into the forest where she happens upon a cottage where seven dwarfs live, and they take her in.

So far, so jolly. Kids (and, let's face it, grown-ups) just love the dwarfs – Sleepy, Dopey, Sneezy, Happy, Grumpy, Bashful and Doc – and the timeless songs like 'Some Day My Prince Will Come', 'Whistle While You Work' and 'Heigh Ho' will have you singing along. But there is some scariness – many adults remember this as the first film that had them hiding behind the sofa – most notably when Snow White flees into the forest and the branches of the trees become menacingly alive, and in the scene when the wicked queen transforms herself into an ugly old crone so she can deliver the poisoned apple to our heroine. If you have small children who may be frightened, don't let them watch those bits alone… and leave the lights on for yourself, too! ★★★★★

SPIRITED AWAY

Voices by Daveigh Chase, Michael Chiklis

2003's Oscar-winner for Best Animated Feature, *Spirited Away* (or *Sen to Chihiro no Kamikakushi* to give it its correct title) can also boast that it is the highest-grossing Japanese movie of all time. An adventure for adults and children, it's the tale of a ten-year-old girl who is moving with her parents to a new house in the suburbs. Her father, however, takes a short cut along the way into a mysterious tunnel, and they find themselves in a seemingly deserted town. As night approaches, faceless spirits appear and the girl realises she is trapped in a spirit realm while her parents have been turned into pigs, and only she can save them by facing her fears.

A superb example of Japanese anime, this is magical, eccentric and beautifully realised. It's quite scary too, thanks to all the creepy witches, gods and monsters in the town, so not recommended for younger children, but older ones who think they have grown out of animated movies will be impressed, amazed and thrilled at this stunning adventure. ★★★★★

THE SWAN PRINCESS

Voices by Jack Palance, John Cleese (1994)

A sweet little animated tale for girls that is loosely based on *Swan Lake*. Young Princess Odette is snatched by evil sorcerer Rothbart (Palance), who turns her into a swan to keep her apart from her love, Prince Derek. She can only take human form when the moonlight glints upon the lake, but at least she has a trio of friends – frog Jean-Bob (Cleese), Puffin and turtle Speed – to help her win the prince and cancel the curse.

The songs here aren't very memorable, but the story and animation is cute enough, and Odette is a determined young thing, not a wussy princess waiting for her prince to come. There are two disappointing sequels, *The Swan Princess II* (1997) and *The Swan Princess III: The Mystery of the Enchanted Kingdom* (1998), both of which are only worth watching for true fans of the first one. ★★☆☆☆

THE SWORD IN THE STONE

Voices by Sebastian Cabot, Karl Swenson (1963)

The legend of King Arthur gets the Disney treatment in this animated tale based on the T H White novel. It's pretty forgettable and a bit dated (the movie was made in 1963 and just doesn't rank as a Disney classic), but there's some fun to be had as magician Merlin and his owl Archimedes meet young Arthur (known as Wart to his pals) and try to teach him about the world in preparation for him becoming king one day. There's interference from a bad guy, of course – in this case Madam Mim – but nothing truly scary or exciting really happens.

Instead there's some jokes and some amusement when Merlin turns Arthur into various cute animals that may entertain smaller viewers. Older kids, on the other hand, would probably rather catch other versions of the Arthur legend, such as John Boorman's grim 1981 *Excalibur* or 2004's grisly *King Arthur* (both films really aimed at adults). ★★☆☆☆

THE THIEF LORD   u/c

Starring Aaron Johnson, Jasper Harris (2005)

Cornelia Funke's popular book for tweenies became a rather lacklustre movie, despite its luscious Venice setting. Orphaned boy Prosper (Johnson) steals his younger mop-haired brother Bo (Harris) from their nasty aunt and uncle, and the pair escape to Venice and a new life. Lost among the winding streets and canals, they are befriended by teenage Scopio (Rollo Weeks), who steals from the rich to support a rag-tag group of kids who live in an abandoned cinema.

Unfortunately none of the kids in this tale have much character to speak of, and the fantasy parts of the film (there's a very special fairground ride that provides the movie's twist) come a little late in the proceedings. Younger viewers may like watching the kids running riot about town, but older ones won't be impressed by the fact all the Italians have English accents or by the sub-*Harry Potter* magical moments. ★★☆☆☆

THREE WISHES

Starring Patrick Swayze, Joseph Mazzello (1995)

In the 1950s, young Tom (Mazzello) is in a car with his mum and little brother Gunny when they accidentally hit a homeless hitchhiker as they swerve to avoid his dog. Instead of popping him off to the local hospital, mum Jeanne (Mary Elizabeth Mastrantonio) decides to take the man in, determined to look after him until his broken leg has healed. (This may sound far-fetched but do remember that the man, Jack, looks quite a lot like Patrick Swayze.) And what a household Jack moves into. Tom's dad is missing, presumed dead, in the Korean War. Tom doesn't fit in with the local kids because he is no good at sport, and Gunny, meanwhile, has a painful stomach and doesn't look very well at all...

As the title suggests, there's magic on the way, though. Jack has an air of the supernatural and tells the boys of a genie with the power to grant three wishes. Older audiences will twig what happens next, but smaller viewers will be enchanted by this sweet little tale that features a nice central performance from Mazzello (best known as the boy in *Jurassic Park*) and a mystical one from Swayze. ★★★☆☆

THUMBELINA   u/c

Voices by Jodi Benson, Gary Imhoff (1994)

There have been various versions of Hans Christian Andersen's classic tale, including rarely seen Brazilian, Russian and Japanese animated ones, but the most accessible for little kids is this adaptation, directed by Don Bluth and Gary Goldman (who also made *All Dogs Go to Heaven* together).

Aimed squarely at little girls under the age of seven, it's the story of a teeny tiny little girl named Thumbelina (Benson, who also voiced Ariel from *The Little Mermaid*) who wants to find a person to love who is just her size. Luckily, there is a prince who fits that description, but our plucky petite heroine first has to fend off the advances of a mean toad looking for a wife for his toady son. All very cute – though not strictly adhering to the Andersen story – but parents should be warned that the accompanying soundtrack is written and performed by (yikes!) Barry Manilow. ★★★☆☆

TIME BANDITS   u/c

Starring Craig Warnock, John Cleese, Sean Connery (1981)

Directed by Terry Gilliam and co-written with another ex-Monty Python member, Michael Palin, *Time Bandits* is a completely bonkers adventure that has deservedly developed something of a cult following among grown-ups. But kids love it too, thanks to the fantastical story, dazzling sets and dark undertones (which probably make it unsuitable for preteens – especially the ending, which won't be revealed here).

Young Kevin (Warnock) befriends a group of dwarfs who appear through a hole in his wardrobe. It's actually a time hole, and the group use it to travel through time, having a series of adventures as they meet such characters as Robin Hood (Cleese), King Agamemnon (Connery), Napoleon (Ian Holm) and God himself (Ralph Richardson). Bitingly funny, as you would expect from Gilliam, brilliantly odd and packed with terrific actors (the cast also includes Shelley Duvall, David Warner and Kenny Baker, better known as R2-D2) – unmissable. ★★★★☆

TOM THUMB

Starring Russ Tamblyn, Terry-Thomas, Peter Sellers (1958)

Russ Tamblyn – whom older viewers will recognise as Riff from *West Side Story* and Dr Jacoby in *Twin Peaks* – has much thigh-slapping fun as the Grimm Brothers' Tom Thumb in this delightful family musical. Jonathan the woodcutter (Bernard Miles) and his wife wish for a son and get one who is just as tall as a thumb. And despite his size, young Tom has some big adventures, thanks to two robbers (Terry-Thomas and Sellers) who use him to steal money and then frame his parents for it.

This is decidedly sweeter than the fairy tale on which it is based, and packed with energetic dancing from Tamblyn and fun songs written by Fred Spielman and Peggy Lee. A fluffy diversion ideal for (pardon the pun) smaller viewers. ★★★☆☆

TUCK EVERLASTING

Starring Alexis Bledel, William Hurt, Sissy Spacek, Jonathan Jackson (2002)

Have tissues at the ready for this enjoyably soppy fable. Based on a novel by Natalie Babbitt, it is the story of young Winnie (Bledel), who in 1914 discovers a family living hidden in the forest called the Tucks. Jesse Tuck (Jackson) in particular is rather appealing, but Winnie soon learns the family's secret – they have all drunk from a magical spring that is, in fact, the fountain of youth, and each is stuck at the age they were when they drank. So Jesse may look like a hunky teenager, but in fact he's over 100 years old. Winnie, who is afraid of dying (and a bit in love already), is unsurprisingly intrigued, but is she prepared to live for ever to be with Jesse, or lose him by living to a normal age?

While cynical viewers will notice a few big plot annoyances (like why the family has stayed in the same woodland home for aeons when they could be making use of their agelessness by travelling the world, and why doesn't Jesse look a bit more frustrated, 104-year-old virgin that he is?), those wanting an old-fashioned romantic fable (yes, this is one for preteen and teenage girls) will have more than a few sniffs during this innocent tale. ★★★☆☆

WILLOW

Starring Val Kilmer, Joanne Whalley (1988)

Based on a story by George Lucas, this fairy-tale-style adventure was a bit of a flop when it was released in 1988, partly because everyone was expecting something on the scale of Lucas's *Star Wars*. While the film is set in a lush, mythical and almost medieval land, some of the story elements are similar – young farmer Willow Ufgood (Warwick Davis, who played Ewok Wicket in *Return of the Jedi*) has to protect a special baby from evil Queen Bavmorda (Jean Marsh). There's a cocky reluctant Han Solo-style hero to help him, too, Madmartigan (Kilmer), as well as a damsel in distress (Whalley).

It's certainly not the epic Lucas probably wanted (it's actually a bit boring and predictable in places) but there are some good effects (one monster and a couple of the grisly swordfights aren't perhaps suitable for younger eyes, though) and enjoyable performances from Davis and Marsh. Kilmer, however, looks pretty uncomfortable, and after sitting through two hours of this so-so film, you probably will be too. ★★☆☆☆

Family Movies and Seasonal Stocking Fillers

There are many movies throughout this book that are just as entertaining for older members of the audience as for the junior ones they were aimed at. This section, however, features those unforgettable films that are not necessarily made solely with kids in mind but are loved by audiences of every age (do note, some are for older children not little ones, but that's clearly mentioned in the relevant reviews). They're the films that crop up on TV during the big holidays, the classics that parents hope their children will enjoy as much as they did when they were first released, the adventures, the musicals, the comedies that everyone can watch together.

And speaking of holidays, there is, of course, one that film-makers particularly like… Christmas. So you'll also find movies set during the festive season here, or at least the ones aimed at families – after all, the great but also expletive-filled and violent *Lethal Weapon* and *Die Hard* were set at Christmas, and you don't want Junior watching those just yet.

BACK TO THE FUTURE   u/c

Starring Michael J Fox, Christopher Lloyd, Lea Thompson (1985)

Michael J Fox went from TV star (in the sitcom *Family Ties*) to mega movie star following his performance in this time-travelling adventure. He's seventeen-year-old Marty McFly (Fox at the time was twenty-four), who despairs of his pushover dad George (Crispin Glover) and spends most of his time with barmy local inventor Doc Emmett Brown

(Lloyd). Doc has invented a time machine – using a DeLorean car and some 'borrowed' plutonium – and Marty soon finds himself zipping back in time to 1955, around the time his parents first met. Through a series of events, he accidentally meets his mum and she falls for him (thinking his name is Calvin Klein after seeing the name on his pants) instead of his dad, so Marty has to somehow get his parents together so he can exist, and locate a younger Doc Brown to help him travel back to 1985.

Refreshingly original, this uses a clever premise to great effect, mixing sci-fi with comedy (the script is hilarious) and adventure and romance. Fox is perfect as Marty (Eric Stoltz originally filmed a few scenes but was replaced early into the production), and his pairing with a manic Lloyd as Doc proved so successful that two terrific sequels followed. ★★★★★

BACK TO THE FUTURE PART II

Starring Michael J Fox, Christopher Lloyd, Lea Thompson (1989)

Filmed back-to-back with Part III, this is the darkest of the three time-travel movies. Having returned from 1955 to 1985, young Marty McFly (Fox) runs into Doc Brown (Lloyd) who has just returned from the future (2015). It seems things are not good – Marty and his girlfriend Jennifer (Elisabeth Shue) are married, but Marty's son is a bit of a disaster. To make matters worse, while they are there the future Biff (the bully from Part I) has got his hands on a reference book featuring the results of many sports events and steals the time-travelling DeLorean to return to 1955 to give to his teenage self, so when Marty and Doc return to 1985 it's a completely different one from the world they left – Marty's mum is married to Biff (who is insanely rich from his betting on events he knew the outcome of) and his dad has been murdered. So Marty has to travel back to 1955, avoiding himself from last time, to retrieve the book before Biff can use it.

Yes, it is all a bit head-scratching, but in a good way – while audiences in 1989 weren't too keen, this actually improves with each viewing (note that it ends on a cliffhanger, so make sure you have Part III to hand). It's not as funny as Part I, perhaps, and younger viewers may not follow all of the time shifts, but it's entertaining viewing nonetheless. ★★★★☆

BACK TO THE FUTURE PART III

Starring Michael J Fox, Christopher Lloyd, Lea Thompson (1990)

A return to a simpler, more comedic format for the third *Back to the Future* movie. Carrying on from where Part II left off, this has (don't read this bit if you haven't seen *BTTF II* yet) Doc stuck in 1885. Marty travels back to rescue him, only to find that Doc quite likes life in the Old West (he's even found a lady friend, played by Mary Steenburgen). Unfortunately, he also discovers Doc may die at the hands of a gunman, who just happens to be related to Biff Tannen, Marty's adversary in 1955 and 1985.

A rousing mix of Wild West fun, comedy and the sci-fi time-travelling adventure from the previous two films, this was a terrific end to a well-written, brilliantly played trilogy. Fox and Lloyd are once again superb, while Steenburgen makes a nice addition to the cast (and nice to see old Doc getting a romantic interest at last!). ★★★★☆

THE BAD NEWS BEARS

Starring Walter Matthau, Tatum O'Neal (1976)

A classic family sports movie, this stars the wonderful Walter Matthau as a beer-sodden baseball coach who ends up trying to whip a Little League team of eleven-year-old kids into shape. They're pretty pathetic players (one is afraid of the ball) until he brings in a star player in the form of pitcher Amanda (O'Neal) and the team actually win a game.

It's fun stuff, in the *Rocky*/*Major League* tradition of losers finally becoming winners, and the film has some real charm and laughs. Two missable sequels (without Matthau and O'Neal) were made, *The Bad News Bears in Breaking Training* (1977) and *The Bad News Bears Go to Japan* (1978) and a slightly raunchier 2005 remake, *Bad News Bears*, in which Billy Bob Thornton stars as the grizzled coach. ★★★☆☆

BEETLEJUICE

Starring Michael Keaton, Geena Davis, Alec Baldwin, Winona Ryder (1988)

A masterful dark comedy from director Tim Burton, this teamed him with actor Michael Keaton for the first time (the following year, Keaton starred in Burton's *Batman*). Not one for your children if they are easily frightened, but a must-see for older kids (there is some swearing and spookiness) who get a kick out of twisted humour.

Wholesome couple Adam (Baldwin) and Barbara Maitland (Davis) die in a car accident and find that they have become ghosts in their own picture-postcard home. Unfortunately a new family moves in – wealthy Charles (Jeffrey Jones), bleak daughter Lydia (Ryder) and step-mother Delia (Catherine O'Hara) – and the Maitlands are horrified when Delia remodels their dream home into a freaky gothic architect's nightmare. Unable to terrify the family themselves (when they appear with sheets over their ghostly selves, Delia thinks it's quaint and decides to invite friends over to witness the apparitions), they call upon Betelgeuse (Keaton), a coarse, belching nasty 'bio-exorcist' who offers to rid their home of the horrible humans – for a price.

Deliciously dark, enjoyably icky and fun throughout, this is one of Burton's best films, and features a tornado of a performance from Keaton, who is only on screen for a third of the film's running time, yet steals the movie from the other excellent actors with his maniacal, hyper turn. Ryder, in her third movie role, is a treat as Lydia ('my whole life is a dark room') and Baldwin and Davis are hilarious too. Just perfect. ★★★★★

BIG 🔺 PG PG

Starring Tom Hanks, Elizabeth Perkins (1988)

When twelve-year-old Josh finds he is too small to go on a fairground ride, he drops a coin into a magic wish machine and wishes he was bigger. Next morning he wakes up to discover his wish has come true (sort of) – while he's still boyish Josh inside, his body is that of a grown man (Hanks). Of course, when his mother (Mercedes Ruehl) sees him, she screams, thinking this stranger has abducted her boy, so Josh heads to the big city and even gets himself a job, testing toys for a big company run by kindly MacMillan (Robert Loggia).

It's hard to imagine now, but Harrison Ford and Robert De Niro were both considered for the lead role in this adorable comedy before Hanks was hired. He's perfect as the boy in a thirty-year-old's body, and brilliantly shows how a young kid would experience things in a man's world – from his first crush and 'sleepover' with co-worker Susan

(Perkins) to his first taste of yucky caviar. With Jared Rushton as Josh's street-smart pal and John Heard as a suspicious work rival rounding out the cast, this is a terrifically played, funny, heart-warming and even weepy slice of family entertainment. ★★★★★

BILLY ELLIOT

Starring Jamie Bell, Julie Walters (2000)

A family feel-good movie that has had lashings of praise heaped upon it since its release in 2000. And it does deserve most of it (though whoever said it was the best British film ever should probably get out and see a few more movies), thanks to not-too-sugary direction from Stephen Daldry and an engaging central performance from Bell.

He, of course, plays Billy, a young lad growing up in a mining community during the British miners' strikes of the 1980s. He's destined for a life down the pit but dreams of being a ballet dancer after switching from boxing lessons to ballet (as taught by Julie Walters's Mrs Wilkinson) – a dream he naturally keeps secret from his friends and his traditional dad (Gary Lewis). From thereon in you can guess the rest, but despite being predictable in places it's an entertaining film with some impressive dance scenes. Parents should note that this film was given a '15' 'R' rating mainly because of some ripe language. ★★★★☆

CHEAPER BY THE DOZEN

Starring Steve Martin, Bonnie Hunt (2003)

A loose remake of the 1950 comedy with Myrna Loy (which was actually based on a true story), this stars Steve Martin as Tom Baker, dad to twelve children. Wife Kate (Hunt) has to leave him in charge when she goes off on a book tour, he's just started a new job as coach to a football team and, as you would expect, one kiddie crisis follows another.

A big enough success to warrant a dire 2005 sequel (in which the entire brood run amok on holiday), this is family entertainment at its most predictable. Steve Martin, who has been so funny in movies like *The Man With Two Brains*, *The Jerk* and *Parenthood* (in which he gives a much better performance as a stressed-out dad, though grown-ups should note it's not a kids' film), here just phones in a performance as the harried dad, leaving the comedy to the kids, played by Hilary Duff,

Smallville's Tom Welling and various cute tots (while Ashton Kutcher pops up as a guy who may be considering marrying into this chaos). Like the similar *Kindergarten Cop* and *Daddy Day Care* (in which Eddie Murphy runs his own day-care centre), this passes the time but isn't worth making too much of an effort to see. ★★☆☆☆

CHITTY CHITTY BANG BANG

Starring Dick Van Dyke, Gert Fröbe (1968)

A cutely quaint film based on Ian 'James Bond' Fleming's book, this has also recently been adapted into a very successful stage musical that has introduced wacky inventor Caractacus Potts to a whole new generation of kids.

Here, the part of Caractacus is played, of course, by Dick Van Dyke, who is just perfect as the eccentric professor who invents a flying car he calls Chitty Chitty Bang Bang (after the sound it makes), which takes him and his children (and babe Truly Scrumptious, played by Sally Ann Howes) to the land of Vulgaria, where the ruthless Baron Bomburst (Fröbe, best known as Goldfinger) decides to get his own hands on it. (Adults who saw this as children should perhaps remember how scared they were of the character the Child Catcher, who roams Vulgaria looking for children to snatch, before they decide whether their little ones should watch this.)

Considered a flop when it was released, this is one of those movies that has gathered many fans as time has passed, and despite being far too long at well over two hours, it does boast effects that, while not amazing, are impressive for the time, as well as some zippy musical numbers. ★★★☆☆

> 'I loved *Chitty Chitty Bang Bang*, which I saw as a child in Ireland in the local cinema where they showed films in two parts and always had an interval. When the car with magical properties took off and spread its wings, interval was called and we had to wait for ages to see where it was going to go.' KENNETH BRANAGH

COOL RUNNINGS ⒶⓅⒼⒼ

Starring John Candy, Leon, Doug E Doug (1993)

It sounds unbelievable, but it's true – in 1988 a team from Jamaica competed in the Winter Olympics bobsleigh event, even though they had never seen snow before. This comedy, which does play a little fast and loose with the facts, is based on their story, and is a feel-good delight.

When runner Derice (Leon) fails to qualify for the Jamaican Olympic team as a sprinter, he decides he's going to compete in the Winter Olympics by forming a bobsleigh team with the help of a coach, Irv (Candy). No matter that there is no snow in Jamaica (a bath-tub with wheels becomes the alternative to a real bobsleigh) or that he doesn't have a team (he rounds up an old go-karting pal and two other misfits) or that they are laughed at by all the other teams when they arrive in Calgary to compete. It's funny stuff about a quartet of plucky underdogs, and for those who scoff that it couldn't possibly have hap-pened, there's also some footage of the real team included in this sweet little movie. ★★★★☆

FLUBBER ⒶⓅⒼⒼ

Starring Robin Williams, Marcia Gay Harden (1997)

Even die-hard fans of Robin Williams, who chortled through *Mrs Doubtfire* and *The Birdcage* while the rest of us were rolling our eyes in despair, may be disappointed with this simplistic update of 1961's *The Absent-Minded Professor* in which the humourmeister pulls a few funny faces but is upstaged at every turn by a dancing green blob of goo and a talking flying saucer named Weebo.

Philip Brainard (Williams) is a very absent-minded professor who can't even remember the date of his upcoming wedding because he's busy working on a new form of energy. What he comes up with instead is an emerald-coloured rubbery substance (flubber) with its own personality which, when smeared on any object, makes it fly through the air at breakneck speed. Throw in some evil dudes who want the formula, a slimy colleague who's after Brainard's girl and a five-minute flubber dance number and you have a flimsy, weakly humorous film with some nice effects that will probably just about sat-isfy very junior viewers but test the patience of everyone else. ★★☆☆☆

GHOSTBUSTERS

Starring Bill Murray, Dan Aykroyd, Harold Ramis, Sigourney Weaver (1984)

Stars Ramis and Aykroyd wrote this comedy (Aykroyd originally wanted pal John Belushi to co-star, but he sadly died in 1982) about a trio of paranormal 'experts' (actually science professors, kicked off campus for their various antics) who set up a ghostbusting business in an old New York firehouse. Ladies' man Venkman (Murray), nerdy boffin Spengler (Ramis) and bumbling Stantz (Aykroyd) suddenly find business booming as ghosts pop up all over Manhattan, and things take a seriously spooky turn when one client, Dana Barrett (Weaver), turns into some sort of hound of the devil and a local accountant (Rick Moranis) turns out to be the key to a spectral bad guy turning up in town.

Packed with great special effects – including icky green ghost Slimer and the memorable giant Stay Puft marshmallow man who lumbers through the streets of the city (but shouldn't scare smaller viewers, although the nasty hounds might) – this is a superb mix of ghostbusting and comedy, with Murray stealing the show as the sleazy but lovable Venkman. Not surprisingly, this became the most successful comedy of all time until the title was snatched six years later by *Home Alone*. ★★★★★

GHOSTBUSTERS II

Starring Bill Murray, Dan Aykroyd, Harold Ramis, Sigourney Weaver (1989)

Five years after the phenomenally successful *Ghostbusters* came this fun sequel. Blamed for the destruction of much of New York, the guys have been banned from working as ghostbusters – Ray Stantz (Aykroyd) and fourth ghostbuster Winston (Ernie Hudson) perform for kiddie parties, Venkman (Murray) hosts a psychic TV show and Egon Spengler (Ramis) continues in his studies. They're brought back together when Venkman's ex, Dana (Weaver), reports that mystical weirdness is happening around her baby son, Oscar, and when ghostly sightings occur all around the city, the team are allowed to go back into action.

While the plot isn't as fresh as in the first film (apparently, it's Manhattanites' bad vibes that are causing lots of ghostly ectoplasmic goo to flow under the city and create all the problems) and the bad guy not as unique (it's some grumpy guy in a painting, who first possesses Peter MacNicol's annoying museum artist Janosz), this still has some laughs and good comic effects, and is certainly worth a look if you are a fan of Part I. ★★★☆☆

HOME ALONE

Starring Macaulay Culkin, Joe Pesci, Daniel Stern (1990)

The movie that made Macaulay Culkin a star when he was just ten years old, this also became the most successful comedy of all time (earning over $500 million worldwide). He stars as eight-year-old Kevin, whose parents accidentally leave him behind when they head off with his siblings for a Christmas trip to France. His initial joy at having the house to himself is short-lived, however, as two inept burglars (Stern and Pesci) turn up and Kevin has to resort to extreme cartoonish measures to keep them at bay.

One of those movies you'll love or hate depending on whether Culkin's character grates on you or not and whether you think the cartoon violence borders on the sadistic, this certainly does move with a rambunctious speed that kids will love, while Kevin's various tricks against the bad guys will have them cheering along. A missable sequel, *Home Alone 2: Lost in New York*, followed in 1992 (this time when Kevin is separated from his family – who should clearly be reported to the NSPCC – he's let loose in Manhattan and runs into Pesci and Stern's burglars again), while *Home Alone 3* was made in 1997 with annoying tyke Alex D Linz playing a new kid taking on some spies. (There was also a dire TV movie, *Home Alone 4*, with another actor, Mike Weinberg, playing Kevin.) ★★★☆☆

HONEY, I BLEW UP THE KID

Starring Rick Moranis, Marcia Strassman (1992)

Wacky scientist Szalinski (Moranis) has done it again. After reducing his kids to the size of ants in *Honey, I Shrunk the Kids*, in this sequel he accidentally enlarges his two-year-old son until he is over 100 feet high. It could happen to anyone – Szalinski is working on a new experiment when his son wanders into the path of the laser beam. Soon, every time the kid comes into contact with electricity, he grows a little bit more, and what's worse is he's heading for Las Vegas, the biggest source of electricity in America.

This comedy is very much like the original, but does have some new jokes and funny moments as Moranis and his wife try to find a way to shrink their son back to his normal size. It's predictable, but not a bad way to spend an evening. A forgettable video/DVD sequel, *Honey, We Shrunk Ourselves*, followed in 1997. ★★★☆☆

HONEY, I SHRUNK THE KIDS

Starring Rick Moranis, Marcia Strassman (1989)

Shrinking people until they are teeny-weeny had been done before – in the fun Dennis Quaid/Meg Ryan comedy *Innerspace* (1987) and the sci-fi adventures *The Incredible Shrinking Man* (1957) and *Fantastic Voyage* (1966), which are all worth a look – but this Disney movie is the best for kids, with its slick balance of comedy, adventure and family entertainment.

Slightly nutty professor Wayne Szalinski (Moranis) accidentally miniaturises his kids (and the neighbour's two boys as well) with his new invention and, not realising what he has done, also manages to throw them out with the trash. The four children have to make their way back across the garden, a trek that involves the microscopic kids avoiding giant insects and dodging a life-threatening lawn mower and lawn sprinkler, which to their small bodies delivers heavy rain akin to a hurricane. Featuring clever special effects and fun performances from the kids, this is a treat. ★★★★☆

INDIANA JONES AND THE LAST CRUSADE

Starring Harrison Ford, Sean Connery (1989)

The third (but not final – a fourth movie is promised for 2008!) Indiana Jones movie, this one is a delight as it introduces adventurous archaeologist Indy's dad, Professor Henry Jones (played with relish by Connery). Beginning with a terrific flashback to Indy as a boy (as played by the late River Phoenix) that explains the origins of his hat, whip and fear of snakes, the movie then brings us up to date (well, the late 1930s), as Indy (Ford) joins his dad in a hunt for the Holy Grail.

With many of the series' much-loved characters returning, from bumbling Brit Marcus Brody (Denholm Elliott) to the exuberant Sallah (John Rhys-Davies), some great locations (Venice, Berlin, Egypt), adventures (a Zeppelin ride, a chase on the Venice canals) and bad guys (those nasty Nazis again), this is as enjoyable as the other two movies, and perhaps funnier thanks to the inspired teaming of Connery and Ford as bickering father and son. Terrific. ★★★★★

INDIANA JONES AND THE TEMPLE OF DOOM

 PG (MA)15+

Starring Harrison Ford, Kate Capshaw (1984)

A follow-up to the phenomenally successful adventure *Raiders of the Lost Ark*, this more violent prequel from Steven Spielberg, set prior to *Raiders* in 1935, actually had a new rating – PG-13 – created especially for its release. Our fedora-wearing, whip-carrying hero Indiana Jones (Ford) finds, after a series of adventures that include being on a plane abandoned by its pilots, that he has ended up in India (with cabaret singer Willie and cute kid Short Round in tow), where desperate locals ask him to find a mystical stone that belongs to their village. The search for the stone leads him to a palace, with a cult, slave labour and lots of other nastiness (including creepy-crawlies) in the catacombs below.

Parents should note that this is more gruesome than the first film – especially a scene in which an unfortunate man has his heart ripped out and you then see it still pulsating in the hands of the bad guy – and darker too, which is perhaps why it is often the favourite of grown-ups! There are jokes, of course (the opening scene in the nightclub is a hoot), terrific action sequences (the rope bridge, the mine cart chase) and a cute sidekick (Ke Huy Quan as Short Round) – in fact, the only thing that stops this movie being as good as the wonderful *Raiders* is a slightly hysterical performance from Kate Capshaw (now Mrs Steven Spielberg) as the over-dramatic Willie. ★★★★☆

JACK ⚠ PG-13 PG

Starring Robin Williams, Diane Lane, Jennifer Lopez (1996)

A twist on the boy-in-a-man's-body tale from *Big* – here, parents Karen (Lane) and Brian (Brian Kerwin) are told that their new baby Jack suffers from a rare ageing disorder (which doesn't exist in real life, of course, just in this film), causing him to age four times faster than normal, so that when he is just ten years old his body is that of a forty-year-old man (who looks remarkably like Robin Williams).

A movie about a boy/man starting fifth grade, making friends and trying to be 'normal' seems an odd choice for *Godfather*/*Apocalypse Now* director Francis Ford Coppola, and it's certainly not his best work by any means. It's a big old shameless weepie that relies heavily on Williams's comic talents to keep it on track, and while there are poignant moments as both Jack and the audience realise he may not live longer than his teens, ideas about how he would spend his days, and his interaction with the kids and adults around him, are sadly wasted. A missed opportunity, and one for Williams fans only. ★★☆☆☆

JUMANJI ⚠ PG PG

Starring Robin Williams, Kirsten Dunst (1995)

As a small child, Alan Parrish finds a mysterious-looking board game named Jumanji and begins to play it, only to find himself sucked into the game's jungle world. Twenty-six years on, brother and sister Judy and Peter (Dunst and Bradley Pierce) discover the game and after unleashing a group of screeching monkeys and a ravenous lion into their home, release Alan – now a grown-up Robin Williams – from his captivity. And he tells them they have to win the game in order to end the chaos once and for all…

Basically an excuse for some wonderful effects – herds of elephants rampaging through the town, giant spiders, etc – this is a fun family film that only falls down when you start to pay too much attention and realise there's very little plot to speak of. All the cast are capable enough (although you can't help feeling that anyone could have played the Robin Williams part) and director Joe Johnston (*The Rocketeer*) keeps everything moving at a fair old speed. Note that very young viewers may find it a little scary (as may arachnophobes). A spin-off animated TV series was also made in 1996. ★★★☆☆

JURASSIC PARK

Starring Sam Neill, Jeff Goldblum, Richard Attenborough (1993)

In the same year he released the far more serious *Schindler's List*, Steven Spielberg also delivered this action adventure packed with phenomenal dinosaur special effects that paved the way for later spectaculars such as 2005's *King Kong*. Based on Michael Crichton's science-gone-wrong bestseller, this was such a hit it has even been credited with increasing the number of students around the world who study palaeontology.

It seems billionaire John Hammond (Attenborough, in his first acting role in over a decade) has created a new kind of theme park on a remote island – using the DNA sucked by an ancient mosquito found fossilised in amber, his scientists have managed to recreate dinosaurs that now roam 'Jurassic Park', ready for the first visitors to see them. Before the park opens, Hammond offers a sneak preview to palaeontologists Alan Grant (Neill) and Ellie Sattler (Laura Dern), sarcastic scientist Ian Malcolm (Goldblum) and Hammond's own grandchildren, Tim and Lex (Joseph Mazzello and Ariana Richards). Unfortunately, since his scientists have created such nasty dinosaurs as velociraptors and a great, drooling and toothy tyrannosaurus rex, bad things are bound to happen. And they do.

And, despite being included in this family section and only getting a 'PG' rating, it is truly scary stuff, partly because the dinosaurs (a mix of computer animation and animatronics) are so jaw-droppingly realistic. Spielberg racks up the tension, clearly delights in putting the kids in peril (one scene, when they are hunted by raptors in the kitchen, is trouser-wettingly tense the first time you see it) and keeps the story going when other directors would have simply been blinded by the impressive dino-effects. It's gripping, funny, edge-of-the-seat stuff, and essential viewing for anyone over ten who has a cushion nearby to hide behind. ★★★★★

JURASSIC PARK 2: THE LOST WORLD

Starring Jeff Goldblum, Julianne Moore, Vince Vaughn (1997)

You thought all the nasty dinosaurs that terrorised everyone in *Jurassic*

Park had died? Well, think again. Turns out there is a second island, 'site B', where the dinosaurs were reared before being transported to the park, and it seems the little blighters are getting ready to chomp on some human meat again. With Richard Attenborough as Hammond, the billionaire who created Jurassic Park, sidelined this time, it's up to Goldblum's Ian Malcolm to return and save the day with his pals – but to complicate things even further, a rival team is on the island (led by Pete Postlethwaite's barmy hunter), hoping to bag a T-rex as a trophy.

With Postlethwaite chewing more scenery than any dinosaur, this is sillier than the original movie, especially when the T-Rex is captured and transported to the US, where it escapes and goes on a rampage while Goldblum pursues it in a car. The action sequences are terrific, of course, and there are some scary bits (especially when the velociraptors are about), and the obligatory child in peril (one wonders about Spielberg's psyche), but this just isn't as thrilling as the first film. ★★★☆☆

JURASSIC PARK 3

Starring Sam Neill, William H Macy, Tea Leoni (2001)

Steven Spielberg, who directed *Jurassic Park* and its sequel, handed the camera over to Joe Johnston (who had helmed episodes of the Spielberg-produced *Young Indiana Jones Chronicles*) for this third adventure. It's eight years since he escaped Jurassic Park, but Dr Alan Grant (Neill) is convinced to return by businessman Paul Kirby (Macy) in return for a large donation to Grant's research project. What he doesn't know is that Kirby's son Eric has disappeared on the island, and he and his wife (Leoni) need Grant's help to find him.

With a few other potential dinosaur-fodder characters in tow (including Alessandro Nivola as Grant's assistant), this is another romp in monster land, with the added tension of some scary new creatures and Grant's idea-coming-true that the raptors have developed intelligence, making them even more deadly. The first movie is still the best, but this is a fair romp for fans of the series. A fourth movie is currently in the works. ★★★☆☆

KINDERGARTEN COP

Starring Arnold Schwarzenegger, Penelope Ann Miller (1990)

A comedy thriller for older kids and adults, this is definitely not one for littler eyes, despite the title. For Arnie plays a tough big-city cop who has to go undercover at a small-town kindergarten (nursery school) to stop a killer, so while he does eventually find his soft and squishy side by being with the little cuties, that doesn't stop him waving his gun around if there's a bad guy in the vicinity (the big finale is quite violent and the plot point of a kidnapped child would disturb younger viewers).

Before all that, there are some very funny moments as Arnie attempts to teach a group of little tykes ('they're like little terrorists'), and adults who know the muscleman better for hard-hitting action roles will get a kick out of watching him twirl a hula-hoop. Probably Arnie's funniest (at least intentionally) movie. ★★★☆☆

THE KING AND I

Starring Yul Brynner, Deborah Kerr (1956)

The lavish Broadway musical – based on Margaret Landon's book *Anna and the King of Siam* and featuring songs by Rodgers and Hammerstein – was translated into a colourful and even more spectacular screen version that won Yul Brynner an Oscar for his performance as the king. He's the gruff ruler of Siam with a large brood of cute children, while the 'I' of the title is, of course, governess Anna (Kerr), who not only takes care of them all, but also warms the king's heart when not clashing with his Eastern ways.

Younger viewers will love the spirited songs – 'I Whistle a Happy Tune', 'Getting to Know You', 'Shall We Dance' – and little girls especially will delight in the story and the gorgeous costumes (some of Kerr's were so heavy she lost weight wearing them). Just yummy. ★★★★☆

LAST ACTION HERO

Starring Arnold Schwarzenegger, Austin O'Brien (1993)

A complete misfire when it was released, this action adventure comedy is nonetheless worth a look as it has some clever moments and a neat premise, even if the execution is a bit heavy-handed.

Young Danny (O'Brien) is a huge fan of the movie character Jack Slater (Schwarzenegger). He's watching the new Slater movie when the 'magic ticket' he is holding transports him into the movie itself, a world where the good guys always win, of course. However, when movie bad guy Benedict (Charles Dance, going seriously over the top) realises what Danny's ticket can do, he snatches it so he can travel back to the real world and kill the actor who plays Slater (Schwarzenegger, of course), so Slater no longer exists in the movie world.

It's clever (and often head-scratching) stuff, but one of the problems here is having a kid protagonist who appeals to junior viewers (while annoying grown-ups), yet making the film so explosive and violent it gets a '15' PG13. Kids old enough to watch it will enjoy the adventure, however, while grown-ups will get a few laughs from some of the movie in-jokes peppered throughout the film. ★★★☆☆

MARY POPPINS   u/c

Starring Julie Andrews, Dick Van Dyke (1964)

The first Walt Disney movie to be nominated for a Best Picture Oscar (and there wasn't another until *Beauty and the Beast* was nominated in 1991), this is a delightful, old-fashioned musical based on the P L Travers books. Julie Andrews deservedly won an Oscar for her portrayal of lighter-than-air nanny Mary Poppins, who floats into the lives of Mr and Mrs Banks (David Tomlinson and Glynis Johns) and their two boisterous children Jane and Michael.

Many of the song and dance sequences will enchant young and old – 'Supercalifragilisticexpialidocious', 'A Spoonful of Sugar' and 'Chim Chim Cheree' especially – and the mix of live action and animation still looks pretty impressive four decades on. Grown-ups may scoff at Dick Van Dyke's appalling attempt at a Cockney accent as chimney sweep Bert, but the uncritical can just sit back and enjoy a funny, toe-tapping film that boasts the best dancing penguins ever. ★★★★☆

MEET ME IN ST LOUIS

Starring Judy Garland, Margaret O'Brien (1944)

Like *The Wizard of Oz* or *The Sound of Music*, this is one of those musicals that has really stood the test of time. It's the movie on whose set Judy met director Vincente Minnelli (they married soon after and had daughter Liza) and she stars as Esther, just one member of a warm family happily living in St Louis who is shocked when their father announces they will be moving to New York.

Set in 1903 as the family await the arrival of the next year's World's Fair, this provides a pretty depiction of the old South, with gentleman callers, trailing flowers and horse and cart rides. It's not all flowers and parasols, however, as Esther falls in love with the boy next door just before dad makes his monumental announcement, and little Tootie (O'Brien) shows she's darker than your average movie cutie by morbidly diagnosing all her dolls with terminal diseases. Simply lovely stuff that will mainly appeal to girls, this features Garland belting out 'The Trolley Song' and delivering an unforgettable rendition of 'Have Yourself a Merry Little Christmas'. ★★★★★

MILLIONS

Starring Alex Etel, Leslie Phillips (2004)

Director Danny Boyle – best known for directing gritty grown-up movies like *Shallow Grave* and *Trainspotting* – delivered his first family film here, a fun tale of two young brothers, seven-year-old Damian (Etel) and nine-year-old Anthony (Lewis McGibbon), who find the loot from a bank robbery and then realise that, because the cash is in pounds sterling, they only have a week to spend it before Britain converts to the euro.

Fantastical in places (one of the duo has saintly visions and believes the money is from God), funny throughout, this boasts two terrific child performances from Alex Etel and Lewis McGibbon and nice support from James Nesbitt as their dad. ★★★★☆

MONSTERS, INC

Voices by John Goodman, Billy Crystal (2001)

If you've got kids who believe there are creatures lurking in their wardrobes, this could be the best (or worst?) movie to show them. For *Monsters, Inc*, the terrific computer-animated adventure from Pixar (who also made *Toy Story* and *Finding Nemo*), proves that monsters really do come into children's rooms through their closets to scare them (oh dear), but also shows they're actually nice cuddly creatures (hurrah!) when they're not 'working'.

It's the tale of big blue beast-like monster Sulley (Goodman), who is the best at scaring children (in the monster world, you see, they get their energy from human children's screams), and his planet-shaped sidekick Mike (Crystal). One night, Sulley accidentally allows a cute kid to follow him back home through her wardrobe door to Monstropolis, causing chaos (monsters are afraid of human children, you see). Packed with laughs (Crystal, especially, is a hoot), well-known voices to amuse adults (James Coburn, Steve Buscemi) and stunning animation – Sulley's fur looks as if you could reach out and ruffle it, perhaps because it features over two million computer-drawn hairs – it's a real treat for grown-ups and kids. And if your little one grows attached to the cute monsters, make sure she watches till the end of the credits, where it helpfully assures us that no monsters were harmed in the making of the film. ★★★★★

MRS DOUBTFIRE

Starring Robin Williams, Sally Field, Pierce Brosnan (1993)

Based on a novel by Anne Fine and directed by *Home Alone*'s Chris Columbus, *Mrs Doubtfire* is really a showcase for Robin Williams's fast and furious comic talents. Here he stars as Daniel Hillard, a divorced dad who doesn't see as much of his kids as he would like, and who has a strained relationship with his ex-wife, Miranda (Field). So when he hears she is looking for a nanny to take care of the children while she's at work, he does what any dad would do... gets his make-up artist brother (Harvey Fierstein) to design a prosthetic female face, then grabs some thick tights, a grey wig and a frumpy dress and transforms himself into Mrs Doubtfire, a lovable Scottish nanny, whom Miranda naturally hires.

Williams sat in the make-up chair for over four hours each day to be transformed into Mrs Doubtfire, but that doesn't seem to have dampened his comic spirit, as he operates on full throttle throughout this comedy. A huge success when it was released, this does have some slow-moving sections and isn't on a comic par with the more grown-up *Tootsie* (in which Dustin Hoffman was the man in drag), but it's amusing enough and should delight kids and Williams fans. A sequel follows at the end of 2006. ★★★☆☆

THE MUMMY

Starring Brendan Fraser, Rachel Weisz (1999)

Get ready for a daft but rip-roaring adventure with this *Raiders of the Lost Ark*-style mix of humour, stunts and special effects, based on the 1932 classic of the same name. Rachel Weisz (sporting some very strange pencil marks where her eyebrows should be) is the 1920s librarian who gets her hands on an Egyptian map which she hopes will lead her to a lost city of the dead. With her brother (an enjoyably dippy John Hannah) and muscle-for-hire Brendan Fraser in tow, she finds the long-buried tombs, but also accidentally reawakens a rather pissed-off (and larger than life) Egyptian priest who was buried alive thousands of years before as punishment for romancing the Pharaoh's missus. He's back to reincarnate her soul, and – in between subjecting various members of the party to yucky deaths – sees Ms Weisz as the perfect body to put his love's spirit into.

Ridiculous and hilarious at the same time, this old-fashioned tale romps along at a cracking pace, while boasting a small helping of gore (making the film unsuitable for under-tens and those of a nervous disposition) and some impressive special effects that shouldn't be missed. Silly but fun. ★★★★☆

THE MUMMY RETURNS

Starring Brendan Fraser, Rachel Weisz (2001)

The title says it all, really. Rick (Fraser) and Evelyn (Weisz) are now married with a young son, Alex (Freddie Boath), but that doesn't stop them going on adventures looking for ancient artefacts. Unfortunately, the Mummy Imhotep whom they thought they had vanquished in Part One is back too, and he kidnaps their boy, sending the pair off in hot pursuit.

This time around, the story is a bit weak – some nonsense about Evelyn being the reincarnation of Nefertiti – but there is plenty of action and some nifty battle scenes featuring the Scorpion King (played by The Rock, who later starred in a spin-off action movie) as well as impressive set pieces featuring a gold pyramid and a flying galleon. Another rip-roaring adventure. ★★★☆☆

THE NUTTY PROFESSOR

Starring Eddie Murphy, Jada Pinkett (1996)

A remake of that classic Jerry Lewis side-splitter from 1963, about a weedy college professor who takes a potion to turn himself into a he-man so he can win the girl of his dreams, this stars Eddie Murphy in something of a comeback performance after a series of duds earlier in the nineties.

In Murphy's and director Tom Shadyac's (*Ace Ventura: Pet Detective*) update, professor Sherman Klump isn't weedy, he's HUGE. Weighing in at over twenty-eight stone, he has tried every diet and exercise imaginable when he uses the serum and becomes Buddy, a smart-mouthed, arrogant Casanova – but it's not long before Sherman realises his other half may be going out of control.

Murphy – who plays Sherman, Buddy and four members of the Klump family (including mama and grandma) in a couple of hilarious dinner table scenes – is hysterical from the opening scene to the out-takes shown over the final credits. Certainly, this is one of the few remakes that is as good as – or maybe even better than – the original, and it is also a triumph for Murphy (although he did later disappoint by making a forgettable, low-on-laughs sequel, *The Klumps*, in 2000). ★★★★☆

ONE OF OUR DINOSAURS IS MISSING

Starring Peter Ustinov, Helen Hayes, Derek Nimmo (1975)

A good old-fashioned British caper movie, this is an entertaining romp for the family. Lord Southmere (Nimmo) escapes from China with a valuable microfilm, and while evading the bad guys he hides it in the bones of one of the dinosaurs on display at London's Natural History Museum. He's been followed, however, so when he bumps into his old nanny, Hettie (Hayes), he asks her to retrieve it before the Chinese spies (led by Ustinov) get hold of it.

Worth watching for the bizarre sight of a dinosaur skeleton being transported through London by Hettie and her nanny pals while being chased by the baddies, this is enjoyably slapstick stuff (if you can get past the caricatures – the nannies are prim, the Chinese are evil… oops) from director Robert Stevenson, who also made family favourites *Mary Poppins*, *That Darn Cat!* and *The Love Bug*. ★★★☆☆

PIRATES OF THE CARIBBEAN: THE CURSE OF THE BLACK PEARL 🔞 PG-13 Ⓜ

Starring Johnny Depp, Orlando Bloom, Keira Knightley (2003)

This sounded like such a bad idea – basing a movie on the Pirates of the Caribbean ride at Disneyland – but it turned out to be one of the best blockbusters of 2003, thanks to some rollicking action and a truly genius performance from Johnny Depp as pirate Jack Sparrow.

Young blacksmith Will Turner (Bloom) hankers after the lovely Elizabeth (Knightley) and finally gets a chance to prove his worth when she is captured by spooky pirates from the ship the *Black Pearl*. With the (reluctant) help of boozy Jack Sparrow – who used to be the *Pearl*'s captain – he sets off to rescue her in an adventure packed with witty one-liners, gallant deeds and sword fights. Of course, Depp, with his braided hair, eye make-up and Keith Richards accent, steals the movie from everyone else, and that's a tough thing to do when you consider the cast also includes Jonathan Pryce (great as Elizabeth's dad), *The Office*'s Mackenzie Crook and Geoffrey Rush as the new captain of the *Black Pearl*, Barbossa.

The director, Gore Verbinski, has since filmed two sequels back to back, 2006's *Dead Man's Chest* (in which Jack owes his soul to the mythical Davy Jones, who comes to collect) and 2007's *Pirates of the Caribbean 3* (Elizabeth is captured by an Oriental pirate, played by Chow Yun-Fat). ★★★★★

RAIDERS OF THE LOST ARK

Starring Harrison Ford, Karen Allen (1981)

Most actors are lucky to have one iconic role during their career, like Sean Connery's James Bond or Anne Bancroft's Mrs Robinson, but Harrison Ford can boast two – Han Solo and, of course, the character he first showcased here, Indiana Jones, that tweed-clad professor of archaeology who scours the globe (when he isn't teaching drooling girls) for artefacts and antiquities.

A homage to the Saturday matinee serials of the 1930s from Steven Spielberg and George Lucas, this is a cracking adventure – Indy is hired by the American government to try and track down the Ark of the Covenant (in which Moses supposedly stored the tablets of the Ten Commandments) before the Nazis get their hands on it – that is a true rollercoaster ride from the much-imitated opening (the bit with the booby-trapped cavern and rolling boulder) to the effects-laden finale. It's nail-biting, funny, whip-smart and action-packed, with Ford making a perfect antihero (Indy gets bruised and battered and isn't that nice to tough-damsel-in-distress Marion, either), a man who treasures ancient artefacts but doesn't think twice about stealing them, either. One of the most enjoyable and memorable escapist adventures ever made, *Raiders* was followed by two cracking sequels (*Indiana Jones and the Temple of Doom, Indiana Jones and the Last Crusade*) and a third is rumoured for release in 2008. ★★★★★

THE RAILWAY CHILDREN

Starring Jenny Agutter, Dinah Sheridan (1970)

A lovely classic English movie, based on the novel by E Nesbit (*Five Children and It*). In 1905, the Waterbury family live in comfort until one night when some mysterious men take away father Charles (Iain Cuthbertson), and so mother (Sheridan), with no money to speak of, has to take the children to a ramshackle Yorkshire cottage to live. Once there, the children, who have no idea what happened to their beloved daddy, become fascinated with the local railway and befriend the stationmaster (Bernard Cribbins).

An absolutely gorgeous story about love, loyalty, charity and growing up, this is a terrific adaptation of a much-loved story, featuring sweet performances from Agutter as oldest child Bobbie and Sally Thomsett as sister Phyllis. One of those movies that makes us wish for a childhood we never had and a luscious green-field England that hardly exists any more, this is a must for everyone, as long as you have tissues handy for the finale when Bobbie calls out 'Daddy! My Daddy!' ★★★★★

THE ROOKIE

Starring Dennis Quaid, Brian Cox (2002)

Dennis Quaid stars as Jimmy Morris, a Texas high school baseball coach who had dreams of playing in the minor leagues as a teenager until a shoulder injury forced him to quit. His pupils, however, have other ideas – they strike a deal with him that if they win the state school baseball championships (a seemingly impossible task, considering they are always beaten), he has to agree to try out for a major league team even though he is twenty years older than all the other players.

You can guess what happens next (this is a Disney movie, so there won't be an unhappy ending), but what makes this so enjoyable is that it's actually based on a true story (the real Jim, who ended up pitching for a major league team, has a cameo role as an umpire at one of the games). Quaid is just wonderful as the man who thinks his big dream has slipped through his fingers, and who has made a life for himself with a wife (Rachel Griffiths) and family that always comes first, and there's nice support from Brian Cox as Jim's gruff father. A warm, fuzzy treat. (Do note that there is a dreadful Clint Eastwood/Charlie Sheen thriller with the same title that should be avoided!) ★★★★☆

THE SCHOOL OF ROCK

Starring Jack Black, Joan Cusack (2003)

Jack Black – who was so superb as the manic record store assistant in *High Fidelity*, but disappointing in movies like *Shallow Hal* and *Saving Silverman* – finally got the leading role to suit his wisecracking talents in this terrific comedy. He plays slacker/wannabe rocker Dewey Finn, who cons his way into a substitute teaching job at a prestigious school because he needs money to pay the rent. Of course, he has nothing to pass on to the kids except his almost psychopathic love of rock music, so it's not long before normal lessons are abandoned and he is teaching the group of ten-year-olds how to form their own band, play guitar like Hendrix and enter a local Battle of the Bands competition.

Directed with zeal by Richard Linklater, this is the perfect forum for Black's manic persona, but the true stars here are the kids, all of whom play their own instruments and rock the house just as well as any grown-ups. Terrific stuff. ★★★★☆

THE SOUND OF MUSIC

Starring Julie Andrews, Christopher Plummer (1965)

Like *The Wizard of Oz* and *It's a Wonderful Life*, *The Sound of Music* is as much a part of a family Christmas as mince pies and rows over who gets the skin off the custard. As enjoyable now as it was back in 1965, it is, of course, the wholesome tale of young Maria (Andrews, in a role originally envisaged for Audrey Hepburn), who leaves an Austrian convent to become governess to the von Trapp children. Plummer is perfect as the stern Baron von Trapp (can you imagine Yul Brynner or Sean Connery in the role, as they were both considered), whose heart is slowly melted by Maria's songs and jolliness, just in time for the pair to gather up the family and flee across the Alps to evade the Nazis.

Yes, everything you could want in a film is here – sing-along songs ('Do-Re-Mi', 'My Favourite Things', 'Sixteen Going on Seventeen' and the weepy 'Edelweiss', to name a few), cutesy kids, teen romance, nasty Nazis, more songs, and the gorgeous picture-postcard scenery. Definitely one for all the family to enjoy (though older kids and teens will probably gag at the sheer loveliness of it all) – altogether now: 'Doe, a deer, a female deer...' ★★★★★

TALL TALE PG PG

Starring Patrick Swayze, Oliver Platt, Nick Stahl (1995)

If your tot is interested in Westerns, but you think most are a little old for him/her, this could be a good kiddie alternative. Set in 1905, it's the story of twelve-year-old Daniel (Stahl), whose father has been fighting developers (led by the evil JP Stiles, played by Scott Glenn) who want to take over the family farm. When his dad is badly injured by Stiles's heavies, Daniel is left to fight alone, but when he flees the farm with the deeds Stiles wants so badly, he meets the hero of the stories his dad used to tell him, straight-shooting Pecos Bill (Swayze). Pecos Bill agrees to help Daniel get home and face the bad guys, and suggests they enlist the help of two of his pals, strongman John Henry (Roger Aaron Brown) and Paul Bunyan (Platt).

It doesn't matter that young kids may not have heard of the legendary Western characters that Daniel meets (including Calamity Jane, who also pops up) – each of the actors delivers a full-bodied performance (Platt, especially, as a tree-hugging Bunyan, is a hoot) that requires no previous knowledge of them or their stories. There's plenty of action and adventure, too, that should entertain Western fans of all ages. Yee ha! ★★★★☆

TOY STORY

Voices by Tom Hanks, Tim Allen (1995)

A rip-roaring computer-animated adventure that is, quite frankly, far too intelligent, funny and beautifully made to be just for a junior audience.

Six-year-old Andy doesn't know that his playthings come alive when he's not in the room. Led by Woody (Hanks), a cowboy doll that's always been Andy's favourite, the toys (including Bo Peep, Mr Potato Head and Rex the dinosaur) gather to await Andy's birthday, where he may get – oh no! – a new toy that he likes more than all of them. And this year, Andy gets the super-duperest toy ever: Buzz Lightyear (Allen). Woody realises he has to get rid of Buzz to be Andy's favourite once again, and his machinations lead the pair into terrible danger in the world outside Andy's bedroom. A witty script and wonderful, almost 3-D animation, plus Hanks and Allen's spot-on characterisations, make this a hugely enjoyable treat. Cute, comic and completely unmissable, this set the standard for all future computer-animated adventures. ★★★★★

TOY STORY 2

Voices by Tom Hanks, Tim Allen (1999)

The cute characters from *Toy Story* return for a second animated adventure in which cowboy doll Woody (Hanks) gets kidnapped by a toy collector who wants to sell him to Japan, and Buzz Lightyear (Allen), dinosaur Rex and pals have to go to the rescue.

Just as fun as the original for both grown-ups and the kids it's supposedly aimed at, this suffers only slightly from the fact that the best two characters – Woody and Buzz – don't interact together very much (after all, their bickering was the funniest part of the original *Toy Story*), but junior audiences won't be disappointed. Eagle-eyed viewers should watch out for cameos from some of the cast of *A Bug's Life* – Heimlich the caterpillar can be seen in one scene munching on a leaf. There are also spot-on homages to *2001: A Space Odyssey* and *Star Wars* – plus the Barbie dolls who dance in one scene are apparently copying moves by Ann-Margret in 1964's *Viva Las Vegas*. ★★★★☆

UNCLE BUCK

Starring John Candy, Macaulay Culkin (1989)

One of the late John Candy's most family-friendly films, he stars as the unreliable, slobbish Uncle Buck, who is asked by his brother and sister-in-law to look after their kids while they are out of town. Unfortunately, as well as cute little Maizy (Gaby Hoffmann) and precocious Miles (Culkin), there's also teenager Tia (Jean Kelly), who sees her parents' absence as the perfect time to sleep with her boyfriend. Throw in a randy neighbour (Laurie Metcalf) and Buck's own long-suffering girlfriend (Amy Madigan) and it looks like Buck may have bitten off more than he can chew.

Parents should note that a series of crude gags make this unsuitable for the under-twelves (although they'd probably love the coarseness), as does a scene in which Buck goes a little over the top while attempting to keep Tia's boyfriend at bay (he gags him and then stuffs him in the boot of his car). But older kids will get a kick out of Candy's antics, even if in the end this just isn't as funny as it could have been with such a talented comic actor in the lead. ★★★☆☆

WALLACE AND GROMIT: THE CURSE OF THE WERE-RABBIT

Voices by Peter Sallis, Helena Bonham Carter (2005)

Fantastic, BAFTA award-winning (it won Best British Film, beating the more highbrow *Pride and Prejudice*) and Oscar-winning (Best Animated Movie) family entertainment from those whizzes with 'claymation', Aardman Animations, who also made *Chicken Run* and the *Creature Comforts* TV series. Dotty inventor Wallace (voiced by Sallis) and his bemused dog Gromit – who we previously met in the short films *A Close Shave* and *The Wrong Trousers* – are on the trail of a giant angry rabbit who is terrorising locals and eating their treasured vegetables days before the annual Giant Vegetable Competition is to be held at Tottington Hall.

As well as this adventure, there's also time for some romance for Wallace, in the form of glamorous Lady Tottington (voiced by Bonham Carter), and a love rival, Victor Quartermaine (brilliantly voiced by Ralph Fiennes). An inventive and witty slice of entertainment that provides adventure and giggles for young viewers and smart laughs for grown-ups. Cracking stuff, eh, Gromit?! ★★★★★

WHO FRAMED ROGER RABBIT

Starring Bob Hoskins, Christopher Lloyd (1988)

Live action has been mixed with animation before and since (Tom and Jerry dancing with Gene Kelly in 1945's *Anchors Aweigh*, Bugs Bunny and pals playing ball with Michael Jordan in 1996's *Space Jam*) but this superb adventure really set a high standard that has yet to be bettered. LA private detective Eddie Valiant (Hoskins, in a role apparently previously offered to Robert Redford and Harrison Ford) doesn't like Toons, the animated creatures who live in the suburb of Toontown. So he's not happy when movie boss Marvin Acme (Stubby Kaye) hires him to investigate whether sexy animated star Jessica Rabbit (voiced by Kathleen Turner) is cheating on her hubby Roger (voiced by Charles Fleischer), and even less amused when Acme is murdered and excitable bunny Roger is the prime suspect.

A brilliant mix of cartoon and live action, this is hilarious as a double act between Hoskins and the animated Roger, and as a surreal kiddie adventure when the pair enter the cartoon world of Toontown (fans of Disney and Warner Brothers cartoons will spot many favourite characters along the way, including the Mel Blanc-voiced Daffy Duck, Bugs Bunny and Sylvester, as well as Betty Boop, Donald Duck and Yosemite Sam). Superb fun for all ages (though little ones may be scared by Lloyd's sinister Judge Doom and his torturing of cartoon characters). ★★★★★

THE WIZARD OF OZ

Starring Judy Garland (1939)

This is one of those movies that everyone has seen a little bit of (usually Garland singing 'Over the Rainbow'), even if they have never seen the actual film. It's the stuff of Hollywood legend – made in 1939 when Judy was seventeen (her budding cleavage had to be taped down so she'd be more convincing as a prepubescent girl), it's a magical fantasy adventure that was actually considered a financial disappointment when it was first released.

Dorothy realises she isn't in Kansas any more after a tornado whisks her off to the magical Technicolor Land of Oz, where she meets the Cowardly Lion, the Scarecrow and the Tin Man, who accompany her down the yellow brick road that leads to Emerald City and the mysterious Oz. Any little girl watching will covet the glittery red slippers Dorothy is given by Glinda the good witch, while kids and grown-ups may find themselves cowering behind the couch when the Wicked Witch appears (even freakier are the Munchkins, while some adults have very traumatic memories of the first time they saw the flying monkeys). Brightly coloured, funny and even frightening, this is a magical, mesmerising fantasy that's a must-see for every kid with a sense of wonder, and a nostalgic trip back in time for every parent. ★★★★★

Seasonal Stocking Fillers

All I Want for Christmas

Starring Thora Birch, Ethan Randall (1991)

All Hallie (Birch) and Ethan (Randall) want for Christmas is for their divorced parents to get back together again. And this being a Yuletide feel-good movie, do you think they'll get their wish, kiddies?

Meant as a comedy for preteens, this will infuriate any grown-ups watching with its scrappy script and daft plotting (the kids' plan is to lock mum's new beau in an ice-cream truck and then fake being sick so Dad and Mum will end up in the same room together, and of course it works), while kids will be bored by the lack of jokes and funny moments. Only of interest if you want to see co-stars Leslie Nielsen (as Santa) and screen legend Lauren Bacall (as the kids' grandma) giving the worst performances of their careers. Bah humbug. ★☆☆☆

Christmas with the Kranks

Starring Tim Allen, Jamie Lee Curtis (2004)

Based on a story, *Skipping Christmas*, written by John Grisham (the author better known for thrillers like *The Firm* and *The Client*), this weak comedy stars Tim Allen and Jamie Lee Curtis as Luther and Nora Krank, who decide to skip this year's Yuletide festivities since their daughter won't be at home with them, and spend the money on a cruise instead (they usually decorate inside and out, with the neighbours all competing to see who can have the most lavish display). The neighbours aren't too happy with the Kranks letting the side down, however, and begin a campaign to convince them to deck their hall and spray fake snow on their roof.

If you think your family has lost sight of the true meaning of Christmas (you know, that it's not just about presents, too much mulled wine and flashing Santa lights), this film is to be avoided as it's about the spirit of shopping, not the spirit of goodwill to all

men. And if you still have warm Yuletide sentiments in your household, you're better off avoiding this humourless, mean movie too, as it will just make you want to strangle the nearest Santa.
★☆☆☆☆

Elf 🎬 PG 🅖

Starring Will Ferrell, James Caan (2003)

A cracking Yuletide comedy that's not just for kids. Little orphan Buddy crawls into Santa's (Edward Asner) sack one Christmas and finds himself transported to the North Pole. He's raised by one of the elves (Bob Newhart), and it's not till he's a fully grown man that he realises he may be a little different from all the pint-sized people around him. So Santa tells Buddy the truth – his mum died when he was born, and his father, Walter (Caan), doesn't know he exists – before sending the innocent man-child (still in his green elf outfit) off to New York so he can find his dad.

A showcase for Ferrell's comic talents, this has some very funny moments, from Santa's advice to Buddy before he goes to the big city ('you see gum on the street, leave it there. It's not candy. And if you see a sign that says "Peep Show", that doesn't mean that they're letting you look at presents before Christmas'), to his adventures in the Big Apple (surprise, surprise, he gets a job in a department-store Santa's grotto). Best of all, though, is the lovely warm and fuzzy feeling this film will give you as Manhattan, and Caan's crabby Walter, finally remember the true meaning of Christmas. Aaah.
★★★☆☆

GREMLINS 🔞 PG PG

Starring Zach Galligan, Phoebe Cates (1984)

This black comedy may not seem a Christmassy film, but it is set during the festive season. Young Billy (Galligan) is given a cute cuddly little creature called a mogwai by his dad, who found it in a quirky Chinese shop. Billy names him Gizmo, and has to follow three important rules with his new pet: he mustn't feed Gizmo after midnight, he mustn't have bright lights around, and he mustn't allow the furry cutie near water.

Of course, it's not long before Billy has inadvertently broken a couple of those rules and, in doing so, causes adorable Gizmo to pop off a few dozen offspring. Unfortunately, they're not sweet like he is – they are mischievous, malevolent creatures called gremlins who seem intent on causing destruction throughout the town.

Surprisingly dark for a family film (although a scene in which one town resident is killed by the creatures was cut, do note the film has a '15' certificate), this has a wicked and almost gruesome sense of humour about it that appeals to older kids as well as grown-ups (it's not suitable for young children though, as they may find the gremlins a little too scaly and scary). ★★★★☆

Gremlins 2: The New Batch ⑫ PG PG

Starring Zach Galligan, Phoebe Cates (1990)

Six years after *Gremlins*, and Billy (Galligan) has moved to the big city with his girlfriend Kate (Cates). They both work for media mogul Daniel Clamp (John Glover, doing a semi-Donald Trump impersonation) in his ultra-modern new skyscraper. But when Billy brings little Gizmo the mogwai to work and he's captured by a scientist who doesn't know what can happen, it's not long before he's spawning those evil gremlins again and they are causing havoc (and this time they can talk, too).

Almost as inventive as the original, this sequel spoofs old TV shows and movies (see Gizmo as Rambo!) and is packed with laughs. In fact, the gremlins themselves are funnier and less scary than in *Gremlins*, making this more of an all-round family film. ★★★★☆

The Grinch (aka How the Grinch Stole Christmas) PG PG

Starring Jim Carrey, Taylor Momsen (2000)

Dr Seuss's tale about the grumpy creature who decides to steal

Christmas from the residents of Whoville got the big-screen treatment (it had previously been made as a cartoon for TV) and it's splashed with colour, flashy and loud, but lacking in the warmth and fuzziness you expect from a Christmas movie.

Jim Carrey clearly has a ball as Grinch, a green, furry creature who lives in a mountain cavern overlooking the cheerful town of Whoville, home of the Whos, with their odd (but slightly more human) faces and annoying love of Christmas. Tired of their infernal jollity, he decides to steal Christmas from them, taking their presents, but a little girl named Cindy Lou Who decides all the Grinch needs is a little love to turn him into a nice guy. While the sets are amazing and the cast quirky, this is really a showcase for Carrey's manic shtick (which is perhaps a little too crazed for very young viewers, who may find him scary) – if you like him, then it's terrific, but if you don't, this could grate a bit. ★★★☆☆

I'll Be Home for Christmas

Starring Jonathan Taylor Thomas, Jessica Biel (1998)

College guy Jake (Taylor Thomas) finds the true meaning of Christmas after he is dumped in the desert as a practical joke and has to make his way across country to be reunited with his family and girlfriend in New York. There's an added bonus if he makes the celebrations too – Dad (Gary Cole) so wants the family to be together for the holidays, he has bribed his errant son with the promise of a shiny red Porsche. Doesn't that just warm your heart?

A sort of kiddie version of *Planes, Trains and Automobiles* (but sadly lacking the comedic talent of a Steve Martin or John Candy), this falls apart thanks to an unlikeable lead character and a series of implausible situations. Preteens may have a few giggles at the daftness of it all but you'll have had to have had a lot of Christmas spirit to really enjoy this lacklustre movie. ★★☆☆☆

It's a Wonderful Life

Starring James Stewart, Donna Reed, Henry Travers (1946)

If you live in the US, on Christmas Day there will be at least one TV channel showing this Frank Capra-directed classic – it's more traditional to an American Yuletide than turkey and crackers. It's often listed as one of the best films ever made, yet it never won any Oscars.

A film about the good in everyone, it's based on the short story 'The Greatest Gift' by Philip Van Doren Stern, and is the tale of George Bailey (Stewart, who nearly turned the role down, tired after returning from the war), an all-round nice guy who grows up in the small friendly town of Bedford Falls but dreams of travelling the world. Instead, he marries Mary (Reed) and has a brood of cute kids, but the stress of his job and the disappointment of never fulfilling his dreams leads him on Christmas Eve to attempt suicide by jumping from the local bridge. However, an angel named Clarence (Travers) comes down from heaven to show George what life in Bedford Falls would have been like if he hadn't existed, and naturally it transpires that it would have been a much darker world without him. A beautiful film that is perhaps a little too bleak for very young viewers, but a must for everyone else. ★★★★★

> *'I love Frank Capra's It's a Wonderful Life when they all get together at the end and the bells go and James Stewart, one of the actors who has influenced me most in my life, says an angel has got his wings. Everyt time I hear a bell ring, I think of some angel getting his wings.' EWAN MCGREGOR*

Jack Frost

Starring Michael Keaton, Joseph Cross (1998)

A sweet, old-fashioned (yes, okay, it's also a bit lame) Christmas film, this stars Keaton as Jack Frost, a rock singer with a wife (Kelly

Preston) and child (Cross) whose music career is on the verge of hitting the big time. That's why he spends so much time away from home, to the annoyance of son Charlie, but Jack intends to spend Christmas with his family – until his car goes off the road in a snowstorm and he's killed. A year later, Charlie builds a snowman in the driveway and when he blows the harmonica which his dad claimed was 'magic', lo and behold, the pile of snow comes alive and Jack finds himself reincarnated as a snowman.

Cute stuff for preteens (with a Hanson and Spice Girls-peppered soundtrack that dates it somewhat), and thanks to a fun vocal performance from Keaton in snowman-mode, not a bad afternoon's viewing for adults either. ★★★☆☆

Jingle All the Way 🔞 PG PG

Starring Arnold Schwarzenegger, Sinbad, Jake Lloyd (1996)

Not sure which is worse – Arnold Schwarzenegger in a comedy, or a movie that celebrates the fact that Christmas is an excuse for commercialism and greed. The big Austrian oak stars as Howard Langston, a dad who doesn't spend enough time with his bratty son (*The Phantom Menace*'s annoying tyke, Jake Lloyd). He thinks all will be made better, however, if he gets his hands on the toy his son wants for Christmas – the much sought-after (and sold out) Turbo Man. Of course, he's not the only one after the toy – a deranged postman (Sinbad) wants one for his kid too, so Howard goes from being Mr Polite to Mr Angry in his quest to buy his son's love.

There's not much else to this comedy, apart from some cartoon-style violence. Kids may cheer as Arnie goes to any length to get his hands on the toy (including chasing a child through one of those play-tunnel things they have at kids' restaurants), while adults will just wish he would turn into the Terminator and blast all the other irritating parents and kids (and the scriptwriter for good measure) out of the way. ★★☆☆☆

Miracle on 34th Street ⚠ 🄶 ⚠

Starring Maureen O'Hara, Natalie Wood, Edmund Gwenn (1947)

A Christmas classic, this was actually released in the US in May 1947 (producers hoped that the ambiguous title wouldn't tip off movie-goers to the fact it was a Yuletide movie). Kris Kringle (Gwenn, who won an Oscar for his performance) gets a job as Santa Claus at Macy's, the famous New York department store. It's there he meets little Susan (an eight-year-old Natalie Wood), who tells him she doesn't believe in Santa, because her mother (O'Hara) has brought her up to think fairy tales and fantasies are nonsense. But Kris says he is actually the real Santa, a claim that first sees him sent to a mental institution and then to court, where he has to prove he is sane, and indeed the real Mr Claus.

A film positively brimming over with festive spirit, this manages to be a terrific feel-good movie without being remotely sickly or saccharine. One for the whole family (including cynics who don't believe in Father Christmas!), this was remade in 1994, starring Richard Attenborough as Kris and Mara Wilson as Susan (fictional store Cole's replaced Macy's, who wouldn't let their name be used for the remake). It's not bad at all (and worth a look if you can't find the 1947 one), but nothing beats the original. ★★★★☆

The Muppet Christmas Carol ⚠ 🄶 ⚠

Starring Michael Caine, Frank Oz (1992)

Charles Dickens's classic Christmas story gets the Muppet treatment, and what a treat it is. Michael Caine – truly getting into the spirit of things – is marvellous as miserly old Scrooge, who makes his poor employee Bob Cratchit (Kermit the Frog, with voice provided by Steve Whitmire, as creator Jim Henson died before the movie was made) work every hour of the day until the Ghosts of Christmas Past, Present and Yet to Come visit him to show him the error of his ways.

With Miss Piggy 'playing' Cratchit's wife, Gonzo narrating the story as Dickens and many other familiar Muppets popping up (including Fozzie Bear, Rizzo the Rat, Animal and the Swedish Chef), this is an enjoyable romp that's a must for Muppet fans (do bear in mind for very young viewers that there are a couple of spooky moments when the ghosts visit Scrooge, rattling their chains) and surely a must-see every Christmas. The Muppets also made a seasonal TV movie, *It's a Very Merry Muppet Christmas Movie*, co-starring William H Macy and Whoopi Goldberg, in 2002, that's worth a look. ★★★★★

The Nightmare Before Christmas

Voices by Danny Elfman, Chris Sarandon (1993)

Fed up with the enforced jolliness of the Yuletide season? Tim Burton's *The Nightmare Before Christmas* – conceived by the director (actually based on a poem he wrote), and helmed by Henry Selick, who also made *James and the Giant Peach* – is the perfect antidote to all that mistletoe and wine. Featuring stop-motion animation, it's the dark, twisted and definitely creepy tale of Jack Skellington, a ghoulish character from the nasty Halloweentown who discovers there's a place called Christmastown that offers something quite different ('There's children throwing snowballs instead of throwing heads. They're busy building toys and absolutely no one's dead!').

Although made by Disney, this is definitely not an adventure for young children – Jack kidnaps Santa, for a start! – but should delight older kids and anyone who enjoys Burton's wickedly dark sense of humour. A fantasy/adventure/musical/horror/comedy that's essential fare for scrooges. ★★★★☆

The Polar Express

Voices by Tom Hanks, Peter Scolari (2004)

Based on a slim children's book, this is the simple tale of a boy who has begun to doubt the existence of Santa. On Christmas Eve, however, a steam train pulls up outside his house and a conductor ushers him aboard, telling the boy and the other kids inside (stereotypes like the greedy kid, the poor boy and the dewy-eyed girl) that the choo-choo is bound for the North Pole, where they will all get to meet Mr Claus himself and hopefully discover the true meaning of Christmas along the way.

So far, so cute. What distinguishes this from other family films isn't its well-meaning if slightly naff story, but how it is told. The film is animated – well, sort of. In a cinematic first, all the performances are by actors who acted out the parts in bodysuits covered in digital sensors, so their motions could be fed into computers and realised on screen in CGI. So, as well as the impressive backgrounds being computer-animated, so are the actors, in an attempt to make the characters as real as possible. Unfortunately, it doesn't quite work – the characters (five of which, including the boy and the conductor, are voiced by Tom Hanks) look more like freaky mannequins come to life than real people, so are unlikely to instil the warm and fuzzies into the tots watching, while Santa himself, when he finally appears, isn't fat and jolly but creepily scrawny instead.

The often jaw-dropping effects go some way to addressing the balance. As the train, en route to the North Pole, hurtles on a rollercoaster-ride track, speeding through forests and across icy plains, it's truly breathtaking and thoroughly entertaining. It's these effects that make *The Polar Express* worth catching, so while – unlike the kids in the movie – you and your family may not eventually believe, you should at least be mildly entertained. ★★★☆☆

Prancer 🔺 G ⚠

Starring Sam Elliott, Rebecca Harrell (1989)

A magical little family film about nine-year-old Jessica (Harrell), who finds a wounded reindeer and naturally assumes it is Prancer, one of Santa's helpers. While she's tending to the injured deer, her father (Elliott) struggles to keep the family farm from going under, and considers whether he should send Jessica to live with her aunt (Jessie's mother has died).

While this isn't suitable for very young children – Jessica's relationship with her harsh father may upset younger viewers – this has some cute moments and a lovely central performance from Harrell as Jessica, who in the end even manages to make some of the town believe in Santa as she tries to heal Prancer before he's needed on Christmas Eve. Aaaah. A DVD sequel, *Prancer Returns*, was made in 2001. ★★★☆☆

Santa Claus: The Movie

Starring Dudley Moore, John Lithgow (1985)

A disappointing Christmas movie, this has cheap flying effects, is low on laughs and adventure and, perhaps worst of all, relegates Santa to a supporting player, despite being called *Santa Claus: The Movie*!

For while the first half is almost sweet, as it tells us how Santa became Santa (he was rescued from a wintry death by elves and whisked off to the North Pole where he was made immortal so he can deliver the presents the elves make each year), the second half is about a disgraced elf named Patch (Moore) who meets an evil businessman (Lithgow) who just happens to make toys, and dangerous ones at that. Unfortunately, the entire film – which unsurprisingly was a box-office disaster – is severely lacking in charm, features an eye-wincingly awful over-the-top performance from Lithgow and has a script littered with bad puns ('elf-help' etc, etc). ★☆☆☆☆

The Santa Clause

Starring Tim Allen, Judge Reinhold (1994)

Tim Allen – a big TV star in the US for the sitcom *Home Improvement*, but best known everywhere else for being the voice of Buzz Lightyear – is divorced dad Scott Calvin, who finds a whole new lease of life after investigating a noise on the roof of his house. It seems Santa and his reindeer are up there, but after Santa trips and is killed, Scott finds himself putting on the iconic red and white suit. Unfortunately, he doesn't realise that anyone wearing Santa's suit becomes the real Santa, and has a bit of a shock when he discovers the next day that he has already gained lots of weight and is sprouting a Santa beard.

An inoffensive Christmas comedy, this is quite fun for kids who don't believe in Santa any more (kids that do may have their illusions shattered), as the plot offers up fun explanations as to how Santa can visit every child in just one night and how he can squeeze into tight chimneys. Allen is enjoyable to watch as his hair turns white and he has to deal with an ex-wife who thinks he has gone insane, and there is nice support from Reinhold, Peter Boyle and David Krumholtz as Bernard the elf, whom Scott meets when he goes to the North Pole. A fair sequel, *The Santa Clause 2*, followed in 2002, in which Scott has to find a Mrs Claus, and a third in 2006, in which Santa/Scott has to stop Jack Frost taking over Christmas. ★★★☆☆

Scrooge ⚠Ⓤ Ⓖ ⚠

Starring Alastair Sim, Mervyn Johns (1951)

There have been more than twenty film and TV versions of Dickens's *A Christmas Carol* (including the Muppets' take on it, *The Muppet Christmas Carol*), with everyone from George C Scott, Patrick Stewart, Tim Curry (in an awful animated version) and Michael Hordern taking on the role of miser Ebenezer Scrooge. The best version, and the best known, is this 1951 British production, in which Alastair Sim stars as Scrooge (and does it better than anyone before or since), who is visited by the ghosts of Christmas Past (Michael Dolan), Christmas Present (Francis De Wolff) and Christmas Yet to Come (C Konarski) one fateful Christmas Eve, in the hope that the apparitions will make him change his mean ways.

With a cast that includes George Cole (as young Ebenezer), Michael Hordern (here playing Jacob Marley) and Hattie Jacques, this is cracking stuff, both as a terrific introduction to Dickens's classic ghost story (the ghostly bits aren't suitable for very young eyes), and as a movie to get you in the Yuletide mood. Avoid the colourised version that's available, and revel in the rich black and white movie the way it was meant to be seen. ★★★★☆

Sci-Fi and Comic-Book Adventures

••

Many kids love science-fiction movies and comic-book adventures, but do remember that, in the main, science-fiction movies are often dark (hey, they are set in deep space!) and comic-book adventures boast not only superheroes, but also the nasty bad guys they have to face. When choosing a film, it's worth bearing in mind that they are often aimed at older kids and adults rather than very young viewers, so if you're picking one of the '12' or '15' UK certificate movies included in this section, it's probably worth checking out its content before subjecting your child to a year's worth of nightmares. And just because one super-hero movie is suitable for your tots, don't assume they all are (hence the inclusion below of the dark but not too creepy *Batman*, but the exclusion of the more violent and sinister *Batman Begins*, which is really for grown-ups).

That said, there's still plenty on offer if your sci-fi/comic fan is under ten – you can't go too wrong with fun movies like *Casper*, *ET*: *The Extra-Terrestrial*, *The Incredibles* or *George of the Jungle*. And if you want a really junior adventure, don't forget *Muppets From Space*…

20,000 LEAGUES UNDER THE SEA

Starring Kirk Douglas, James Mason (1954)

Jules Verne's classic adventure story has been captured on film before (in 1907 and 1916) and since (an animated version in 1973 and for TV in 1997 and 2002), but this Disney version is perhaps the most enter-taining, featuring a cast that includes Kirk Douglas, James Mason and Peter Lorre.

A professor (Paul Lukas) is determined to discover whether a rumoured sea monster that attacks boats really exists, but when his

Kiddie Comics

For the most junior viewers there are a few comic strips that have been made into movies that are ideal. *Garfield* is reviewed here, while fans of Peanuts can get to know pooch Snoopy and his human pals Charlie Brown, Linus and co in the feature-length animated adventures *A Boy Called Charlie Brown* (1969) and *Snoopy Come Home* (1972), which both stay true to Charles Schulz's original drawings. (There are, of course, numerous shorter Peanuts cartoons, originally made for TV and now available on DVD, including the classic *A Charlie Brown Christmas* from 1965.)

Little boys will no doubt love naughty *Dennis the Menace* (1993), in which little tyke Dennis (an American comic-strip character, not the football-loving British one from the *Beano* comics) foils a (rather menacing for younger viewers) burglar, *Home Alone*-style. There are also two inferior straight-to-DVD sequels, *Dennis the Menace Strikes Again!* (1998) and the animated *Dennis the Menace in Cruise Control* (2002).

Or, while it is pretty awful for anyone over the age of eight, there's also *Richie Rich* (1994), in which a fifteen-year-old Macaulay Culkin tries to hide the fact his voice has broken in his portrayal of the wealthiest kid in the world, who has everything a boy could want except friends (boo-hoo). Luckily, he gets some just in time for them to help him fend off a bad guy, in what was to be Culkin's last 'little boy' film (he then took a nine-year hiatus before returning to the screen as club kid/drug addict Michael Alig in the very adult *Party Monster*).

own ship sinks, he, harpoon master Ned Land (Douglas) and Conseil (Lorre) discover the supposed monster is actually an atomic submarine called the *Nautilus*, captained by the brilliant but megalomaniac Nemo (Mason).

There's lots of macho posturing from Douglas, a deliciously bonkers performance from Mason and some very impressive sets depicting the

Nautilus (the film won Oscars for Art Direction and Special Effects), but kids and grown-ups alike will get most enjoyment out of the classic battle with a giant squid that's not to be missed. ★★★★☆

AT THE EARTH'S CORE

Starring Doug McClure, Peter Cushing (1976)

A camp seventies sci-fi adventure, based on Edgar Rice Burroughs's novel, and made by the same producing and directing team behind *The Land That Time Forgot*. Legendary horror actor Peter Cushing (playing it wonderfully tongue-in-cheek) is Dr Abner Perry ('You cannot mesmerise me! I'm British!' he says, just before being hypnotised), who, along with brawny David Innes (McClure), has devised a contraption called the Iron Mole which bores through solid rock. You can guess what happens next.

Adults will snigger as our heroes and their big drill end up in a strange land at the earth's centre full of prehistoric creatures and scantily clad cave girls, but boys will love the (unscary) monsters, assuming they don't notice the wires, while girls will enjoy the hokey romance between macho David and a slave girl (Caroline Munro). Yes, it's as bad as it sounds. But in a good way. ★★★☆☆

ATLANTIS: THE LOST EMPIRE

Voices by Michael J Fox, James Garner (2001)

A drab, over-complicated and utterly forgettable Disney adventure. There aren't even any songs or cute cuddly creatures in this waterlogged tale that tries to be *20,000 Leagues Under the Sea* with cartoon explosions. Instead, we get the plodding tale set in 1914 of Milo Thatch (nicely voiced by Fox), a young man who believes in the legend of Atlantis and, thanks to a journal written in Atlantean that only he can translate, has a pretty good idea where it is. Luckily for Milo there's an eccentric millionaire who believes in Atlantis too, and is funding an expedition to rediscover it. Soon our eager hero is mucking in with the crew of a submarine (led by crusty Commander Rourke, voiced by Garner), on his way to find the lost city.

While the underwater world is beautifully realised, the animation of the characters is surprisingly blocky (check out the square fingers and triangular fingernails – what's that about?) and will no doubt get the thumbs-down from kids more used to the colourful and three-dimensional animation of *Toy Story* or *Shrek*. Equally, it's hard to imagine younger viewers sitting still through a film that waffles on about New-Agey 'life forces' and gets all deep and meaningful around the time Milo realises the army he has been sent down to Atlantis with may not have the Atlanteans' best interests at heart. Even sci-fi-style effects that pepper the film regularly enough to stop you slipping into unconsciousness don't raise this to the level of one of Disney's lesser films of the last twenty years. After all, even the dire *The Fox and the Hound* had a cute fluffy puppy... ★★☆☆☆

BATMAN

Starring Michael Keaton, Kim Basinger, Jack Nicholson (1989)

Orphaned when his parents were shot in front of him by a laughing robber when he was a child, Bruce Wayne (Keaton) has a split personality. By day he is a suave millionaire, but by night he dons a cape and rubber mask to become Batman, a superhero on the edge, dedicated to ridding the streets of Gotham of criminals. Helped by his trusty butler, Alfred, our hero has gadgets galore (including, of course, the Batmobile) hidden in the caves beneath his imposing home (actually Knebworth House in Hertfordshire) and they come in handy when a new bad guy comes to town, the cackling Joker (Nicholson).

Director Tim Burton was the perfect person to make a dark, stylish version of the *Batman* comics for the big screen, and he made a terrific choice hiring Keaton, who is just right as the conflicted, brooding crimefighter. It's certainly nothing like the campy sixties TV series (and because of some creepy moments, probably isn't suitable for the under-elevens – when released at UK cinemas it had a '12' certificate), instead it's a beautifully realised adventure, featuring a glamorous Basinger as reporter Vicki Vale, a brilliantly bonkers turn from Nicholson and a catchy soundtrack from Prince. ★★★★★

BATMAN FOREVER

Starring Val Kilmer, Nicole Kidman, Jim Carrey, Tommy Lee Jones (1995)

The third nineties Batman movie (following on from *Batman* and

Batman Returns), this was the first not to be directed by Tim Burton and it shows – it's not as dark (shame) and instead, thanks to director Joel Schumacher, it is brasher, flashier and, well, a bit over the top. Stepping into Batman's cape and mask (taking over from Michael Keaton) is Val Kilmer, who looks rather bland and a bit sulky as the hero with a split personality. Nicole Kidman isn't given much to do as love interest Dr Chase Meridian, so it's left to Jim Carrey, as the manic Riddler, and a quite frightening Tommy Lee Jones, as Two-Face, to liven things up a bit.

It's certainly lavish and splashy in terms of effects and sets, but it's simply not as good as the first two films. The introduction of Chris O'Donnell as Robin is a disaster (adult viewers will just want to punch him, while kids will groan at his annoying persona), and the addition of nipples to the Bat costumes is downright disturbing. What's next, a jockstrap over Superman's tights? ★★★☆☆

BATMAN RETURNS

Starring Michael Keaton, Danny DeVito, Michelle Pfeiffer (1992)

Even darker than *Batman*, this sequel from Tim Burton is many a man's favourite, thanks to Michelle Pfeiffer's sultry, PVC-clad turn as Catwoman. The real bad guy of the piece is the Penguin (DeVito), a man with flippers for hands, whose parents abandoned him to the sewers as a baby (quite a distressing scene for younger viewers), where he was raised by penguins. Now he's back, and with the help of businessman Max Shreck (a scene-stealing Christopher Walken), he wants to take over the city. Can our hero save the day, or is he too busy romancing secretary Selina (Pfeiffer), little knowing she slips into her own costume at night and is in fact Batman's enemy?

As good as, if not better than, the first film, *Batman Returns* is packed with action, dark humour and stunning set pieces. Be warned, though, that the penguins featured in the film are surprisingly creepy, and the film's overall sinister tone (and DeVito's rather icky Penguin) is likely to upset preteen children. ★★★★★

BATMAN AND ROBIN

Starring George Clooney, Uma Thurman, Arnold Schwarzenegger (1997)

While *Batman Forever* wasn't a wholly successful follow-up to *Batman* and *Batman Returns*, the fourth Batman film of the nineties was a complete disaster, boasting an all-star cast and a script that sounds as if it was written during someone's tea break.

George Clooney (who, girls young and old will agree, looks dreamy) just isn't right as Bruce Wayne/Batman – he's better in character roles than in a big comic-book blockbuster like this and is overshadowed by a bonkers performance from Arnold Schwarzenegger as bad guy Mr Freeze. Poor Arnie has to spout dialogue like 'Ice to see you!' but Uma Thurman has an even worse time as former dowdy scientist turned Poison Ivy, awkwardly slinking around, mainly because there's not much else to do. But the big boos and hisses should go to the double act of Alicia Silverstone as Batgirl and Chris O'Donnell as Robin, both blander than over-boiled chicken and just as appetising.

While pubescent boys may get a kick out of Alicia and Uma in clingy outfits, they're the only ones likely to be amused by this dull adventure (although adults can while away the time by spotting the numerous homoerotic moments). ★★☆☆☆

THE BLACK HOLE

Starring Maximilian Schell, Anthony Perkins (1979)

Following the success 20th Century Fox had with *Star Wars*, two years later Disney did sci-fi with this impressive-looking but silly adventure that features mad scientist Hans Reinhardt (Schell), a crew of robots and, as the title suggests, a supposedly perilous journey into a black hole.

Star Wars fanatics will hate it, as it borrows heavily from the film – there's even a whiny-voiced robot (voiced by Roddy McDowall) who sounds like C-3PO's cousin – while everyone else will just be bored as the impressive cast – Perkins, Ernest Borgnine, Yvette Mimieux – wanders around the vast ship on the edge of the black hole, presumably searching for a decent script. ★★☆☆☆

CARAVAN OF COURAGE: AN EWOK ADVENTURE ⚠ 🆄 **G** PG

Starring Warwick Davis, Eric Walker (1984)

Star Wars fans who found those fuzzy teddy bear creatures in *Return of the Jedi* almost as irritating as Jar Jar Binks should perhaps give a wide berth to this kiddie spin-off featuring the little munchkins. Wicket the Ewok (the one who befriended Leia in *Jedi*) and his pals come to the rescue of two human children whose spaceship has crash-landed on the forest moon of Endor. Their parents have been captured by a nasty creature, so the Ewoks decide to help them find them, even if it means a long, perilous journey. And, er, that's about it.

Made for TV in the US (but released theatrically elsewhere), this looks much cheaper than a *Star Wars* movie but doesn't mess with the franchise too much (although fans may be annoyed that the chattering Ewoks can now speak English). Clearly aimed at little kids, it passes the time and was followed by a sequel, *Ewoks II: The Battle for Endor*, in 1985, and an animated TV series, *Ewoks*. ★★★☆☆

CASPER ⚠ PG PG

Starring Christina Ricci, Bill Pullman, Eric Idle (1995)

Casper is the cutest ghost you're ever likely to see on film. Based on the old American cartoon and comic book *Casper the Friendly Ghost*, the movie is a terrific mix of live action and the superb wizardry of Steven Spielberg's Amblin Entertainment and George Lucas's Industrial Light & Magic.

Casper is a ghost who haunts Whipstaff Manor with his three odious uncles, Stretch, Stinkie and Fatso. All Casper wants is a friend, and his wish is granted when Kat (Ricci) and her 'ghost therapist' father Dr Harvey (Pullman) move into the manor. There are some wonderful comic moments as the spectral uncles try to get rid of the 'fleshies', and the comedy is successfully mixed with the impressive ghostly effects that will enchant both adults and children alike. An animated TV series followed in 1996, and three so-so video/DVD follow-ups, the prequel *Casper: A Spirited Beginning* (1997), *Casper Meets Wendy*, starring a young Hilary Duff (1998), and the animated *Casper's Haunted Christmas* (2000), aimed at very junior viewers. ★★★★☆

DICK TRACY

Starring Warren Beatty, Madonna, Al Pacino (1990)

Martin Scorsese, Tim Burton and John Landis were among the directors who were considered to bring comic book Dick Tracy to the screen at one time or another, but when Warren Beatty was offered the chance to direct he said yes, with one stipulation – that he be the star, too. The end result is an odd movie – not a blockbuster, not an action picture, and yet not an arthouse movie either – that will most likely appeal to older (teens and up) viewers (younger ones will probably be bored, and perhaps are a little young to see co-star Madonna oozing all over Mr Beatty).

Coloured in the bright shades of the comic (red, blue, yellow, purple, green and orange) and populated with impressive character actors like Mandy Patinkin, Paul Sorvino, Charles Durning, Seymour Cassel and Pacino, this is the stylised tale of detective Dick Tracy and his various encounters with bad guys like Big Boy Caprice (an over-the-top Pacino) and a smouldering Madonna as chanteuse Breathless Mahoney ('You don't know if you want to hit me or kiss me. I get a lot of that.'). It has great songs (from Stephen Sondheim), but ultimately it looks and sounds great yet doesn't have a pacy plot to keep you gripped until the end. ★★★☆☆

ET: THE EXTRA-TERRESTRIAL

Starring Henry Thomas, Drew Barrymore (1982)

A classic weepie of the highest order, this is a terrific sci-fi film for all the family (and was, in fact, the winner of a 2005 poll to find the best family film ever). Instead of scary invaders from Mars (*The War of the Worlds*) or ravenous, hideous beasts (*Alien*), this arrival from outer space is cute and cuddly and (pass the tissues) has accidentally been abandoned on earth by his pals, who have zipped off home in their spaceship.

A homage to childhood from director Steven Spielberg, this has lonely young boy Elliott (Thomas) befriending the pot-bellied creature (played in many scenes by a small person in an ET suit, while the character's face was supposedly imagined after the production team superimposed Einstein's forehead and eyes onto the face of a baby) and introducing him to such earthly customs as beer drinking, candy eating, and dressing up in Elliott's sister Gertie's (Barrymore) clothes. But it's not all warm and lovely – soon government men are on their trail, ready to experiment on our little space traveller.

Appealing to the little kid in all of us, this is packed with nicely written and well-played sentimental moments that will turn even the most cynical viewer into a pile of blubbering mush, especially when ET's life is in danger (the scene when he goes all white and chalky may be too distressing for little viewers) or he memorably tells Elliott (tissues again, please) he wants to 'phone home'. An anniversary edition, released in 2002, has computerised changes to ET's facial expressions (subtle differences Spielberg was unable to achieve in 1982) and, most notably, the digital replacement of the government agents' guns with walkie-talkie radios. ★★★★★

EXPLORERS

Starring Ethan Hawke, River Phoenix (1985)

Sci-fi fan Ben (Hawke) has a dream in which he sees a giant circuit board, so along with pal and young wannabe scientist Wolfgang (Phoenix) he miraculously builds a sphere of energy that can travel through space (it seems aliens have sent the blueprints telepathically). Teaming up with loner Darren (Jason Presson), they're soon zapping around above their town, until the aforementioned aliens whisk them up into space for a meeting.

Directed by B-movie fan Joe Dante (who often alludes to the kitsch fifties films he loves, in movies like *Gremlins* and his segment of *Twilight Zone: The Movie*), this was a flop at the box office, perhaps because it was quite quirky (the aliens have learnt everything about earth from TV, so greet the kids by saying 'What's up, Doc?') and never lives up to the fun of the first hour (before the kids are on the ship). Nonetheless, it's his most kiddie-friendly film (no scares here) and while kids can identify with the boys' dreams of space travel, grown-ups can catch fifteen-year-old Hawke in his first screen performance. ★★★☆☆

FANTASTIC FOUR

Starring Ioan Gruffudd, Jessica Alba, Julian McMahon (2005)

While many of the comic-book adaptations mentioned here are aimed at teenagers (the ones with the most cash to spend at the cinema) and adults, *Fantastic Four* will probably be best enjoyed by younger viewers looking for action and adventure (but, alas, very little plot). Reed Richards (Gruffudd), Sue Storm (Alba), Ben (Michael Chiklis), Johnny (Chris Evans) and businessman Victor von Doom (McMahon) are exposed to cosmic radiation (oops) while in space and find they all have superpowers on their return to earth. Stretchy Reed becomes Mr Fantastic, Sue is Invisible Woman, poor Ben, thanks to some rock-like disfigurement, is The Thing, and Johnny is the Human Torch (handy when the heating's on the fritz). Doom, meanwhile, just seems to have got grumpier, and becomes the bad guy mainly because he wants to marry Sue and she's not interested.

The chief reason this will appeal to younger viewers is the effects, which are pretty fantastic, from Gruffudd's elasticky body to Johnny's flamey-ness, and the light tone of the whole film (aside from Ben being clearly upset that he's now a big hunk of rock, everyone else has fun with their new powers). It's certainly not a great comic-book movie, but it zips along and if you think your kids are a little young for *Batman*, *X-Men* or *Spider-Man*, this isn't a bad choice. ★★★☆☆

FLASH GORDON

Starring Sam Jones, Max von Sydow (1980)

Camper than a field full of tents, this 1980 adventure is mainly remembered for the rock anthem 'Flash' by Queen that thunders across the soundtrack. Directed by Mike Hodges (better known for grittier films like *Get Carter* and *Croupier*), it's a brightly coloured adventure as New York Jets quarterback Flash Gordon (Jones) travels with his pals to the planet Mongo to face off against the evil Ming the Merciless (Von Sydow), who is going to destroy the earth.

Former set decorator Jones and ex-model Melody Anderson (as Flash's pal Dale) are both pretty appalling, Von Sydow chews and spits out the kitsch scenery, while actors including Timothy Dalton and Brian Blessed just look bemused at their outlandish costumes. It's all terribly silly, but nonetheless an enjoyable romp for all ages, one of those films that's so bad it's actually pretty good. ★★★☆☆

FLIGHT OF THE NAVIGATOR

Starring Joey Cramer, Veronica Cartwright (1986)

Grease director Randal Kleiser was the man behind the camera for this kid-in-space adventure. Young David (Cramer) falls down a ravine in 1978, but when he comes round a few minutes later and goes home, he finds a different family living there. It seems it's now 1986 and he's been missing for eight years (though hasn't aged a day), and when NASA gets involved they realise that David was kidnapped by a UFO that has since crashed and has data in his brain that can fly the contraption. Of course, the NASA scientists want to observe David further but he has other ideas, and plots his escape with the help of a young woman (Sarah Jessica Parker) who works there.

While this has comic moments that will remind you of *Back to the Future*, *Flight of the Navigator* is a fun film in its own right, even when it becomes a straight chase movie (featuring the flying saucer with David at the controls) towards the end. It has dated a bit (check out Parker's hair) but is a cutely enjoyable junior romp nonetheless. ★★★☆☆

GEORGE OF THE JUNGLE

Starring Brendan Fraser, Thomas Haden Church (1997)

The lone survivor of a plane crash in the jungle when he was a sprog, muscle-bound George (Fraser) swings through the trees like Tarzan (except the few-bananas-short-of-a-bunch George tends to crash into most of them) and keeps company with a pet elephant named Shep and a professorial talking ape (voiced by John Cleese). That is, until the day he saves heiress Ursula (Leslie Mann) from a lion, and ends up travelling back with her to the United States to meet her upper-crust folks.

There's a funny subplot about inept poachers with their eye on the talking ape, and another involving Ursula's pain-in-the-butt fiancé (Haden Church, who grown-ups will recognise from his praised turn in *Sideways*), but the film – based on a comic strip and TV series – really belongs to the hilariously daft Fraser. Made for all ages, this hasn't exactly got a taxing plot and is sometimes too silly for words, but both young and old will no doubt revel in the utter stupidity of it all. A poor DVD sequel, unimaginatively titled *George of the Jungle 2* (2003), sent our hero to Las Vegas to help his pal Ape. Church and Cleese returned, but alas there's no Brendan Fraser – his role is played by Christopher Showerman. ★★★★☆

HULK

Starring Eric Bana, Jennifer Connelly (2003)

Anyone who remembers the enjoyably daft seventies series *The Incredible Hulk* – in which Bill Bixby turned into a big green he-man, as played by bodybuilder Lou Ferrigno (who cameos as a security guard in this version) – will be disappointed by this 21st-century big-screen reworking of the *Marvel* comic, while kids will just be bored by it.

It's a shame, as the Hulk was always a fascinating antihero, a mushy-pea-coloured Jekyll and Hyde, who only came into being when Bruce Banner (played here by Bana) got grumpy. But here, that doesn't even happen until well over half an hour in, by which point your sense of anticipation will have been dulled by the movie's subtexts (father/son angst with Nick Nolte clearly bonkers as Banner senior, some self-important twaddle about the ethics of science). Of course, when he does romp across the screen as the not-very-jolly green giant, bouncing from rock to rock, battling mutant dogs or swatting at helicopters, it's a treat, but because it's been so drearily ponderous up to then, you're unlikely to be awake enough to care. And they still don't explain how Bruce can transform from nerd to Hulk without splitting his trousers. ★★☆☆☆

THE INCREDIBLES

Voices by Craig T Nelson, Holly Hunter (2004)

After dashing superhero Mr Incredible (voiced by Nelson) saves a person who didn't want to be saved, he and his fellow superheroes (including Samuel L Jackson as Frozone) find themselves buried under a barrage of legal complaints and compensation demands that drive them all underground and out of business. So instead of saving the day, Mr Incredible and his wife Elastigirl (Hunter) have to assume the identities of 'normal' people – Bob and Helen Parr – and live ordinary lives. Bob becomes an insurance salesman, Helen a housewife and mother to their children Dash, Violet and Jack Jack, but Bob still dreams of his glory days and jumps at the chance when a mysterious stranger asks him to climb back into his (now rather too small) super-suit for a final adventure.

The Incredibles is sometimes an odd mix of adult sitcom and family adventure. The early part of the film – as Bob goes about his mind-numbing day job – has gags and humour clearly aimed at grown-ups and an almost melancholy feel as the characters are slowly fleshed out, so it's only when the entire family are roped into Bob's adventures – and the two kids get to try out their own superhero skills – that younger members of the audience are likely to chuckle with glee.

Of course, when things do get going, it's a terrific romp that should enchant kids whose bums haven't been numbed by the almost two-hour running time. While they soak up the action, older viewers can delight in guessing who the hilarious fashion designer Edna (voiced by the film's writer/director, Brad Bird) – who provides the family with their new costumes – is modelled on: Isaac Mizrahi, Edith Head, Coco Chanel and *Vogue* editor Anna Wintour are just some of the names people have suspected. ★★★★☆

THE ISLAND AT THE TOP OF THE WORLD

Starring David Hartman, Donald Sinden (1974)

A 'lost world' romp in the same vein as *The Land That Time Forgot* and *Journey to the Center of the Earth*. In this one, based on Ian Cameron's novel *The Lost Ones*, Sir Anthony Ross (Sinden) recruits an archaeologist (Hartman) and airship captain (Jacques Marin) to travel with him to the Arctic in search of Ross's missing son. Instead, they find an island hidden under the clouds populated by a race of lost Vikings, but things don't look too friendly when the Vikings decide our intrepid explorers are actually a sign that the world is coming to an end.

The story is pretty preposterous – as is the inclusion of a French poodle along with the explorers, who belongs to the airship captain – while the film-makers' decision to have the Vikings speak in Norse, and then not always translate it, is just odd. But the sets are terrific and the airship miniature doesn't look as awful as you'd expect for a film

made in 1974, a fact which just about rescues it from the reject pile.
★★☆☆☆

JOURNEY TO THE CENTER OF THE EARTH

Starring Pat Boone, James Mason (1959)

A Jules Verne story that has been filmed many times (an alternative
worth watching is the 1999 TV version with Treat Williams and Jeremy
London, and look out for a Disney version featuring kids who discover
Verne's manuscript in 2007). James Mason stars as Professor
Lindenbrook, who is determined to find the world's centre by popping
down into an Icelandic volcano. There are rival explorers to worry
about, but it's the giant mushrooms and dinosaurs roaming down
below that he and his team should really watch out for.

Fans of the Verne novel filled with dank, spooky caves won't enjoy
this colourful adaptation that depicts the centre of the earth as a big
sparkly jewel. But kids will like the splendid look of the film and the
sense of silly adventure, while adults can laugh at the casting of naff
singer Pat Boone as the movie's 'hero'. ★★★☆☆

THE LAND THAT TIME FORGOT

Starring Doug McClure, John McEnery (1975)

The first in a kitsch series of British movies made by director Kevin
Connor in the seventies and starring Doug McClure (the others are *At
the Earth's Core*, *The People That Time Forgot* and *Warlords of Atlantis*),
this is based on an Edgar Rice Burroughs novel set during the First
World War. When a German U-boat sinks an American submarine, the
Yanks manage to sneak onto the enemy ship. After a few onboard con-
frontations, the Germans and Americans agree to a truce until they
can reach land... but they somehow take a wrong turn at sea and end
up in a land named Caprona (actually the Canary Islands and
Pinewood Studios) where dinosaurs and cavemen have survived.

Yes, the dinosaurs aren't exactly of *Jurassic Park* standard, the dialogue is ropey and it's all a bit silly. But men who were boys back in
the seventies when this first came out loved it, and boys nowadays will

still get a thrill as the U-boat passengers first glimpse the strange volcanic land. *The People That Time Forgot* is a sequel to this film – sadly the third book in Burroughs's 'Caprona' trilogy, *Out of Time's Abyss*, was never filmed. Older kids who enjoy this will no doubt love *The Planet of the Apes* and its sequels (though they aren't thought of as family/kids films due to dark themes and Charlton Heston's disturbingly greased-up naked torso). ★★★☆☆

MEN IN BLACK

Starring Tommy Lee Jones, Will Smith (1997)

Little did we know, but aliens have been living among us for decades disguised as humans (mainly in Manhattan apparently, but that's no big surprise). Hidden in a complex in New York's Battery Tunnel are the halls of immigration which monitor the comings and goings of these strange creatures from other worlds, while it is the job of a secret government agency known as the Men in Black (MIBs) to keep the human population unaware of their existence (they have a special zapper which erases the memory of people who've had alien encounters), and to police any law-breaking mean green mothers from outer space while they're on earth.

One of these black-suited, Ray-Ban-wearing MIBs is K (Jones), who's on the lookout for a new partner to help him catch an extremely ugly extra-terrestrial named Edgar (Vincent D'Onofrio) who's illegally landed on the planet. The man he chooses is a smart-talking street cop (Smith), who, once recruited, must give up his old identity (he's rechristened 'J') and have his fingerprints and all details of his former existence erased for ever.

Scintillating special effects, sharp one-liners and hilarious aliens abound as J and K set about their mission, which has something to do with preventing Edgar from threatening life on earth as we know it. There's not a huge amount of story to speak of, but this is one of the few movies in which it doesn't matter, as too much plot would detract from Jones (who knew he could be so great at comedy?) and Smith's on-the-money performances and Barry (*The Addams Family*) Sonnenfeld's cool, slick, fun direction.

Daft and fast, this film (based on the *Marvel* comic) may offend die-hard alien conspiracy theorists who think the subject should be treated seriously and reverently, but it is a truly hilarious sci-fi treat for everyone else. (Very young viewers may find Edgar the alien a bit nasty, though.) ★★★★☆

MEN IN BLACK II

Starring Tommy Lee Jones, Will Smith (2002)

The Men in Black are back to save the universe once more. This time around, Agent K (Jones) has 'retired' from the MIB and works in a post office, unaware of his previous life hunting bad-guy aliens living on earth. But when Agent J (Smith) needs his pal's help, he restores K's memory so the pair can fight the evil Serleena, a Kylothian monster cunningly disguised as a lingerie model (Lara Flynn Boyle).

The plot isn't up to much but all the sci-fi comedy ideas that made the first film a huge hit are here – the great teaming of Smith and Jones, Frank the talking pug, Rip Torn as the man in charge, the funny script ('Silly little planet. Anyone could take over the place with the right set of mammary glands') and the bonkers special effects (including a giant, angry worm). The first one is far better, but this is still worth a look for fans. ★★★☆☆

MIRRORMASK

Starring Stephanie Leonidas, Gina McKee, Rob Brydon (2005)

Graphic novel writer Neil Gaiman (*The Sandman*) delivers a dark, strange-looking adventure along with illustrator/director Dave McKean that's best left to the teens it is probably aimed at. Young Helena (the terrific Leonidas) is sick of her life – her parents (McKee and Brydon) own and work in a travelling circus, while she just yearns for a more normal existence. After her mum is rushed to hospital, Helena falls asleep among the many drawings she has made of a strange fantasy world, and then finds herself transported into that world, where a beautiful queen (also McKee) lies in a coma and an evil queen (McKee again!) threatens to turn the world to darkness.

Visually stunning (with creatures made by Jim Henson's Creature Shop) as Helena wanders through the world of her drawings like an Alice in a twisted Wonderland, looking for a magical mask that may save the Queen of Light and also send Helena home, this unfortunately never engages on a narrative level and seems much longer than it actually is. Yes, it's inventive, and teens interested in graphic art and design will be fascinated, but everyone else will wonder what the fuss is all about. ★★★☆☆

THE PEOPLE THAT TIME FORGOT

Starring Doug McClure, Patrick Wayne (1977)

A sequel to *The Land That Time Forgot*, this fantasy adventure starred Patrick (son of John) Wayne as Major Ben McBride, who decides to organise a mission to find his lost friend, Bowen (McClure), who has been missing for years (well, since *The Land That Time Forgot!*). You see, McBride received a message in a bottle from Bowen describing a strange land filled with prehistoric creatures and women in skimpy leather outfits, so naturally he wants to check it out and hopefully find his pal. Uh oh. So McBride and plucky photographer Lady Charlotte Cunningham (Sarah Douglas), plus a few expendable supporting actors, find Caprona and discover Bowen could be alive – but will they get to him before either he is sacrificed into a volcano or they are attacked by pterodactyls?

If you compare this with another 1977 sci-fi release, *Star Wars* (and look out for Darth Vader himself, aka Dave Prowse, as an executioner here), its special effects look, well, awful, but it's nonetheless a rollicking fantasy adventure that should entertain (and certainly not scare) young fans of dinosaurs and prehistoric romps. ★★☆☆☆

THE PHANTOM

Starring Billy Zane, Kristy Swanson, Catherine Zeta Jones (1996)

Completely forgettable adventure based on the comic strip of the same name. Billy Zane (who is much better as a bad guy, as he was in *Titanic*) stars as Kit, the latest in a long line of men who have donned the mask and unflattering purple bodysuit of the Phantom to right wrongs and fight injustice with the help of trusty steed Hero.

Unfortunately, not much else happens that's very interesting. Treat Williams gets a few good lines as bad guy Xander Drax, and there are some exotic locations for Zane to gallop around on his horse, but Zeta Jones is under-used as the sultry bad girl pilot and Swanson is just wet as Kit's love interest. And that purple jumpsuit is really ugly, too. ★★☆☆☆

ROBOTS

Voices by Ewan McGregor, Robin Williams (2005)

The team that brought us the cute animated adventure *Ice Age* deliver another enjoyable kids' movie featuring impressive computer-generated animation that should entertain adults almost as much as tots. The story – set in a robot world populated by, you guessed it, robots – is simple enough. Mr and Mrs Copperbottom take delivery of a baby robot named Rodney (McGregor), who – in a nice twist on labour – they have to assemble in their living room. The family isn't rich, so as Rodney grows he is given hand-me-down body parts, but he dreams of the day when he can rise above his station (Dad is a dishwasher – literally – at the local eaterie) and present his own inventions to big businessman Bigweld (Mel Brooks). Of course, when Rodney finally travels to Robot City, things aren't as he imagined. Bigweld has disappeared, and the sleek, crafty Ratchet (Greg Kinnear) has taken over the company and is planning a nefarious scheme that threatens patched-together robots like Rodney and his newfound pals, including Fender (Robin Williams, doing his first voice-over since the Genie in *Aladdin*) and Piper (Amanda Bynes). Can our small-town boy save the day?

A possible love interest for Rodney comes in the form of Bigweld employee Cappy (Halle Berry) but this cartoon romp is more about the slick animation (check out the set-piece ride Rodney has when he arrives in town) and Rodney's growing up from idealistic tin can to a robot made of stronger stuff than anything too cute and cuddly (it's likely this will appeal more to boys than girls for this reason). Clever rather than warm, it's an enjoyable diversion for most kids (the film received a PG rating on its cinema release for a few menacing moments) but ultimately not a classic one. ★★★☆☆

THE ROCKETEER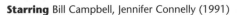

Starring Bill Campbell, Jennifer Connelly (1991)

One of those films that's great to look at but never quite takes off in every other department, *The Rocketeer* was expected to be a big smash in the summer of 1991 but instead was trampled on by cinemagoers in the stampede to see *Robin Hood: Prince of Thieves* and *Terminator 2*. It's the 1938-set story of bland stunt pilot Cliff (played by a bland Campbell), who sees a way to distinguish himself from the crowd and impress his gal, Jenny (Connelly, displaying enough cleavage for this to warrant a parental warning), when he stumbles across a prototype rocket jet pack that blasts him into space but, strangely, doesn't set fire to his trousers. Soon he's transformed himself into the Rocketeer, complete with cool leather jacket and a helmet that hides his identity, and is off skywards to do battle with everyone from gangsters to nasty Nazis.

It's not a patch on *Raiders of the Lost Ark* (from which it borrows heavily), but there are some stunning sets and nice performances from a cast that also includes Alan Arkin (as Cliff's helmet-designing buddy), Timothy Dalton (as an Errol Flynn-esque egomaniacal movie star with his eye on Jenny) and *Lost*'s Terry O'Quinn (as Howard Hughes) to make up for Campbell's lack of screen presence and a dull, action-free first half. ★★☆☆☆

THE SHADOW   PG

Starring Alec Baldwin, Penelope Ann Miller (1994)

Based on the 1930s radio series (which was followed by a series of pulp novels), *The Shadow* is an odd adventure for older kids – younger ones will find the facially creepy Shadow a bit disturbing (as will fans of Alec Baldwin!) – that mixes Eastern mysticism with comic-book-style action. Baldwin stars as Lamont Cranston, who has spent time in Tibet becoming all deep and meaningful, and arrives in New York ready to cloud men's minds with his mystical powers in order to fight crime. The bad guy is Shiwan Khan (John Lone), Genghis Khan's last remaining descendant, who wants to kill the Shadow and take over the world ('Khan conquered half the world – my task is to finish the job,' he says in that deep matinee-movie voice only bad guys seem to have).

Beautiful to look at, if a little low on action for this type of film (although there is one great fight sequence involving mirrors), this stays true to the Shadow's 1930s origins. It has flaws, however, such as the casting of a forgettable Miller as the sassy dame, but overall is well worth a look. ★★★☆☆

SHORT CIRCUIT ⒫ PG PG

Starring Ally Sheedy, Steve Guttenberg (1986)

A family high-tech comedy (although, two decades on, it doesn't look very high-tech, and it isn't hilariously funny either) that's most appealing for younger viewers. A military robot, designed as a killing machine, gets zapped with lightning and, through the magic of static electricity, becomes a friendlier sort, complete with wacky quips (as voiced by Tim Blaney, who also voiced Frank the pug dog in *Men in Black*). Ally Sheedy is the gal who takes the odd robot (named 'Five' because he was fifth on the production line), while Guttenberg is Five's designer, desperate to track down the sweet little machine before the military do.

It's fairly cute stuff for young-'uns with a few neat one-liners (on spying Sheedy in the bath, the now self-aware robot comments 'nice software') that has an unnecessary romantic subplot between Sheedy and Guttenberg but otherwise passes the time amiably enough. A dreadful sequel, *Short Circuit 2*, in which the robot is loose in New York, was released in 1988. ★★☆☆☆

SKY HIGH ⒫ PG PG

Starring Kurt Russell, Kelly Preston (2005)

The superhero adventure is crossed with a coming-of-age comedy in this terrific film for all ages. Young Will Stronghold (Michael Angarano) is a pretty normal teenager – except both his parents are superheroes. Dad (Russell) is 'The Commander' and Mum (Preston) is 'Jetstream', and they are both eagerly awaiting the day that Will gets his own superpowers so that he can join them in the fight against crime. The trouble is, while some of Will's young friends have already discovered what their superpower is, Will has had no signs at all, a problem he has kept to himself but which is bound to come out when he starts at Sky High, the school for superhero kids that is hidden in the clouds. Poor Will has to survive his first year at school – where he is soon relegated from 'Hero' class to the class for sidekicks – while dealing with the sports teacher from hell (Bruce Campbell), the school bully and an evil bad guy on the loose.

This all comes together as a thoroughly enjoyable romp, enlivened by deliciously tongue-in-cheek performances from Preston and Russell as the superhero parents, and smart turns from the kids. Comic fans will love the references littered throughout the film, while Lynda Carter (aka Wonder Woman) as the school principal and Campbell make it all even more fun. Part camp spoof, part teen adventure, this is a total treat. ★★★★☆

SPACECAMP

Starring Kate Capshaw, Lea Thompson (1986)

Intended to be a fun space adventure about kids who are accidentally launched in the space shuttle, *SpaceCamp* was the victim of bad timing – it was originally scheduled for release in the US in early 1986, but then in January of that year the unthinkable happened, and the real space shuttle *Challenger* exploded, killing the seven astronauts on board. When the film was released six months later it wasn't a hit, which is a shame as it's actually like a (very dated!) junior version of *Apollo 13*, and it co-stars a twelve-year-old Joaquin Phoenix (then credited as Leaf) in his first big-screen role.

He plays Max, one of a group of teenagers attending a summer camp in which they get to experience the space shuttle on flight simulators. And after Max befriends an intelligent robot (which actually looks pretty clunky by today's standards), it's not long before he and his pals find themselves in the real shuttle *Atlantis*, which is accidentally sent into orbit with them on board. With a cast that also includes *The OC*'s Tate Donovan and Mrs John Travolta, Kelly Preston, it's fascinating for adults to see what these actors looked like a couple of decades ago, while younger kids with a passion for space travel will get a kick out of seeing teens in space. ★★☆☆☆

SPIDER-MAN

Starring Tobey Maguire, Willem Dafoe (2002)

Who would have thought that Sam Raimi, the director of cult horror movie *The Evil Dead*, would be the right man to turn *Marvel* comic hero Spider-Man into a blockbuster movie? He certainly was, however, and his choice of leading man – Tobey Maguire, better known at the time for serious fare like *The Ice Storm* – was spot on, too.

While younger viewers may find the early scenes a little slow, the rest of us can enjoy the Spider-Man myth unfold as Raimi reveals just how student Peter Parker (Maguire) goes from nerdy teenager to muscly superhero after a bite from a genetically modified spider. We're also introduced to potential love interest Mary Jane (Kirsten Dunst), Aunt Mae (Rosemary Harris) and Uncle Ben (Cliff Robertson), who Peter lives with, and Peter's friend Harry (James Franco) and Harry's multi-millionaire dad, Norman Osborn (Dafoe), who, after an experiment goes wrong, turns into Spidey's nemesis, the Green Goblin.

Packed with impressive CGI effects, this is a fun adventure that shouldn't scare smaller viewers (Dafoe's goblin looks a bit nasty but seems more mad than bad), although it really is aimed at older comic-book fans (and has a '12' certificate in the UK). ★★★★☆

SPIDER-MAN 2

Starring Tobey Maguire, Kirsten Dunst (2004)

An enjoyable sequel to 2002's blockbuster. This time around, Spider-Man's alter ego Peter Parker (Maguire) is having something of a mid-life crisis. At the end of the first film, he chose duty over his love for Mary Jane (Dunst), but he is still hankering after her and his conflicting emotions are even causing a bit of performance anxiety – sometimes when he flicks his wrist (stop sniggering at the back), the webs that usually shoot from his hands refuse to materialise. What's a superhero to do? Well, it looks like he may ditch his red and blue spandex costume and resume a normal life, but then along comes nuclear scientist Octavius (Alfred Molina). He's working on some newfangled thingie for Peter's old pal Harry (James Franco), now the head of Osborn Industries since the death of his dad (Willem Dafoe) in the first film. But something goes wrong with an experiment, and the formerly genial Octavius ends up fused to an eight-legged metal contraption that turns him into an angry, rather powerful and impressively mobile bad guy intent on squishing the webbed one like a bug.

All in all, this is a decent follow-up that should satisfy young and old fans of Spider-Man. Perhaps a bit too much time is spent on Peter/Spidey's crisis of faith to keep young viewers engaged (also, the scarier bits are probably not suitable for viewers under eight anyway), but the action picks up in the second half in two terrific sequences: a showdown at an old pier and, most notably, a battle between Doc Ock (as the *Daily Bugle* dubs Octavius) and Spider-Man on an out-of-control subway train. Maguire and Dunst renew their on-screen chemistry, while Molina makes a terrific baddie, growling and looking suitably crazed. ★★★★☆

STAR KID

Starring Joseph Mazzello, Alex Daniels (1997)

It's tough being a twelve-year-old boy, as Spencer (Mazzello, best known for his role in *Jurassic Park*) well knows. He's ignored by his dad and sister, they've just moved to a new town and the school bully has singled him out for punishment. So it's handy that Spencer has just found a talking space suit then, isn't it? And it's even more useful when Spencer climbs inside and discovers he can control (to some extent) the 7ft-tall contraption and become a kind of superhero in the process.

It's fairly simple but cute stuff, aimed squarely at kids interested in sci-fi but who are too young to watch 'grown-up' science-fiction movies. The robot suit isn't exactly high-tech and the effects aren't top-notch, but the cast are winning and the finale (in which some bad-guy aliens come to earth to grab the suit for themselves) is fun and frantic. ★★★☆☆

STAR WARS EPISODE I: THE PHANTOM MENACE

Starring Liam Neeson, Ewan McGregor (1999)

For more than a decade we had waited and then when the prequel to the first three *Star Wars* movies came along, what a crushing disappointment it was. Juvenile, boring (what's all that political and Trade Federation nonsense?) and devoid of any humour, it seems more like an advert for the wonders of CGI than a well-rounded movie.

Okay, that's the bitterness over with. On the plus side, there are moments (between the boring bits) clearly aimed at a new (junior) *Star Wars* audience – after all, the story does centre around little boy Anakin (Jake Lloyd, who parents will find teeth-grindingly annoying). One day, he'll become the evil Darth Vader (see *Revenge of the Sith*, below), but for now he's a blond mop-topped cutie eager to be trained in the ways of the Jedi by Qui-Gon Jinn (Neeson) and a young Obi-Wan Kenobi (McGregor, playing the role performed by Alec Guinness in Episode IV). There's an (overly long) pod race that looks like something kids would play on a computer game, a terrific battle between our heroes and nasty Darth Maul (smaller viewers may find the result of this fight upsetting, and Maul himself, with the black and red make-up, is quite scary to behold), and some very impressive backdrops that are a feast for the eyes. It's nowhere near as good as the other *Star Wars* films, of course, and most adults won't like it. But more innocent, accepting children may even find something good to say about Jar Jar Binks... ★★☆☆☆

STAR WARS EPISODE II: ATTACK OF THE CLONES [PG] [PG] (MA)15+

Starring Ewan McGregor, Hayden Christensen (2002)

'Great effects, shame about the script' pretty much sums up this sequel to 1999's *The Phantom Menace*. Anakin Skywalker (aka the boy who will be Vader) is now a petulant teenager (as played by Christensen) who refuses to listen to his mentor, Obi-Wan Kenobi (McGregor), and instead makes googly eyes at Padmé Amidala (Natalie Portman) when he should be training to be a Jedi. There is some interesting stuff that adds to the *Star Wars* legends – Obi-Wan meets bounty hunter Jango Fett, dad of Han Solo's nemesis, Boba, and a new bad guy is introduced, Christopher Lee's Count Dooku (is that the worst character name ever?). But there's also an annoying romance between Anakin and Padmé, and a really irritating chase that seems similar to one from *Chicken Run*.

Aimed at preteens and teenagers (though surely boys – the biggest *Star Wars* fans – will hate the naff love story), this has some impressive action sequences and is worth a look simply for the light-sabre battle between Dooku and a flying, angry Yoda. ★★★☆☆

STAR WARS EPISODE III: REVENGE OF THE SITH

Starring Ewan McGregor, Hayden Christensen (2005)

George Lucas's final *Star Wars* movie is a massive improvement on the disappointing prequels *The Phantom Menace* and *Attack of the Clones*, and neatly sets the stage for the events that take place in the original (and still the best) three *Star Wars* movies: *A New Hope*, *The Empire Strikes Back* and *Return of the Jedi*.

Definitely the darkest of the series after *The Empire Strikes Back*, this has petulant youth Anakin Skywalker (Christensen) being lured to the dark side, risking his marriage to Padmé Amidala (Natalie Portman) and friendship with Obi-Wan Kenobi (McGregor) in the process. Parents should note it's quite scary stuff, too, from Anakin's first shocking act when he goes bad, which involves trainee Jedi kiddies and could really upset younger viewers, to the jaw-dropping battle with his former mentor Obi-Wan on a volcanic planet that leaves him disfigured (and you do see this in detail). Padmé's fate isn't much cheerier, but it's all gripping stuff and it brings the *Star Wars* universe to a fitting finale (although the *Clone Wars* animated TV series and a rumoured live-action one keep the legends alive) for both kids and parents who grew up with the original films. And, yes, we do get to see Anakin pop on the mask that symbolises his final transformation into the movies' ultimate bad guy, Darth Vader. Cool. ★★★★☆

STAR WARS EPISODE IV: A NEW HOPE

Starring Harrison Ford, Mark Hamill, Carrie Fisher (1977)

Despite being Part IV in George Lucas's *Star Wars* saga, this is, of course, the one that started it all back in 1977 – an amazing, visually jaw-dropping, science-fiction adventure story of heroes, villains and other worlds (its title was lengthened from just '*Star Wars*' when Lucas began work on the three prequels). It has stood the test of time very well, so even young kids brought up on splashy CGI effects will be impressed and thrilled by the story of young Luke Skywalker (Hamill).

Following the death of the aunt and uncle who raised him,

'I have always loved all the *Star Wars* films for the drama, the effects and the action. I would love to be the queen of the Jedis.'
X-FILES STAR GILLIAN ANDERSON

headstrong Luke teams up with an old man named Ben Kenobi (Alec Guinness), two creaky robots, a cocky spaceship pilot called Han Solo (Ford) and his furry Wookie pal Chewbacca to rescue damsel-in-distress Princess Leia (Fisher) from the evil Darth Vader (played by former Green Cross Code Man Dave Prowse, with voice provided by James Earl Jones).

Packed with odd creatures, robots (including, of course, the famous C-3PO and R2-D2), faraway planets and gadgets (the *Millennium Falcon* spaceship which Lucas imagined would look like a flying hamburger, the sword-like light sabres), plus the quasi-religious legend of Jedi knights, *Star Wars* isn't just a film, it's a cinematic universe, brimming over with adventure, heroes, bad guys and excitement. A classic for all ages. ★★★★★

STAR WARS EPISODE V: THE EMPIRE STRIKES BACK U PG PG

Starring Harrison Ford, Mark Hamill, Carrie Fisher (1980)

As any fan of the *Star Wars* universe will tell you, this 1980 sci-fi epic is the best of the six movies. It's the darkest (although the final film made, *Revenge of the Sith*, is almost as bleak), it has the best lines and it also has the entirely believable budding romance between arrogant Han Solo (Ford) and icy Princess Leia (Fisher) – after all, who else would put up with either of them?

The action begins shortly after *A New Hope* left off. The rebels are hiding out on the remote ice planet Hoth, planning their next attack on the evil Empire. But they are discovered – cue a superb battle sequence as giant walking machines (AT-ATs to aficionados) trudge through the snow – and the group are soon hurtling off to different parts of the galaxy. Luke and pint-sized robot R2-D2 set out to find Yoda, a Jedi Master who will school him in the ways of the Force, while a bickering Han and Leia, along with Wookie Chewbacca and droid C-3PO, take off in the *Millennium Falcon*.

With *that* revelation ('Luke, I am your father') at the end, which was jaw-dropping to audiences at the time, top-notch effects and some truly edge-of-the-seat moments, this is superb stuff, though perhaps a bit too scary for little children (unlike the original, *A New Hope*, or the overly cute *Return of the Jedi*). ★★★★★

STAR WARS EPISODE VI: RETURN OF THE JEDI

Starring Harrison Ford, Mark Hamill, Carrie Fisher (1983)

The cuddliest of all the *Star Wars* movies – this one is a favourite among younger viewers for the cute 'n' furry Ewoks (basically, child-size teddy bears) who populate the planet of Endor. It's there that Han Solo, Luke Skywalker and Princess Leia (along with, of course, trusty companions R2-D2, C-3PO and Chewbacca) start their adventures this time around, in their latest battle against the evil Empire and super bad guys Darth Vader and the Emperor.

While Han and Leia get friendly with the Ewoks on the forest planet (and, although many *Star Wars* fans scoff at them, you can't deny they're huggable fuzzy creatures – awww), Luke flies off for another chat with Jedi Master Yoda before his ultimate confrontation with his dad. All the loose ends are tied up a bit too sweetly by the end credits, but nonetheless this is a better *Star Wars* movie than, say, the dull *The Phantom Menace* or computer-game-like *Attack of the Clones*. So there. (Fact fans should note this was originally called *Revenge of the Jedi*, until George Lucas decided those good-guy, Force-using Jedi knights cannot seek revenge.) ★★★★☆

SUPERGIRL

Starring Helen Slater, Peter O'Toole (1984)

Made the year after *Superman III*, *Supergirl* is riddled with plot holes – the first being, why doesn't her cousin, Superman, pop up at any point to help? – but is nonetheless worth a look on a wet Sunday afternoon, especially if you want your little girl to catch one of the few superhero movies in which most of the big roles are played by women.

Kara (played by Helen Slater) leaves her outer-space home (actually a chunk of the planet Krypton that survived) to track down something called an omegahedron, which is a valuable power source. Of all the planets in the galaxy it could have ended up on, the omegahedron plopped down on earth and is in the hands of a witch named Selena (Faye Dunaway). So Kara – renaming herself Linda Lee when she isn't flying around in a Supergirl costume – enrols in boarding school, falls in love and, finally, remembers that she's supposed to be getting the omegahedron back.

Dunaway overacts to the point of absurdity, but Slater is amiable enough as Supergirl, and there's nice support from Brenda Vaccaro, Mia Farrow and Peter O'Toole. ★★☆☆☆

SUPERMAN

Starring Christopher Reeve, Marlon Brando, Gene Hackman (1978)

There have been numerous big- and small-screen versions of *Superman*, from the 1940s animated adventures and 1950s black-and-white TV series starring George Reeves, to the teen-friendly TV shows *Lois and Clark: The New Adventures of Superman* (1993–97) and *Smallville* (from 2001). But this movie version remains the one against which all others will be compared, and deservedly so.

The planet Krypton is dying, so Jor-El (Brando, who reportedly got $4 million for just ten minutes of screen time) packs his baby son into a pod and sends him into space, and the little tot ends up on earth, where he is raised by Jonathan and Martha Kent (Glenn Ford and Phyllis Thaxter). Of course, little Clark Kent (as he becomes known) is stronger, faster and more super than your average kid, so when he grows up and moves to Metropolis to become a reporter, he dons that iconic red and blue bodysuit and cape to fly around and battle bad guys like Lex Luthor (Hackman) while saving the always-in-jeopardy Lois Lane (Margot Kidder).

Beautifully bringing the back story of Clark/Superman to the screen (and Jeff East as the young Clark is a cutie), then adding action and adventure for the second half (and Oscar-winning flying effects), this is a terrific movie for everyone. The cast is a who's who of stars – alongside Brando (who, rumour has it, refused to learn his lines, and during one scene read his dialogue off baby Superman's nappy), Hackman and Ford, there's Susannah York, Ned Beatty, Jackie Cooper, Trevor Howard, Terence Stamp and Valerie Perrine – and Reeve was perfectly cast as the Man of Steel. ★★★★★

SUPERMAN II

Starring Christopher Reeve, Terence Stamp, Gene Hackman (1980)

If it's possible, this sequel to 1978's *Superman* is even better than the original. Richard Donner, who directed the first one, had filmed some footage for this sequel while making Part I but was replaced by Richard Lester, who re-shot most of it (some of Donner's original footage apparently remains, and there has been a petition online for it to be released at cinemas).

This time Clark/Superman (Reeve) has to decide whether his love life or being a superhero is more important. He's in love with Lois Lane, and prepared to give up his powers to be with her, but his timing is a bit off – just as he relinquishes his powers, three Kryptonian bad guys are freed from their one-dimensional prison and head to earth to cause some havoc. Oh Superman, please save us!

Packed with action and adventure, and more comedy than *Superman* (especially when Lois decides to test whether Clark is really Superman by throwing herself into Niagara Falls in the hope he will save her), this also boasts three terrific villains in the form of Terence Stamp's General Zod, Sarah Douglas's S&M vamp Ursa and Jack O'Halloran's thuggish Non. A super treat. ★★★★★

SUPERMAN III

Starring Christopher Reeve, Richard Pryor (1983)

If you've read the *Superman* reviews above, you'll know that the 1978 and 1980 movies were great. This, the third *Superman* movie to star Christopher Reeve, is not, however. The first big problem is that the producers hired comedian Richard Pryor as the bad guy (a computer geek who teams up with multimillionaire Robert Vaughan to do vaguely bad stuff) and he wasn't a good enough actor to make the most of an underwritten part. Meanwhile, Margot Kidder (as Lois Lane) only pops up in a blink-and-you'll-miss-her cameo performance, leaving the romantic stuff to Clark's old flame Lana Lang (Annette O'Toole, who went on to play Mrs Kent in the TV series *Smallville*).

It all adds up to a silly adventure as Superman is zapped with red kryptonite and is split into two people, one good and one evil (as a prank, the bad Superman straightens the Leaning Tower of Pisa in one of the movie's rare fun scenes). But with much of the Superman mythology left out, this is only worth watching if you're truly a completist. ★★☆☆☆

SUPERMAN IV: THE QUEST FOR PEACE

 PG u/c

Starring Christopher Reeve, Gene Hackman (1987)

Oh dear, oh dear, oh dear. The last *Superman* movie to star Christopher Reeve should probably be seen as a disaster from which even our favourite superhero couldn't rescue any survivors. With a limited budget that meant the film-makers had to reuse special effects from the earlier films, a terrible nuclear-disarmament plot that Reeve had a hand in, and the whole production filmed in Milton Keynes (yes, really – the United Nations building is actually Central Milton Keynes train station, while catalogue company Argos's headquarters doubled for a Metropolis hotel), it really is a disappointing end to the franchise.

It seems Superman has decided to round up all the nuclear weapons and throw them into space. Unfortunately, this creates Nuclear Man (Mark Pillow), an android programmed by Lex Luthor (Hackman) and his nephew Lenny (Jon Cryer) to wreak havoc on earth. It's cheap-looking (you'll recognise it's London Underground doubling for a Metropolis subway train out of control), nonsensical and worth avoiding at all costs. ★☆☆☆☆

THE TIME MACHINE

Starring Rod Taylor, Yvette Mimieux (1960)

An absolutely yummy adaptation of H G Wells's time-travel adventure, this is kitsch stuff but great fun too. Victorian scientist George (Taylor) builds a time machine, and, despite the warnings of his best pal ('If that machine can do what you say it can do, destroy it, George! Destroy it before it destroys you!'), sets off into the future, zipping past three world wars until he gets to the year 802,701. There he discovers the peaceful Eloi people (including dumb blonde babe Weena, played by Mimieux), who seem to sit around all day sunbathing, and learns that they are under threat from another tribe descended from humans, the brutal Morlocks.

While the cannibalistic Morlocks may be a bit much for younger viewers (eight and under), this is otherwise a treat for the whole family, thanks to Taylor's tongue-in-cheek performance, the clever set design (the time machine itself is gorgeous) and smart direction, especially in the sequences when George accelerates forward in time and we're shown the changing fashion in shop windows, flowers blooming and dying at speed – all amazing when you realise director George Pal had only $750,000 to work with (the film deservedly won an Oscar for its special effects). Fans should note that the DVD includes a thirty-minute epilogue to the movie, starring Taylor, that was filmed in 1993. An incredibly tedious remake, starring Guy Pearce and an over-the-top Jeremy Irons, was made in 2002, but is too dark and dull to be considered a family film. ★★★★☆

TITAN AE

Voices by Matt Damon, Bill Pullman (2000)

The AE of the title stands for 'After Earth', as our little planet has been obliterated by some nasty aliens in this animated adventure. Some humans have survived, and one in particular, Cale (Damon), is pretty important as he holds the key to the survival of the human race – it seems he has the map of a ship called the *Titan* tattooed on his hand, and if he and a group of space travellers can find it, humanity will be saved. Hurrah!

Made by former Disney animator Don Bluth (who also did *The Land Before Time* and *An American Tail*), this has some dazzling animated sequences and breathtaking backdrops, but is a bit too dark and serious for younger viewers. Teens disappointed by the newer *Star Wars* movies will find something to like though, as this is a fascinating space adventure, filled with nice vocal performances (the cast also includes Drew Barrymore, John Leguizamo and Nathan Lane), action, adventure and icky aliens. ★★★☆☆

WARLORDS OF ATLANTIS

Starring Doug McClure, Peter Gilmore (1978)

Incredibly silly but enjoyable fantasy adventure that marked the final teaming of director Kevin Connor with star Doug McClure (they also worked on *The Land That Time Forgot* and its sequel, and also *At the Earth's Core*). Also known as *Seven Cities of Atlantis*, it follows the exploits of a professor, his son Charles (Gilmore) and engineer Greg Collinson (McClure), who descend into the murky sea depths in Collinson's experimental submerging contraption. Of course, their expedition goes pear-shaped when they are attacked by a giant octopus and dragged down to one of the cities of Atlantis. Held captive, they discover that the Atlanteans are actually from Mars and are using their super brains to manipulate history!

A rollicking adventure that boasts actress/dancer Cyd Charisse (*Singin' in the Rain*) and *Cheers'* John Ratzenberger in the supporting cast, this is one for fans of hokey British fantasy and a must for all monster-loving little boys. ★★★☆☆

X-MEN (12) PG-13 (M)

Starring Hugh Jackman, Patrick Stewart (2000)

A cracking movie version of the popular comic about a group of mutants with special talents brought together by Professor Xavier (Stewart). He runs a school that's a safe haven for kids and adults with extraordinary powers, which is perhaps a good thing as Senator Kelly (Bruce Davison) wants to persecute them, believing they should all be registered rather than allowed to live incognito in regular society. Unfortunately, another mutant, Magneto (Ian McKellen), wants to take matters into his own hands by taking over the world, so the good guys – Wolverine (Jackman), Storm (Halle Berry), Cyclops (James Marsden), Dr Jean Grey (Famke Janssen) and young Rogue (Anna Paquin) – have to try and stop him.

The effects are terrific – especially Wolverine's painful razorlike claws – and the cast impressive (McKellen and Stewart are perfect as the former friends who have become adversaries, while Paquin gives the movie heart as the girl whose touch can send the recipient into a coma), so you almost don't notice the slim plot. A terrific adventure for teens and grown-ups. ★★★★☆

X2: X-MEN 2   (M)

Starring Hugh Jackman, Patrick Stewart (2003)

A follow-up to the hugely successful *X-Men* that reprtedly cost a whopping $120 million, much of which must have been spent on Alan Cumming's brilliantly effective costume as the creepy-looking (but deep down, he's sensitive) mutant Nightcrawler, who kicks the film off in bang-crash style by trying to kill the American president. Which is just the excuse military man General Stryker (Brian Cox) needs to target the mutants that live among us. (If you remember from Part I, there are nice mutants who are peaceful and led by Patrick Stewart's Professor X, and nasty mutants who hang around with Ian McKellen's witty Magneto.)

Once again the special effects are great and there are some terrific set pieces to behold as Wolverine flexes his claws, young Pyro (Aaron Stanford) starts fires and Storm (Halle Berry) whips up a few weather problems. All the mutants are well cast, from Jackman's brooding Wolverine to Rebecca Romijn's eye-catching Mystique, and it all looks so brash and amazing on screen that you'll probably not notice the lack of coherent plot. ★★★★☆

X-MEN: THE LAST STAND □/⊂ □/⊂ □/⊂

Starring Hugh Jackman, Patrick Stewart, Halle Berry (2006)

The third instalment in the *X-Men* series (and judging by the title, possibly the last), this adventure directed by Brett Ratner (*Rush Hour*) continues the story of Professor Xavier (Stewart) and his band of nice mutants, Storm (Berry), Wolverine (Jackman) and pals, and the bad mutants led by Ian McKellen's Magneto.

Unfortunately, the tension wanes somewhat as the government have discovered a 'cure' for mutations – meaning mutants who want to be like normal human beings (whatever that means) can do so. Magneto doesn't like the idea as it's tantamount to extermination, fuzzy-wuzzy mutant Beast (Kelsey Grammer) isn't sure, and Xavier is too busy dealing with the risen-from-the-dead Jean Grey (Famke Janssen), who is just a tad unhinged (but sporting a nice, dark red hairdo and matching outfit). A few plots are abandoned in mid-course, leaving the whole affair feeling like it was slashed with Wolverine's claws, while the cast are given little to do except dodge explosions and dreary dialogue. A disappointing finale. ★★☆☆☆

ZATHURA: A SPACE ADVENTURE

Starring Jonah Bobo, Josh Hutcherson (2005)

An adventure along the same lines as *Jumanji* (kids find themselves trapped in a game come to life), which is hardly surprising as they both have the same author, Chris Van Allsburg (who also wrote the book on which *The Polar Express* was based). Luckily, it's less of a mess than *Jumanji*, and is a thoroughly imaginative and entertaining adventure for kids and grown-ups.

Left in the house with their sleeping teenage sister (Kristen Stewart) by dad (Tim Robbins), siblings Danny (Bobo) and Walter (Hutcherson) come to blows when the younger Danny keeps getting on his big brother's nerves. But they'll have to find a way to get along together sharpish, as Danny has just discovered a game called Zathura hidden under the basement stairs, and when he starts to play, their house rips away from its suburban street and starts hurtling through the galaxy. It seems the boys have become part of the game, and have to play to the end – together – if they are going to get home. And that means dodging meteor showers, strange aliens and an out-of-control robot, and encountering a mysterious astronaut who may be able to save them all if they can just stop bickering.

Far more character-driven than *Jumanji* (which just seemed like a series of special effects strung together), this features excellent performances from the kids and Dax Shepard as the astronaut. It's fun stuff (although a little long, perhaps, at almost two hours), with a few moments that look as if they could scare younger viewers, but will probably thrill them instead. ★★★★☆

Television Treats

If a TV series is a hit, it's no surprise that Hollywood comes calling to turn it into a guaranteed (in theory) big-screen smash. Some of the spin-offs reviewed below were made around the same time as the TV show on which they were based (like the film versions of the Nickelodeon cartoon series *Rugrats* and *The Wild Thornberrys* or the early Muppet movies) and by the same teams involved in the original show, so if you – or your young ones – like the TV series, chances are the movie will satisfy, too.

However, some films come along a lot later than the TV series on which they are (often loosely) based, and the rule of thumb that if you like the show you'll like the movie doesn't apply here. For every *Addams Family* or *Magic Roundabout* that stays true to a series' humour, style and fun, there's a *Thunderbirds* or *Inspector Gadget* that takes a terrific idea and bludgeons it with a mallet. We can only hope that one of the most eagerly awaited TV spin-offs of all time – *The Simpsons* movie, due late in 2008 – falls into the first category...

For more kids' movies based on TV shows that are aimed at very young viewers, see Tiny Tots.

THE ADDAMS FAMILY

Starring Anjelica Huston, Raul Julia, Christopher Lloyd, Christina Ricci (1991)

Meet the strange and spooky Addams Family: vampish Morticia (Huston) and her husband Gomez (Julia), their children Wednesday (Ricci) and Pugsley (Jimmy Workman), Frankenstein-lookalike butler Lurch (Carel Struycken), and the hand with a life of its own called Thing. Not your average family to be sure – Wednesday sleeps with a headless doll and tries to kill her brother by strapping him to the

Classic Kids' TV Series on DVD

With 'grown-up' TV series such as *Buffy the Vampire Slayer*, *Friends* and *The Office* selling as many copies on DVD as movie blockbusters, it's no surprise that lots of children's TV shows are also enjoying DVD releases. Here are some recommendations.

1) **The Muppet Show.** Jim Henson's classic puppet series that began in 1976 is finally on disc, and the first-season DVD features Henson's pitch to TV companies when he was trying to get the show made. Fans of Henson's terrific work should note that compilation discs featuring music and entertainment from his series *Fraggle Rock* and *Sesame Street* are also available. Unfortunately, *The Storyteller*, his series featuring John Hurt as an old man reciting fairy tales, is currently only on Region 1 (USA) DVD.

2) **Bagpuss.** Every episode of *Bagpuss*, that pink and cream cat that came to life along with Madeleine the rag doll, Professor Yaffle and the mice, is available on DVD, so you can see just why little girl Emily loved him so much. And if you're a fan of British seventies kids' shows, note that *Mr Benn*, *Mary, Mungo and Midge*, *Bod*, *Roobarb and Custard*, *Pipkins*, *Jamie and the Magic Torch* and *Fingerbobs* are all on DVD. (*The Magic Roundabout*, sadly, is not currently available, and neither is *The Banana Splits*.)

3) **Thomas the Tank Engine and Friends.** Forget the film (reviewed below), the series narrated by Ringo Starr is far cuter. And the littlest viewers may also enjoy *Pingu*, the mischievous penguin, the funky *Bear in the Big Blue House*, those animated *Rugrats*, and *Fairly Odd Parents*. Episodes of *DuckTales* aren't currently available.

4) **Danger Mouse.** One for all ages, but older kids (over eight) especially adore crime-fighting Danger Mouse and his reluctant sidekick Penfold (brilliantly voiced by David Jason and Terry Scott). And, of course, other animated adventures on DVD for the entire family include *The Simpsons*, *SpongeBob SquarePants*, *The Flintstones*, *Willo the Wisp* and *What's New, Scooby-Doo?* At the present time, *Top Cat* is only available on Region 1 DVD.

family's electric chair or chasing him with an axe, Morticia snips the heads off roses and puts the stems in a vase, while Gomez casually hits golf balls off the mansion's roof into the house next door.

The plot involves the return of Uncle Fester (Lloyd), who disappeared years before only to return to claim his half of the huge Addams estate – but forget the story, it's the scenes showing this weird group who literally 'raise the dead' and enjoy pouring the contents of a bubbling cauldron over unsuspecting carol singers that are the best part of this hilarious film.

It's based, of course, on the cult TV series of the sixties (itself based on Charles Addams's cartoons), but this new version has the added attractions of a five-star performance from a very young Christina Ricci as Wednesday and – hey! – MC Hammer singing 'The Addams Groove'. Dark and very funny, but because of its spooky nature, perhaps not suitable for very young viewers. ★★★★☆

ADDAMS FAMILY VALUES

Starring Anjelica Huston, Raul Julia, Christopher Lloyd, Christina Ricci (1993)

An enjoyable follow-up to the hugely successful *Addams Family* movie that delivers more of the familiar ghoulish laughs. This time around, Uncle Fester (Lloyd) finds love in the form of Debbie Jellinsky (Joan Cusack), little suspecting that she is actually after his money. Meanwhile, kids Wednesday (Ricci) and Pugsley (Jimmy Workman) are sent away to a 'normal' summer camp after they try to kill Morticia and Gomez's new baby Pubert, leading to a hilarious Thanksgiving play that descends into chaos, driving the camp counsellors (the marvellous Peter MacNicol and Christine Baranski) close to the edge of sanity.

With Wednesday developing her first crush, Fester abandoning his family and embracing suburbia for his gold-digging love, and Debbie resorting to increasingly silly methods of bumping him off, this has even more laughs than the original movie and a scene-stealing turn from Cusack. A third film, *Addams Family Reunion*, featuring none of the original cast, was made in 1998 for video/DVD but is best left on the shelf. ★★★★☆

BATMAN: THE MOVIE

Starring Adam West, Burt Ward (1966)

Zap! Bang! Kapow! Yes, a feature film version of the most ridiculous show to grace our TV screens does exist, Batfans. Originally planned as the pilot episode to the sixties show *Batman*, it was actually released as a movie following the success of the first series. Adam West and Burt Ward are, of course, the leotard-wearing, utility-belt-sporting Dynamic Duo, protecting the people of Gotham City with gizmos like the BatBoat (designed especially for the film) from a quartet of bad guys: the Joker (Cesar Romero), the Riddler (Frank Gorshin), the Penguin (Burgess Meredith) and Catwoman (Lee Meriwether).

As camp as you'd expect, this is desperately silly stuff that should have kids and adults in stitches as daft dialogue is spouted ('Penguin, Joker, Riddler… and Catwoman, too! The sum of the angles of that rectangle is too monstrous to contemplate!'), our heroes are placed in danger and the bad guys are foiled once again. It's also an ideal choice if your kids are into superhero stories but you don't think they're old enough for the more recent *Batman* movies yet. ★★★☆☆

BEAN

Starring Rowan Atkinson, Peter Egan (1997)

Mr Bean was one of those TV shows, like *Big Brother*, which has millions of adoring viewers, yet has an equal number of people who hated it with a vengeance. If you fall into the latter category, this version of Rowan Atkinson's bumbling comic creation is akin to the most drawn-out, eye-piercing torture you can think of. However, if you're a Bean fan, this will probably hit the right notes, as it's also a slick, well-performed comic confection which stays true to the format of the series, and keeps the laughs sweet enough to amuse the smallest of viewers, who are probably more familiar with the spin-off cartoon series.

Hapless Bean is transported to Los Angeles, where he's sent to attend the unveiling of a priceless painting at a Californian gallery. Of course, Bean botches it big time, leaving a trail of destruction in his wake as he single-handedly jeopardises both his host's marriage and Anglo-American relations. Atkinson accomplishes every pratfall and inept moment to perfection, and writers Richard Curtis (*Four Weddings and a Funeral*) and Robin Driscoll (*The Fast Show*) keep the daft situations coming. But unless gags so old Benny Hill would have rejected them are your thing, you're better off leaving this one for the little kids and going in another room to watch re-runs of Curtis and Atkinson's witty and clever *Blackadder* instead. ★★★☆☆

BIGFOOT AND THE HENDERSONS

Starring John Lithgow, Kevin Peter Hall (1987)

Four years after this comic movie was made, a spin-off TV series, *Harry and the Hendersons* (also the film's US title), was produced that ran for two years. While the sitcom produced a few laughs, it wasn't a patch on the original in which John Lithgow stars as George Henderson, who, with his family in the car, accidentally hits an animal in the road. That 'animal' turns out to be Bigfoot (7ft tall Hall), so the Hendersons, naming him Harry, take him home to nurse him back to health – seemingly so he can then crash about their house breaking everything in sight with his ungainly paws.

That's about it, really (there's a subplot about a poacher, of course) but there are some terrific laughs to be had if you're a slapstick fan as Harry wreaks havoc, and Kevin Peter Hall (who also played the predator in *The Predator* and its sequel) is expert at Harry's facial expressions behind Rick Baker's (*An American Werewolf in London*, Michael Jackson's *Thriller* video) masterful make-up. A cute, hairy adventure to watch with younger members of the family. ★★★☆☆

DOUG'S 1ST MOVIE

Voices by Thomas McHugh, Fred Newman (1999)

For the uninitiated, *Doug* was a TV animated series that originated in the US on the channel Nickelodeon, who also brought us *Rugrats* and *SpongeBob SquarePants*. It has to be said that – taken as a series or as a movie – *Doug* isn't on a par with either, but if kids like the show they will probably find something entertaining in this feature-length version.

Twelve-year-old Doug (McHugh) and his pal Skeeter (Newman) befriend a monster that lives in the local polluted lake. Calling him Herman Melville, the boys decide the critter's pretty nice, but Doug has other things on his mind apart from saving a friendly monster –

he's trying to pluck up the courage to ask Patti Mayonnaise to the school dance. Hmm – pollution, dating, social status, judging people by the way they look – could this simple little movie be deeper than it looks? Nah. ★★★☆☆

THE FLINTSTONES

Starring John Goodman, Rick Moranis (1994)

Hanna-Barbera's sixties cartoon about prehistoric couple Fred and Wilma, pet dinosaur Dino and neighbours Barney and Betty, was translated into a very silly (but often funny) live-action movie with John Goodman fitting perfectly into the role of dim-witted Fred. Rick Moranis is less successful as Barney (wouldn't Danny DeVito have been better?) and Elizabeth Perkins and Rosie O'Donnell don't make much of an impression as their put-upon wives, but grown-ups will get more than a few chuckles from Elizabeth Taylor's turn as Fred's disapproving mother-in-law, while men especially will enjoy the casting of Halle Berry (playing a character called Miss Stone, a role that was originally offered to Sharon Stone) as secretary to Fred's boss Cliff Vandercave (Kyle MacLachlan, camping it up with glee).

The plot is pretty simple – Fred gets promoted but it's part of scheming Vandercave's evil plan – but kids especially will enjoy the film mainly for the visual gags (check out Fred's garbage disposal beneath the sink), the true-to-the-cartoon sets and vehicles, and creatures provided by Jim Henson's Creature Shop. ★★★☆☆

THE FLINTSTONES IN VIVA ROCK VEGAS

Starring Mark Addy, Stephen Baldwin (2000)

Uh-oh. Always beware a sequel (or in this case, a prequel) in which none of the original main cast return (could it be because they read the script?). Of course, in this case, John Goodman and Rick Moranis and pals were probably too old to play younger versions of Fred Flintstone and Barney Rubble, but even with the miracle of age-defying make-up and computer-generated trickery, it's unlikely either would have signed on for this weak attempt to cash in (six years later!) on the success of *The Flintstones* movie.

Set before Fred married Wilma and Barney married Betty, this adventure relocates the boys (Addy and Baldwin) and their gals (Kristen Johnston, Jane Krakowski) to a casino in Rock Vegas. Fred and Wilma (who has run away from her domineering mother, played here by Joan Collins) fall in love, but Wilma has another suitor, the smarmy and rich Chip Rockefeller (Thomas Gibson) in hot pursuit. Kids who liked the first movie may find a few moments to laugh at, but there's not much to recommend this to grown-ups except a terrifically hammy performance from Alan Cumming as rocker Mick Jagged. ★★☆☆☆

GARFIELD: THE MOVIE

Starring Breckin Meyer, Jennifer Love Hewitt (2004)

Jim Davis's comic strip (which then became a TV cartoon series) about a lazy, lasagne-loving cat gets the big-screen treatment in an adventure aimed at the most undemanding, junior members of the audience.

Garfield (voiced by Bill Murray) hates his owner Jon's (Meyer) new pet, Odie, but when the dog goes missing he braves the big city to find him (isn't that the plot of *Toy Story*?). A live-action movie with Garfield the only CGI character (the other animals are played by real cats and dogs), this doesn't offer much for anyone over the age of seven (though Murray's quips will raise a few smiles) but as a diversion for littler viewers, it is pure catnip. (And it's a must for cat fans, too.) A sequel followed in 2006. ★★★☆☆

THE GREAT MUPPET CAPER

Starring Jim Henson, Frank Oz, Diana Rigg (1981)

The second movie to feature the Muppets, this one's set in Britain (locations include Knebworth House, also used as Wayne Manor in 1990's *Batman*) so features a host of British character actors, including Trevor Howard, John Cleese, Diana Rigg and Peter Ustinov.

Kermit, Fozzie and Gonzo travel to England to interview Lady Holiday (Rigg), whose jewels were recently stolen. There, Kermit falls for her assistant, Miss Piggy, and when she is framed for the theft, the Muppets set out to prove the porcine one's innocence. With dance routines, an Esther Williams-style swimming musical number for Miss Piggy, a lovely bicycle ride through a London park and joke after joke after joke, this is the second best movie to feature everyone's favourite puppets (after the original, *The Muppet Movie*). ★★★★☆

HEY ARNOLD! THE MOVIE

Voices by Spencer Klein, Paul Sorvino (2002)

A popular cartoon series from 1996 to 2004, *Hey Arnold!* is the story of a nine-year-old freaky-haired boy named Arnold (we never learn his surname) who lives in a boarding house with his grandparents and an assortment of characters. When the series finished, the plan was to make three half-hour episodes for the finale, but instead they were put together to make this movie of Arnold's adventures.

The rather dull plot concerns an industrialist who wants to bulldoze Arnold's neighbourhood to make way for a new mall, but most viewers will probably be more entertained by the movie references (to *Speed*, *Scooby-Doo*, *Casablanca* and *Men in Black* among others) and spotting the celebrity voices, including Jennifer Jason Leigh, Christopher Lloyd and Dan Castellaneta (aka the voice of Homer Simpson). One for fans of the series only. ★★☆☆☆

INSPECTOR GADGET

Starring Matthew Broderick, Rupert Everett, Joely Fisher (1999)

Inspector Gadget, you may recall, was an animated TV series (a French, Canadian and American co-production) in the 1980s. Gadget was a bumbling, Clouseau-like police inspector equipped with various bionic attachments (go! go! gadget!) who thought he was solving crimes when in fact his niece Penny and trusty dog Brain were doing all the work. It was cute and fun, but fans of the show (and everyone else) should steer clear of this Hollywood live-action movie version, as there's no evidence of either cuteness or humour at all here.

Broderick – so funny in *Ferris Bueller's Day Off*, but for this he must have given his comic skills the year off – is the security guard who is transformed into Inspector Gadget with an array of attachments including stilts and skis. Unfortunately bad guy Sanford Scolex (Everett, going so wildly over the top you have to admire his nerve) has built an evil robot that looks just like our hero and it's on the rampage. Snore. It's all very silly without being very amusing, and pretty slow and dull, considering it's less than an hour and a half long. ★☆☆☆☆

JETSONS: THE MOVIE

Voices by Mel Blanc, George O'Hanlon (1990)

Devised by Hanna-Barbera as a space-age twist on their own stone-age success, *The Flintstones*, *The Jetsons* ran for a year in 1962 and then was briefly resurrected in the mid-eighties. While it never had the success of its predecessor, *The Jetsons* did develop something of a cult following, which perhaps explains why an animated movie of such a short-lived show was made in 1990.

Husband and wife George and Jane Jetson and their kids Judy and Elroy live in futuristic Orbit City, but when George is promoted, he's relocated to a factory on another planet and his family have to go along, too. There's a plot twist that involves dumber-than-dumb George becoming a pawn in his boss's game, and some teddy bear-like creatures whose existence is threatened by the factory, but none of it will impress sophisticated kids, who expect more cunning plot twists like those you would find in *Monsters, Inc*. Utterly forgettable. ★★☆☆☆

JIMMY NEUTRON: BOY GENIUS

Voices by Debi Derryberry, Patrick Stewart (2001)

A feature-length version of the terrific animated TV series, this was in fact intended as a pilot episode to launch the show on TV, but executives thought it was so good they released it in cinemas first. The title says it all – Jimmy Neutron is a boy genius, forever inventing funky little gizmos to amuse himself and his friends (and viewers, as the contraptions usually work only occasionally). However, in this adventure he may need all of them to save the world after aliens abduct all the adults from his home town of Retroville.

Like the subsequent series, this is funny and fast-paced stuff that should delight younger viewers. It doesn't have as many grown-up references as we've come to expect from animated movies, but there are tons of gags, inventive moments and a huge helping of energetic fun that should amuse even the most jaded of audiences. ★★★☆☆

LOONEY TUNES: BACK IN ACTION (AKA THE LOONEY TUNES MOVIE)

Starring Brendan Fraser, Jenna Elfman (2003)

A collection of shorts was released as *The Looney Looney Looney Bugs Bunny Movie* in 1981, but it wasn't until 1996's *Space Jam* that the much-loved cartoon characters got their own feature-length film. This second adventure for the gang, which again mixes live action and the animated characters, was actually conceived as a straight follow-up to *Space Jam* and was originally dubbed 'Spy Jam'. However, Hollywood rumour has it that director Joe Dante (best known for *Gremlins*) hated *Space Jam*, because he felt it didn't stay true to the Looney Tunes characters, so he dubbed this movie 'anti-Space Jam' while it was being made.

It's certainly a better film, packed with Hollywood in-jokes for grown-ups (including a *Psycho* spoof and numerous sci-fi references) and lots of cartoon fun for the kids. The plot's not exactly Shakespeare – Daffy Duck is tired of being second best to Bugs Bunny, so quits working in films, but Bugs, a studio vice-president (Elfman) and a security guard (Fraser) realise his worth so head to Las Vegas after him – but it romps along at a fair old pace, with favourites like Sylvester, Tweety Pie, Yosemite Sam, Elmer Fudd and Speedy Gonzalez (along with 'live' stars Steve Martin, Timothy Dalton and Joan Cusack) popping up along the way. ★★★☆☆

THE MAGIC ROUNDABOUT

Voices by Robbie Williams, Ian McKellen (2005)

That classic teatime kids' show (narrated and adapted by Emma Thompson's dad, fact fans) from the sixties and seventies gets a 21st-century update with this cute movie-length version aimed at toddlers too cool for *Teletubbies* and *Tweenies*. After Dougal accidentally releases evil Zeebad from his prison, he and his pals Ermintrude, Brian and Dylan embark on a quest away from their enchanted village to find three magic diamonds before Zeebad uses them to encase the world in ice.

Robbie Williams is terrific as the voice of Dougal, while Bill Nighy (as hippy Dylan), Ian McKellen (as Zebedee), Jim Broadbent (Brian the snail), Joanna Lumley (as singing cow Ermintrude) and Tom Baker (as the evil Zeebad) are all great – only Kylie Minogue as Florence lets the side down with an odd Aussie/Brit clipped accent. Sweet and eccentric stuff for little ones and the adults watching with them who have fond memories of the original series. ★★★★☆

MIGHTY MORPHIN POWER RANGERS

Starring Karan Ashley, Steve Cardenas (1995)

A completely bonkers kids' TV series, *Mighty Morphin Power Rangers* ran for three years (1993–96) and told the story of a group of strapping teenagers who have been chosen to wear brightly coloured lycra body-suits and co-ordinating motorcycle helmets to fight evil. Based on a Japanese show, it was made all the more laughable as, while the talking scenes were American, they were mixed with old action footage shot for the original Japanese series. Kids loved it though (parents weren't so keen, because of the violence), so it came as no surprise when a video game spin-off was followed by a feature film.

Paul Freeman (best known to kids for his role as Belloq in *Raiders of the Lost Ark*) was drafted in to play bad guy Ivan Ooze and does so with wit ('Oh, the things that I have missed: the Black Plague, the Spanish Inquisition, the Brady Bunch reunion…'). He's interested in a bit of world domination, especially if it means stripping the Power Rangers of their powers. Slicker than the TV series – all the action here was filmed especially for the movie – this has some flashy special effects and long fight scenes but very little else to recommend it. 'It's Morphin time…' (or not, perhaps). ★★☆☆☆

MR MAGOO

Starring Leslie Nielsen, Kelly Lynch (1997)

The myopic sixties cartoon character Mr Magoo gets resurrected in the form of Leslie Nielsen for this predictable family comedy, which is basically an excuse for Nielsen to turn out his usual *Naked Gun/Police Squad* shtick under a different guise, and is only notable for some above-average action scenes (courtesy of *Rumble in the Bronx* director Stanley Tong) and a superb canine performance from Angus, Magoo's bulldog.

The plot – unsurprisingly – is simple: bumbling millionaire Quincy Magoo unwittingly comes into possession of a stolen gem, and a ruthless jewel thief (Lynch, showing a previously untapped flair for comedy), her incompetent sidekick, the CIA and the FBI are all on the case to get it back. It's exactly what you'd expect – endless bungling – aimed at a junior audience probably unaware of the original Magoo cartoon. So they're unlikely to want to watch this anyway. ★☆☆☆☆

THE MUPPET MOVIE

Starring Jim Henson, Frank Oz (1979)

Those lovable, eccentric puppets the Muppets, who first appeared in their own TV show in 1976, got a big-screen adventure in 1979 featuring all the much-loved characters, including Kermit the Frog, Miss Piggy, Fozzie Bear, Animal, the Swedish Chef and the Great Gonzo. Supposedly based on creator Jim Henson's own journey to Hollywood, the film follows Kermit's adventures as he leaves his swamp and heads to Tinseltown with his pals to seek his fortune, evading a frog's-leg merchant along the way.

It's like a Bob Hope and Bing Crosby road movie as the fuzzy puppets cross the country, and it stays true to the series that anyone over the age of thirty remembers and loves. With a (human) cast that includes Elliott Gould, Dom DeLuise, Bob Hope, Mel Brooks, Steve Martin, Richard Pryor, Telly Savalas and even Orson Welles, it's a grown-up's delight, but kids of all ages will laugh and enjoy the Muppets' fun adventures. A must for everyone. ★★★★★

MUPPETS FROM SPACE

Starring Frank Oz, Jeffrey Tambor (1999)

Gonzo, and not Kermit the Frog, gets centre stage in this Muppet movie. Always unsure of where he came from or what species he is (and who he should blame his hooked nose on), Gonzo becomes convinced he's being contacted by his alien family after he starts hearing voices, so heads off to meet them. With a nasty scientist on his trail, it's up to his fellow Muppets to save poor Gonzo before it is too late.

Packed with celebrity cameos, from *GoodFellas'* Ray Liotta to Andie MacDowell, Hulk Hogan and *Dawson's Creek* stars Joshua Jackson and Katie Holmes, this is a fun adventure that's high on laughs even if it is low on plot. Cute stuff. ★★★☆☆

THE MUPPETS TAKE MANHATTAN

Starring Jim Henson, Frank Oz (1984)

After *The Muppet Movie* and *The Great Muppet Caper* came this third adventure for the gang created by Jim Henson. It's more of the same, of course – this time, after failing to stage a musical on Broadway, the Muppets go their separate ways in New York, only for Kermit to be hit by a taxi and lose his memory.

It's more childish than the first two films, with less humour aimed at grown-ups and a flashback sequence thrown in of the Muppets as babies that later became an animated TV series (*Muppet Babies*). But it's still an entertaining Muppet movie, and includes the long-awaited nuptials of Kermit and Miss Piggy, as well as jokes aplenty, songs and cameo appearances from Gregory Hines, Joan Rivers, Liza Minnelli, Brooke Shields, and ex-New York Mayor Ed Koch. ★★★☆☆

MUPPET TREASURE ISLAND

Starring Frank Oz, Tim Curry (1996)

Robert Louis Stevenson's classic book gets the Muppet treatment in this film directed by Jim Henson's son Brian (Jim sadly died in 1990). Here, young Jim Hawkins (former *Grange Hill* actor Kevin Bishop) is given a map of Treasure Island by dying man Flint, so heads off to find the hidden treasure on a boat captained by Smollett (aka Kermit the Frog). Also along for the ride is Long John Silver (Curry) who wants the treasure for himself, and when the motley crew arrive on the island they find that Flint left behind Benjamina Gunn (aka Miss Piggy), who may be after it herself.

It's all a lot of fun, with Curry going deliciously over the top as

'***Muppet Treasure Island* is great because it is based on a really good series of TV programmes that are lovely to watch. The Muppets and the film give a very healthy message for children, while being very funny and not too annoying for parents.'** DAVID THEWLIS

Silver (probably the best idea when you are acting alongside a frog and a, erm, ham). And while you're laughing, watch out for a bad guy character called Spa'am – Hormel Foods, the company that makes Spam, sued the film company for naming an evil character after their processed meat (the suit was unsuccessful). ★★★☆☆

THE MUPPETS' WIZARD OF OZ

Starring Ashanti, Queen Latifah (2005)

If you think the original classic *The Wizard of Oz* is too scary for your little ones, check out this 21st-century version of the tale as played out by those loveable Muppets. Dorothy (singing star Ashanti) works in her Aunt Em's (Queen Latifah) diner, but dreams of pop stardom. After a tornado hits her town she finds herself transported to Oz, and heads off with the cowardly lion (Fozzie Bear), Scarecrow (Kermit the Frog) and Tin Man (Gonzo) to meet the Wizard and see if he can make her dream come true.

Sticking (loosely) to the original story, this works some of the time as a junior version of the 1939 film, with fun cameos from Quentin Tarantino and Kelly Osbourne, but comes a cropper with some modern-day references (there's a *Passion of the Christ* joke, bizarrely) that would fly over the heads of little viewers and just grate with older ones. While parents of tiny tots may be relieved to hear that the Wicked Witch (as played, of course, by Miss Piggy) is funny rather than frightening, they should also note that Ashanti's skimpy outfits should probably have got a '15' certificate all on their own. ★★★☆☆

MY FAVOURITE MARTIAN

Starring Jeff Daniels, Christopher Lloyd, Elizabeth Hurley (1999)

A sixties sitcom no one remembers is updated into a forgettable nineties family film, as Martin the Martian (Lloyd) crash-lands in

California and ends up taking refuge in down-on-his-luck TV reporter Tim O'Hara's (Daniels) living room. While there are a few neat special-effect gimmicks (Martin can shrink his spaceship, and anyone inside it, and have *Honey, I Shrunk the Kids*-style adventures), the opening gag on Mars looks cheap and the running joke of Martin's spacesuit Zoot (which talks) is irritating rather than amusing.

Dad may be entertained by bitchy reporter Hurley and dippy gal Daryl Hannah's revealing outfits; kids, however, will be yawning before the opening credits have finished. ★★☆☆☆

PEE-WEE'S BIG ADVENTURE

Starring Paul Reubens, Elizabeth Daily (1985)

Before Tim Burton directed *Batman*, and before Paul Reubens's career hit a speed-bump following his 1991 arrest for indecent exposure, the pair teamed up to make this terrific kids' film featuring Reubens's character Pee-wee Herman. Reubens first performed as Herman – a child-like, baby-voiced, well-meaning geek – as part of a stand-up comedy routine, and following an airing on TV, this movie went into production and was followed by a TV series, *Pee-wee's Playhouse*, and a sadly missable movie sequel, *Big Top Pee-wee*.

Here, Pee-wee's big adventure begins when his prized bicycle is stolen. Determined to get it back, he sets off on a bizarre cross-country journey to recover it, meeting a host of quirky people (including escaped cons, bikers and rodeo clowns) along the way. It's all completely bonkers in a way that kids (and adults who enjoy the slightly strange) will love, and a lot of the enjoyment depends on whether you love the man-child that is Pee-wee (and you should!) or find him squeakily irritating. Watch and decide for yourself… ★★★★☆

POKÉMON: THE FIRST MOVIE

Voices by Phillip Bartlett, Veronica Taylor (1999)

Pokémon was the cunning Japanese/American ploy to part parents with their cash as their kids demanded Pokémon trading cards, computer games, toys and books. While the Pokémon characters were first seen in a Nintendo computer game, it was the 1998 TV series (cunningly shown at teatime) that got kids hooked, and was followed quickly by this short (75 mins) movie.

For the uninitiated, Pokémon are pocket monsters, and young Ash (Taylor) wants to be the greatest master of these creatures in the world, which he will achieve by catching all of the little darlings (and there are hundreds of them). In this film, a new Pokémon has been created by scientists, called Mewtwo, who wants to rule the world, so it is up to Ash and his pals to save the day. Unfortunately, the film-makers assume anyone watching is already a Pokémon fan, so don't expect much explanation as to what on earth is going on (and there's not much dialogue either). It looks nice (lots of bright colours and Pikachu the Pokémon is a cutie) but might as well be in Aramaic if you've never seen any Pokémon before. One for fans of the series/game only, this was followed by *Pokémon: The Movie 2000*, *Pokémon 3: The Movie* and *Pokémon 4Ever*. ★★☆☆☆

PUFNSTUF

Starring Jack Wild, Billie Hayes (1970)

Based on a US TV series that ran for just one year, *Pufnstuf* is a real oddity. Jack Wild (aka the Artful Dodger from *Oliver!*) stars as Jimmy, a young boy with a magic flute. Unfortunately, the witch Witchiepoo wants it, and there are numerous other outlandish creatures and contraptions around to help or hinder Jimmy, including Pufnstuf the dragon, a jet-powered broom, a talking boat and Nazi rats.

It's all very trippy (well, what do you expect when the movie's title is basically 'Puffin' stuff'), with most of the creatures played by puppets or men who should know better dancing in big brightly coloured costumes. As an oddity for adults, it passes the time (and features a cameo performance from singer Mama Cass) but kids will probably just roll their eyes at the sheer badness of it all. ★★☆☆☆

THE RUGRATS MOVIE

Voices by E G Daily, Christine Cavanaugh (1998)

Those lovable (or, in the case of bullying Angelica, thoroughly unlikeable) animated babies get their own feature-length cartoon as little Tommy (Daily) takes his friends on all sorts of adventures following the birth of his little baby brother Dill.

There are some surprisingly scary notions here for a film aimed at tots (the babies are separated from their parents and have to find their way home), but then they've probably seen *Jurassic Park* on TV, so this will seem positively tame. The cool soundtrack (Lenny Kravitz, Beck, Lisa Loeb) is more likely to be appreciated by grown-ups watching, but this is nonetheless perfect fare for junior fans of the hugely successful TV series. Two more-of-the-same sequels, *Rugrats in Paris* (2000) and *Rugrats Go Wild* (2003), which teamed the toddlers with the Wild Thornberrys, followed. ★★★☆☆

SCOOBY-DOO

Starring Sarah Michelle Gellar, Freddie Prinze Jr (2002)

A live-action version of the classic Hanna-Barbera ghost-chasing cartoon, with Gellar, Prinze Jr, Linda Cardellini and Matthew Lillard as teenagers Daphne, Fred, Velma and Shaggy (Scooby-Doo is a CGI creation, voiced by stuntman Neil Fanning). The gang of monster hunters have split acrimoniously, but are reunited when they are all individually invited on a trip to Spooky Island, a resort run by Mondavarious (Rowan Atkinson) where, of course, spooky things are happening, and the mystery is just waiting to be solved.

As in the original cartoons, the funniest moments come whenever Scooby-Doo and Shaggy are on screen (although there are some laughs to be had from Freddie Prinze Jr's awful blond wig) and the high jinks do slow down when they're not around. But with the film-makers staying close to the heart of the original series (even the cartoon costumes are copied nicely), it's not as bad as it could have been, and is certainly laugh-out-loud silly (especially for younger viewers) in places. ★★★☆☆

SCOOBY-DOO 2: MONSTERS UNLEASHED

Starring Sarah Michelle Gellar, Freddie Prinze Jr (2004)

Kids who liked Part I will get a few giggles from this so-so sequel to 2002's hit *Scooby-Doo*. The gang – Shaggy, Daphne, Fred, Velma and dim-witted dog Scooby-Doo – are at the opening of a museum dedicated to their crime-solving exploits when one of the exhibits comes back to life to terrorise the crowd. What could be going on?

With Alicia Silverstone joining the cast as a journalist investigating the gang, Seth Green as the museum's creator and the wonderful Peter Boyle as Old Man Wickles, this does have a few things to recommend it. It's not great, by any stretch of the imagination, but perhaps not as awful as it could have been. ★★☆☆☆

THE SMURFS AND THE MAGIC FLUTE

Voices by Michel Modo, Albert Medina (1976)

The only full-length colour animated movie to feature the little blue guys known as Smurfs (there is a new version planned for 2008), this movie was actually made before the 1981 TV series that made them so popular. Based on characters by Belgian author Peyo – in Belgian they are known as 'Schtroumpfs' – it's a simple enough tale of, you guessed it, a magic flute, which the Smurfs have to retrieve from a villain who has stolen it.

If your kids have never seen the Smurfs before, this is a nice introduction, ideal for very young viewers. However, if they are au fait with the world of the Smurf, they may not be too impressed with the animation here (the TV series, made by Hanna-Barbera, was slicker and brighter), a set of different voices, and the absence of characters that were created later, such as Smurfette (who actually was really annoying and whiny, so no great loss) and Gargamel. ★★☆☆☆

SPACE JAM

Starring Michael Jordan, Wayne Knight (1996)

Cartoon favourites Looney Tunes (aka Bugs Bunny, Daffy Duck and pals) got their first feature-length movie in this mixture of live action and animation. Fans of the classic cartoons may not approve, however, as the characters look a bit more modern and lack some of the zaniness of the original shorts, but there is definitely fun to be had as the Tunes are transported to an outer-space amusement park and are forced to play a basketball game against the alien 'Monstars'. If they win, they will be set free, but if they lose, they are doomed to stay on the planet for ever – so the Looney Tunes kidnap basketball star Michael Jordan to help them.

With cameos from basketball players (including Charles Barkley and Patrick Ewing), this will appeal to young fans of the sport, while grown-ups will get a laugh or two from the performances of Bill Murray and Wayne Knight. It's not a classic, perhaps, as many of the short Looney Tunes cartoons were, but it's fun nonetheless, and also notable for one new character – Lola Bunny, Bugs's love interest. Aaah.
★★★☆☆

THE SPONGEBOB SQUAREPANTS MOVIE

Voices by Tom Kenny, Clancy Brown, Scarlett Johansson, Alec Baldwin (2004)

Animated TV show *SpongeBob SquarePants* has developed a huge following, among kids of all ages, who love the brightly coloured sea sponge and his underwater pals, Patrick (the pudgy starfish), Mr Krabs (the miserly crab who runs the restaurant, the Krusty Krab, where SpongeBob works) and Squidward (the grumpy squid), and adults, who pick up on the more grown-up humour littered throughout the series. Like *The Simpsons*, it is fun for all, and this feature-length movie, while a little stretched out over an hour and a half, is packed full of fun.

The story is simple: our little hero SpongeBob has to leave his home town of Bikini Bottom to track down King Neptune's stolen crown. But it's his adventures along the way that make this such a treat for fans, from a hilarious appearance by David '*Baywatch*' Hasselhoff to the jaw-dropping sight of Patrick in fishnet stockings and suspenders (not a moment, perhaps, to explain to very junior members of the audience).
★★★★☆

TEENAGE MUTANT NINJA TURTLES

Starring Elias Koteas, Judith Hoag (1990)

It's hard to imagine now, but back in the late 1980s many kids had

Teenage Mutant Ninja Turtle fever. An animated TV series about a group of pizza-loving turtles who lived in the New York sewers and were a bit mutant due to some toxic substance, the show grew to become a cultural phenomenon as kids shouted the catchphrase 'cowabunga' at each other in the playground, bought comic books, trading cards, video games and toys and decided which one of the group – Leonardo, Michelangelo, Donatello or Raphael – they liked the most.

So it came as no surprise when a live-action movie of the show was made in 1990. And it's pretty fun too, as the 'boys', with their Zen-like master, the rat Splinter, take on the evil Shredder and his henchmen. Packed with wisecracks and ninja moves, it is heavy on the martial arts (the scenes aren't bloody, but if you have a little warrior in the house, be prepared for much kicking and karate-chopping of furniture after he's viewed this) and light on plot, which kids will love even if (and probably because) their parents don't approve. Two pretty awful sequels, *The Secret of the Ooze* and *Turtles in Time*, were also made, and a new Teenage Mutant Ninja Turtles movie is being made in 2007. ★★★☆☆

THUNDERBIRDS

Starring Bill Paxton, Anthony Edwards (2004)

Ex-*Star Trek: The Next Generation* actor-turned-director Jonathan Frakes had a difficult task translating the much-loved British institution that was Gerry Anderson's series to the big screen – especially as the *Thunderbirds* we all know and love was made with 'Supermarionation' (or, in layman's terms, puppets) and this version – shock, horror – features real people.

Of course, it's not really aimed at anyone who remembers the original series, so it's almost mean to complain that it lacks the nostalgic fun and creaky adventure we associate with *Thunderbirds* on TV. This is an only-for-kids film, so Frakes doesn't even allow more than one or two knowing winks about the movie's origins (watch out for a brief glimpse of a string emerging from one of the actor's hands in one scene, and Brains moving like a puppet under the manipulation of the bad guy), instead filling the movie with flimsy adventures that may entertain boys under the age of ten but will leave everyone else feeling almost as wooden as Anderson's discarded puppets.

Beloved characters such as chauffeur Parker (Ron Cook), Lady Penelope (Sophia Myles), Brains (Edwards), Jeff Tracy (Paxton) and his international rescue team do make an appearance. But Paxton and his older kids are soon stuck up in space, leaving his youngest son Alan and two other nondescript adolescents down on Tracy Island to outwit the nefarious The Hood (Ben Kingsley) in what is effectively a rip-off of *Spy Kids*.

The sets are impressive, the sixties design suitably funky, and there is a certain thrill in watching the various craft launch flashily into the sky. But in all other respects, this unexciting Thunderbird never quite gets off the ground. Nostalgia fans should note that a feature length version of the sixties TV puppet series, called *Thunderbirds Are GO!* (1966) probably won't impress the kids but will appeal to grown-ups who'll be tickled by the guest voices (Bob Monkhouse, Cliff Richard) and the Cliff and the Shadows soundtrack.

★★☆☆☆

TOM AND JERRY: THE MOVIE

Voices by Richard Kind, Dana Hill (1992)

It's hard to believe, but this really is the first Tom and Jerry feature film (though they did, of course, have a cameo role alongside Gene Kelly in *Anchors Aweigh*). Unfortunately, after chasing each other since 1940 in terrific cinema shorts and cartoons on the small screen, the hapless cat (Tom) and cunning but cute mouse (Jerry) are stuck in a movie that is only notable for the fact that the two characters talk – and that isn't even new, as it was first tried in some of their cartoons in the 1960s.

Even worse, those lifelong rivals are now (gulp) friends. Which means the cartoon violence that kids (and, let's face it, grown-ups) watch Tom and Jerry for is pretty much absent, and instead the pair team up to help a cutesy-wutesy orphan being victimised by her guardian. What's next? Bart Simpson deciding to run for school president? ★☆☆☆☆

TRANSFORMERS: THE MOVIE

Voices by Leonard Nimoy, Robert Stack, Orson Welles (1986)

Back in the 1980s, all little boys wanted Transformers. Featured in a TV cartoon series that was really an extended advertisement for the toys, Transformers were those robots that could bend and change into, well, other robots. Or trains, planes and other vehicles. That's about all they did, but in the series and this film they got to talk too, and were divided into good robots (Autobots) and bad ones (Decepticons).

The plot here has the Autobots trying to protect their planet from the Decepticons, and particularly an evil being called Unicron (voiced by Orson Welles, who completed vocal work on the film shortly before his death in 1985). It's more exciting than you would expect as the battle begins – and it's also quite violent in places as the robots are melted, blown to smithereens or squished into little pieces. Not one for very small viewers, then. ★★★☆☆

THE WILD THORNBERRYS MOVIE

Voices by Lacey Chabert, Tom Kane (2002)

Created by the same team as *Rugrats*, *The Wild Thornberrys* TV series, which began in 1998, followed the adventures of Eliza (Chabert), who travels the world with her wildlife documentary-maker parents in a mobile home, along with teen sister Debbie, foster brother Donnie and pet monkey Darwin. Thanks to an encounter with an African shaman, Eliza can talk to the various animals she meets, and understand them, which comes in handy here when the family come across a herd of elephants threatened by evil poachers.

Unfortunately, while the plot would work nicely in a half-hour episode, it's stretched a little too thin over nearly three times that length here. Tots who like the series may stick with it, but anyone else should just forward to the last half and the film's entertaining climax as the family take on those nasty elephant snatchers. ★★☆☆☆

WOMBLING FREE u/c

Starring Kenny Baker, Frances de la Tour (1977)

All together now: 'Underground, overground, wombling free, the Wombles of Wimbledon Common are we...' If you were a child of the seventies (the TV series ran from 1973 to 1975 and a more modern version was made in the nineties), you're probably already misty-eyed, remembering those fuzzy creatures who made use of humans' discarded litter and went by the memorable names of Orinoco, Uncle Bulgaria, Tomsk, Bungo and Wellington (not forgetting female Womble Madame Cholet, of course).

This film version, once again featuring author Elisabeth Beresford's cuddly characters, doesn't look quite as, well, adorably creaky as the series – here, it is actors in Womble costumes rather than the puppets we loved on the telly. And, if an eco-message plot wasn't bad enough (Bungo wants to try and make humans understand their littering is getting out of control), this has a scary cast addition in the form of red-haired child star Bonnie Langford. Aaaargh – will the horror never end? Of course, if your children have never seen the original series, they probably won't mind the lack of puppetry (and, hopefully, they will have never heard of Langford before) so they may be entertained. But this does lack the loveliness of the series, so one can only hope one day that will pop up on DVD. ★★☆☆☆

Teen Movies

This section concentrates on teen movies, so grown-ups with preteens should take note that the films featured here are aimed at older children (aged thirteen and over), often for a good reason – there may be some strong language, drug references, sexual (or at least dating) situations and even a small amount of violence in the film's content. However, there are some films featured here that are about teens (and kids going through that life-changing adolescent stage that filmmakers often refer to as 'coming of age') which *are* suitable for slightly younger viewers, such as *Grease*, *Clueless*, *Mean Girls* or the romantic drama *A Walk to Remember* (just look for the ones with 'PG' or '12' certificates).

With one notable exception (the teen classic *Heathers*, which, despite an '18' certificate, is included since it turned teen movies on their heads), none of the films featured have anything higher than a '15' certificate, which is why good-but-raunchy '18' certificate movies like *Risky Business* and *Dazed and Confused*, sex comedies like the *American Pie* movies and tough dramas like *River's Edge* and *Less Than Zero* aren't featured. They may be *about* teens, but they're really most suitable for over-sixteens (and sometimes over-eighteens), unless you're feeling very broad-minded. (Alternatively, since they are all worth a look, just send your fourteen-year-old to bed and then watch them yourself.)

Teen Horror (and Horror Comedies)

Teens and horror movies have always gone hand in hand, especially since a young Jamie Lee Curtis screamed her lungs out while being chased by Michael Myers in John Carpenter's low-budget but very successful *Halloween* back in 1978. But while many horror movies, such as the *Friday the 13th* series, *A Nightmare on Elm Street* and its sequels, *Final Destination* and *Scream*, feature teenagers – usually as the victims – they're not actually meant to be viewed by anyone under the age of eighteen, thanks to the violent content (obviously) and often prolific nudity and sex (usually just before a couple is hacked to pieces). There are, however, some 'horror' movies and horror comedies that are less graphic (and have the '15' certificate to prove it). So if your teenage pride and joy wants to see *I Spit on Your Grave* and you want him to watch *Bambi*, the movies below may be a happy compromise...

Buffy the Vampire Slayer

Starring Luke Perry, Kristy Swanson, Donald Sutherland (1992)

Before he created *Buffy the Vampire Slayer* the TV series (starring Sarah Michelle Gellar), Joss Whedon's idea of a young girl who is chosen to slay vampires was a film script that was made into this 1992 movie. It's not as good as the series by any means (it co-stars Luke Perry for a start), but there's still fun to be had as young cheerleader Buffy (Swanson) finds she has to ditch all things vacuous and discover her inner tough girl when she is visited by Merrick (Sutherland). He reveals to her that she is the chosen one, destined to fight the forces of evil, so soon she's missing cheerleading practice so she can drive stakes through the hearts of fanged creatures of the night.

Desperately silly and lacking in scares (no wonder Whedon made his TV series darker and wittier) but nonetheless tons of fun, this features a tongue-in-cheek performance from Sutherland and a slightly hammy one from Rutger Hauer as the main vampire villain.
★★★☆☆

The Craft

Starring Robin Tunney, Fairuza Balk, Neve Campbell (1996)

Boys have suspected it for decades – when girls get together they become witches. At least, that's what happens when school outcasts Nancy (Balk), Bonnie (Campbell) and Rochelle (Rachel True) befriend new girl Sarah (Tunney), and realise she is the missing fourth girl they need to complete their teenage coven. Soon, the 'bitches of Eastwick' (as their schoolmates have dubbed them) are practising magic instead of doing their maths homework, changing the colour of their hair, levitating and wreaking revenge on their classmates with the help of a little witchcraft.

Despite the fact that none of the actresses were anywhere near teen age while making the film (Tunney was twenty-four, Balk and Campbell were twenty-two, and True was coming up to thirty), they're all pretty convincing as tortured teens expressing their adolescent angst through magic. Of course, they could have conjured up hunky men and millions of dollars to ease their pain, but their mean retributions are far more fun in this occasionally twisted horror comedy. ★★★☆☆

The Faculty

Starring Jordana Brewster, Elijah Wood, Famke Janssen, Robert Patrick (1998)

A daft, flashy teen horror comedy that's a cross between *Species*, *Invasion of the Bodysnatchers* and *Scream* (hardly surprising when you realise the author is *Scream/Scream 2*'s Kevin Williamson). A group of high-school kids begin to believe what we have all suspected is true – their teachers have actually been taken over by aliens. It's up to them to put a stop to it before the whole school – and the town – is taken over, but how can they tell who has an alien inside them (cue a 'testing' scene very similar to the one in John Carpenter's *The Thing*) and who hasn't?

Filled with some corking special effects (including a great decapitation, if you like that sort of thing) and fast one-liners, this is utterly silly, but also completely enjoyable. Do note, however, that there are some horror moments – a few jumps and scares involving sharp implements and dead bodies and the aforementioned decapitation – so this is really only suitable for older teens. ★★★☆☆

The Lost Boys 🔞 R (MA)15+

Starring Jason Patric, Kiefer Sutherland (1987)

When young Sam (Corey Haim), his older brother Michael (Patric) and their mum Lucy (Dianne Wiest) move to the seaside town of Santa Carla to live with the boys' crusty old grandpa, little do they know that they have relocated to the mass-murder capital of the world. For while the town looks okay during the day, at night it plays host to a group of teen bikers led by spiky blond-haired David (a mesmerising Sutherland), who takes a special interest in Michael after the newcomer makes a play for young beauty Star (Jamie Gertz). What Michael doesn't know is that this biker gang are more than just thugs, they are vampires, responsible for the numerous missing children in the town. And when he hangs round with the gang and they get him to drink a bottle of red stuff that we know isn't cranberry juice, it's not long before Michael wants to sleep all day and hide his eyes from bright lights.

A stylish, slick teen horror comedy, this works thanks to a snappy script ('My own brother a goddamn, shit-sucking vampire! Oh, you wait 'til Mom finds out, buddy!'), great performances – Haim was never better than as Sam, who is informed of the ways of vampires by comic book geeks the Frog brothers (Corey Feldman and Jamison Newlander) – and nice twists on the vampire legend (the three boys arm themselves with water pistols filled with holy water). It also looks really cool, from the camera zooming over the water towards the town, to the scene in which the vamps dangle from a bridge, daring Michael to let go and hurtle through the mist with them to whatever is below, and boasts a memorable soundtrack (including Echo and the Bunnymen's appropriately creepy version of 'People are Strange' and Gerard McMann's haunting 'Cry Little Sister'). ★★★★☆

The Monster Squad

Starring Andre Gower, Robby Kiger (1987)

It seems the baddest bad guys – the Mummy, the Werewolf, Frankenstein's monster, Gill Man (aka the Creature from the Black Lagoon) and Dracula – have got together to find an amulet that could destroy the balance of good and evil in the world and turn everything to darkness. Seems simple enough, but first they have to get past a group of kids who found vampire hunter Van Helsing's diary and are now calling themselves the Monster Squad, and who are determined to stop them.

Yes, this is as daft as it sounds – a sort of Abbott and Costello meets Scooby-Doo adventure – but it's fun too (one kid slaps Dracula with the garlic bread he is carrying to make a getaway) for kids wanting a few scares and a few chuckles.★★☆☆☆

Teen Wolf

Starring Michael J Fox, James Hampton (1985)

Scott (Fox) has more problems than your average angst-ridden teenager – when the moon is full he sprouts fur and fangs as part of a family curse that turns the males into werewolves. Will he keep his fuzziness a secret? Or could his wolfish agility come in handy on the basketball court and turn him into a popular kid at last?

An incredibly silly but really rather sweet teen comedy, this pales in comparison with Fox's other 1985 movie, *Back to the Future*, but passes the time quickly enough. A sequel, *Teen Wolf Too*, which starred Jason Bateman (now the grown-up star of TV's cult hit *Arrested Development*), is best left on the shelf. ★★★☆☆

10 THINGS I HATE ABOUT YOU   PG

Starring Heath Ledger, Julia Stiles (1999)

Shakespeare's *The Taming of the Shrew* gets updated to high-school America in this *Clueless*-style romantic comedy from ex-*Seinfeld* and *Ellen* director Gil Junger.

School flirt Bianca (Larisa Oleynik) wants to date local hunk Joey (Andrew Keegan), but her dad won't let her until her older – and extremely antisocial – sister Kat (Stiles) starts dating. New kid Cameron (*3rd Rock from the Sun*'s Joseph Gordon-Levitt) also wants to date Bianca, so a plan is hatched to get Kat a date (in the form of Jim Morrison-esque Ledger) so that Bianca is allowed out of the house. People who have never read the Bard will figure out the outcome before the end of the opening credits, but despite a shaky start this zips along merrily enough and benefits from a very entertaining (and attractive) ensemble cast and a star-making performance from Ledger, who of course has since gone on to receive much critical acclaim for his 2005 performance in *Brokeback Mountain*. ★★★★☆

ADVENTURES IN BABYSITTING

Starring Elisabeth Shue, Maia Brewton (1987)

When her boyfriend cancels their date, Chris (Shue) agrees to babysit the Anderson kids (Brewton and Keith Coogan) for the evening. However, when her best friend (Penelope Ann Miller) calls asking to be rescued from the city bus station, Chris has no choice but to bundle the kids into the car and head into Chicago to pick up her pal, and naturally numerous disasters occur on the way.

It's basically a series of mishaps in the big city as the kids get lost, encounter criminals, end up on stage at a blues club and generally get themselves out of bizarre tricky situations. There are some funny moments to be had though, and Shue is sweet as the babysitter who has an unbelievably eventful evening with her charges. This film marked the directorial debut of Chris Columbus, who went on to make *Home Alone* and the first two *Harry Potter* movies. ★★★☆☆

BEND IT LIKE BECKHAM

Starring Parminder Nagra, Keira Knightley (2002)

There's romance, comedy, culture clashes and, of course, football galore in this terrific film from Gurinder Chadha that made stars of both its leading ladies, Parminder Nagra (who now appears in *ER*) and Keira Knightley, who has gone on to win acclaim for such varied movies as *Pirates of the Caribbean* and *Pride and Prejudice*.

Young Londoner Jess (Nagra, whose leg scar and its real-life origins were written into the plot) is a huge fan of footballer David Beckham and dreams that one day she too will score a winning goal for England. However, because her parents are traditional Sikhs, they frown on her love of football, so when she is spotted playing footie in the park by Jules (Knightley) and is asked to try out for the local women's team, she has to keep her ball-kicking activities to herself. Which won't be easy when she discovers that an important match clashes with her older sister's much-anticipated wedding.

With a love interest supplied by Jonathan Rhys Meyers as the girls' coach and hilarious support from Juliet Stevenson as Jules's mum, this is packed with good performances and smart dialogue, and is brimming over with fun, even if you don't understand the offside rule. Score! ★★★★☆

BETTER OFF DEAD...

Starring John Cusack, Curtis Armstrong (1985)

Life isn't going too well for Lane (Cusack). His girlfriend has left him for the boy who can ski the highest ski run, so he decides maybe suicide is the answer, but when he attempts to take his own life, even that doesn't go as he planned, and he decides the only way to win back the girl is to ski that run for himself. Yes, we're in quirky movie territory: in the background his best friend confuses snow for that other white powder, the local newspaper-delivery boy becomes increasingly unhinged in his search for payment and neighbourhood Japanese drag racers challenge kids in their parents' station wagons.

Cusack nailed the adorable/downtrodden teen role here, and delivers the humour with panache while all hell breaks loose around him. It's crazy stuff with bits of animation sprinkled in that won't be to everyone's taste (and it has dated a tad – check out the hideous fashion), but it's worth a look nonetheless. Cusack and the film's writer/director, Savage Steve Holland, reteamed for the similar *One Crazy Summer* (1986), which also starred Demi Moore and again featured Holland's animation. ★★★☆☆

BILL & TED'S BOGUS JOURNEY PG PG

Starring Keanu Reeves, Alex Winter (1991)

Dude! Everyone's favourite residents of San Dimas, California, Bill (Winter) and Ted (Reeves), returned for a sequel to their excellent adventure. And quite surreal stuff it is too – director Peter Hewitt (who was just twenty-five when he directed this, his debut feature) references Ingmar Bergman's *The Seventh Seal* and Pressburger's *A Matter of Life and Death* while following the boys on their new journey. This time, a bad guy (Joss Ackland) from the future (where the older Bill and Ted rule all) has sent evil robot replicas of our heroes back to the present to bump them off. Can Bill and Ted beat Death (William Sadler) by playing battleships, Twister and Cluedo with him? Can they save their girlfriends from the evil robot dudes? And most importantly, will they be back in time to perform at the Battle of the Bands?

Even better than the original, this is packed with laughs thanks to Matheson's and Ed Solomon's script, and extremely clever bits among all the dumb-dude stuff. Reeves and Winter are both terrific – especially as their evil robot selves, while Sadler almost steals the show as a Death who can rap ('You might be a king or a little street sweeper, but sooner or later you'll dance with the reaper') yet is still worried about how cool he is. Eye-wateringly funny. ★★★★☆

BILL & TED'S EXCELLENT ADVENTURE
PG PG

Starring Keanu Reeves, Alex Winter (1989)

The movie that made Keanu Reeves a star, but also saddled him with a dumb-dude persona that took him a few years (and movies) to shake off, possibly because he is so spot-on as a spaced-out California teen that everyone forgot he was acting! Reeves and Winter star as Ted and Bill, two aspiring rock musicians (their band is called Wyld Stallyns) living in San Dimas who have to write a history paper about how various characters in history would view life in their town in 1988 – a problem when you learn they think Caesar is 'that salad-dressing dude' and Joan of Arc was Noah's wife. Luckily for them, a mysterious phone booth has just popped up, along with time traveller Rufus (George Carlin), and they are soon travelling across time, picking up historical figures (Socrates, Napoleon, Genghis Khan, Joan of Arc, Freud) to help them with their project.

It's bonkers stuff, peppered with infectious Valley-speak ('party on, dude', 'bodacious' and 'excellent!' briefly became teen catchphrases), dopey dialogue ('I'm Dr Freud, but you can call me Siggy') and all the cool teen stuff that grown-ups just don't get. Brilliant… or should that be *excellent*! ★★★★☆

THE BREAKFAST CLUB

Starring Judd Nelson, Molly Ringwald, Ally Sheedy (1985)

Following on from *Sixteen Candles*, writer/director John Hughes delivered a second movie that came pretty close to depicting how teenagers speak and think. The film made Hughes a name to watch (he went on to make *Pretty in Pink*, and wrote *Home Alone* and *Flubber*, to name a few) and introduced the world to the media-dubbed 'brat pack' – a group of young actors who had a score of hit movies in the late eighties.

The story here is simple – five very different teenagers are thrown together for a Saturday detention. There's the jock (Emilio Estevez), the nerd (Anthony Michael Hall), the weird girl (Sheedy, all black eyeliner and shaggy hair), the princess (Ringwald) and the rebel (Nelson), all trying to get through the day (while writing a paper about who they think they are) under the mean eye of school principal Vernon (Paul Gleason). Predictably, by the end they have discovered they're not that different after all, but the fun here is in the banter ('Does Barry Manilow know that you raid his wardrobe?'), performances and, of course, that soundtrack (including Simple Minds' smash '(Don't You) Forget About Me'. A perfect slice of the eighties that is still a treat for teens today. ★★★★★

BREAKING AWAY

Starring Dennis Christopher, Dennis Quaid (1979)

Four high-school pals – Dave (Christopher), ex-football player Mike (Quaid), joker Cyril (Daniel Stern) and Moocher (Jackie Earle Haley) – live in the Indiana college town of Bloomington, where they are doomed to be looked down upon as 'cutters' (a derogatory term for the working-class locals) by the university-attending rich kids. Dave becomes enraptured with cycling, and Italian racing in particular, much to the consternation of his dad ('I'm not "papa", I'm your god-damn father'), while Mike secretly wants to play ball in college, and the other teens share their dreams too.

A look at small-town America as much as it is a movie about teens not knowing what the future holds, this has an edge-of-the-seat climax (the Little 500 bike race) and winning performances throughout. It's surprising that Christopher never became a star following his performance here (he's mainly done stage and TV work in the past couple of decades), while the other Dennis, Mr Quaid, shines so much here that it's obvious he was a talent to watch. ★★★★☆

CHASING LIBERTY

Starring Mandy Moore, Jeremy Piven (2004)

The (marginally) better of the two movies focusing on a rebellious US President's daughter to be released in 2004 (the other, *First Daughter*, is reviewed below), this one stars singer/actress Moore as Anna, the eighteen-year-old who just wants to be treated like any other girl, rather than as the offspring of the leader of the free world. So when she's on a trip to Europe, she gives her Secret Service guys the slip and ends up falling for a hunky Brit (Matthew Goode) she meets along the way.

Ripping off the classic Audrey Hepburn romance *Roman Holiday* at every turn, this certainly isn't original, but there are moments of humour (mainly provided by Piven and Annabella Sciorra as two amorous Secret Service agents) and Moore makes an amiable leading lady. And, as a tour guide to Prague and Venice, it couldn't be better. ★★☆☆☆

CIRCLE OF FRIENDS

Starring Minnie Driver, Chris O'Donnell, Alan Cumming (1995)

Maeve Binchy's novel of girlie friendship set in 1950s Ireland is nicely brought to the screen here by director Pat O'Connor, who also made the Charlize Theron/Keanu Reeves weepie *Sweet November*. Minnie Driver reportedly piled on thirty pounds to play young Benny, who experiences boys, love and betrayal for the first time when she leaves her little old-fashioned village for college in Dublin, along with pals Eve (Geraldine O'Rawe) and the snooty Nan (Saffron Burrows). Each girl experiences romantic entanglements – Benny falls for hunky rugby player Jack (O'Donnell), Nan has a secret affair with local landowner Simon (Colin Firth), while Eve has to fend off her amorous boyfriend Aidan (Aidan Gillen).

It's a little treat of a film, thanks to lovely performances from the leads, especially Driver as the sensitive gal who doesn't want her heart broken ('You mustn't mess me about. I know I may look like a rhinoceros, but I've got quite a thin skin really') and Cumming as the slithery Sean, whom her parents want her to marry. (Parents should note that while sexual situations come up throughout the film, it's all dealt with pretty nicely and discreetly – after all, these are good Catholic girls.) ★★★★☆

CLASS

Starring Rob Lowe, Andrew McCarthy (1983)

Like the more adult *Risky Business* and *The Girl Next Door*, this is one of those films that brings to life many a teenage boy's fantasy. Naive young Jonathan (McCarthy, in his film debut) finds life is never the same again after he befriends the monied Skip (Lowe) at the posh prep school they both attend. Skip helpfully sends Jonathan off to the city to find a woman to lose his virginity with, and Jonathan succeeds with a businesswoman he meets in a hotel (Jacqueline Bisset) who somehow believes he is older than his seventeen years. It's only later, of course, that she discovers he's just a kid and later still when the pair realise they have something in common – she's Skip's mother!

Definitely one aimed at older teens, because of the hormones raging in every scene, this movie can't decide whether it is comedy or drama, so throws in a bit of both. It doesn't quite work, therefore, but there are nice performances from the three leads and some fun stuff throughout. Fact fans should note that, as well as boasting the first film role for McCarthy, *Class* also marked the feature-film debuts for Virginia Madsen and a very young and pimply John Cusack. ★★☆☆☆

CLUELESS

Starring Alicia Silverstone, Brittany Murphy (1995)

Jane Austen's classic *Emma* gets transplanted to nineties LA in this comedy that launched (albeit briefly) a few Beverly Hills catchphrases such as 'I'm audi' (I'm out of here), 'Monet' (someone who looks pretty from a distance but is a mess up close) and 'total Baldwin' (a good-looking guy, as in actors Alec and Billy Baldwin).

Cher (Silverstone) lives with her lawyer dad (mum died in a freak liposuction accident) in a Beverly Hills mansion, has a colour-coordinated wardrobe to die for and a best pal named Dionne (Stacey Dash). At school the pair befriend new girl Tai (Murphy) and decide to give her a make-over so she can snag a cute guy, while Cher sets her own sights on the brooding Christian (Justin Walker). Of course, Cher has a hunky stepbrother at home (Paul Rudd) who's much nicer, but writer/director Amy Heckerling has fun with the smart dialogue and situations Cher encounters along the way to true happiness. Terrific stuff for teenage girls, this was spun off into a TV series featuring Dash, with Rachel Blanchard taking over the role of Cher, that ran from 1996 until 1999. ★★★★☆

CONFESSIONS OF A TEENAGE DRAMA QUEEN

Starring Lindsay Lohan, Adam Garcia (2004)

Anyone male or over the age of fifteen should avoid this teen girl drama that stars *Freaky Friday*'s likeable Lindsay Lohan. It's as predictable as a spot appearing on your adolescent face on date night, as new-girl-in-school Lola (Lohan) tries to impress the suburban girls with her big-city ways, obsess about clothes and fantasise about the lead singer of a rock band (Garcia).

Because it's made by Disney, it's an unrealistic, sanitised look at the life of a fifteen-year-old girl (no sex or adolescent fumbling here), when we only have to watch TV shows like *The OC* to know what girls Lola's age are really thinking about, but that at least makes it suitable (if slightly brain-numbing) viewing for younger teens. ★★☆☆☆

CRAZY/BEAUTIFUL

Starring Kirsten Dunst, Jay Hernandez (2001)

Dunst is the rich girl who falls for a Latino boy (Hernandez) from the wrong side of the tracks, but the twist here is that he is the hard-working, straight arrow (getting up at the crack of dawn to travel across LA on a bus to a good school), while she is the mad, rebellious one (daddy pays no attention, mummy isn't around and stepmum doesn't understand her), brimming over with trouble and teen angst.

Yes, as well as being a romance (complete with cool, MTV-friendly rock/pop soundtrack), this is an 'issues' movie, one of those films packed with messages ('drugs are bad', 'studying is good') that usually turn up on daytime TV. But while the script sometimes thuds with melodrama, the film boasts terrific, classy and moving performances from the cast, notably Hernandez and Bruce Davison (as Dunst's congressman father), and especially a ferocious Dunst. ★★★★☆

CROSSROADS

Starring Britney Spears, Zoe Saldana (2002)

This is, of course, the movie debut of sex kitten pop star Britney Spears, not the naff ITV soap. Britney – whom we first meet lip-synching Madonna songs into her hairbrush dressed in her undies – isn't bad as studious Lucy, who reunites with childhood pals Kit (Saldana) and pregnant Mimi (Taryn Manning) to honour a pact they made as tots to go in search of their destinies after their high-school graduation. Travelling with Mimi's hunky friend Ben (Anson Mount), they intend to head to LA to enter a singing competition, dropping Lucy off in Arizona on the way so she can find her long-lost mother (*Sex and the City*'s Kim Cattrall).

But, as in similarly poppy films like *Flashdance* and *Coyote Ugly*, the plot really isn't what's important. It's getting to see (if you're a teenage boy) Britney in her lacy undies or flashing her toned midriff at every available opportunity. It's Britney winning (surprise surprise) a karaoke competition en route singing 'I Love Rock 'n' Roll', or scribbling down 'poetry' that you know will end up being a song about her feelings. And for those who remember the popster's pledge of remaining a virgin until she got married, it's the dialogue before and after her deflowering on screen that will lead to more than a few knowing sniggers from grown-up viewers. Funny stuff if you're not a member of the Britney Spears fan club. ★★★☆☆

CRUEL INTENTIONS

Starring Sarah Michelle Gellar, Ryan Phillippe (1999)

An over-the-top modern-day teen update of Choderlos de Laclos's *Les Liaisons Dangereuses* (which was also the basis for the movie *Dangerous Liaisons*), this has TV's Buffy, Sarah Michelle Gellar, vamping it up as Kathryn Merteuil, a rich young bitch who lusts after her stepbrother Sebastian Valmont (Phillippe) while getting perverse pleasure out of mentally torturing him. Her latest method is by betting him that he can't seduce and bed young, idealistic Annette (Reese Witherspoon, now Phillippe's real-life wife) who has declared in a magazine article that she is determined to remain a virgin until she finds true love. If he loses the bet, Kathryn gets his Jaguar, and if he wins, he gets Kathryn.

Packed with plot twists as Sebastian and Kathryn ruin reputations and lives for sport, and frank scenes – including the now infamous 'lesbian kiss' between Gellar and Selma Blair (as Cecile, one of Sebastian's conquests) – this is part black comedy and part farce, a raunchy update packed with gorgeous-looking co-stars (Joshua Jackson, Sean Patrick Thomas, Tara Reid) that, while it fluffs the ending somewhat, is a camp treat throughout. For older teens only, though! ★★★★☆

DANGEROUS MINDS

Starring Michelle Pfeiffer, George Dzundza (1995)

To Sir, With Love got a nineties update, with Michelle Pfeiffer in a leather jacket and specs replacing Sidney Poitier as the teacher inspiring inner-city kids to stop shooting each other and learn poetry by the two Dylans (D Thomas and Bob D, geddit?).

A surprise hit – aside from Pfeiffer, the cast is made up of a group of unknown actors and schoolkids – this had audiences lining up not only to see Michelle getting down and dirty as the ex-marine, but also because of the bestselling soundtrack, which includes tracks by Wendy & Lisa, and the hit 'Gangsta's Paradise' by Coolio. In fact, it often seems as if you're watching a feature-length rap video as every inner-city *Boyz n the Hood*-style cliché is trotted out over the music while our Michelle tries to solve problems like gang-involvement and teenage pregnancy (warning to parents – do expect some violence and very frank language). It says something about her talents as an actress that she actually makes this rather preachy and formulaic film watchable, but even she can't stop you from wincing at the Hollywood feel-good ending. ★★★☆☆

THE DELINQUENTS

Starring Kylie Minogue, Charlie Schlatter (1989)

Wanting to sex up her goody two-shoes image post-*Neighbours* (and before she became one of the biggest-selling female singers thanks to some raunchy music videos), Kylie Minogue took on the lead role in this *Rebel Without a Cause* wannabe set in 1950s Australia. She stars as Lola, who has the hots for young Brownie (Schlatter). Trouble is, they are both under age and have hideous parents, so they have to risk everything to be together alone in the big city. (More traumatic perhaps is Kylie's bleach-blonde hair in the movie's second half – scary.)

It's terribly soapy stuff, performed by two unconvincing leads, and it's littered with every troubled-teen cliché you can think of. In fact, it's truly abysmal, and only a fevered Kylie fan should attempt to sit through it without sniggering or throwing something at the TV in disgust. ★☆☆☆☆

DON'T TELL MOM THE BABYSITTER'S DEAD

Starring Christina Applegate, Joanna Cassidy (1991)

A sort of teenage *Home Alone*, as Sue Ellen (Applegate) finds herself up to her neck in trouble when her mother goes to Australia for two months, leaving an aged babysitter in charge. Of course, said carer drops down dead, Sue Ellen and her siblings take the poor woman to the mortuary – and then discover the money their mother had left for them while she was away is in the babysitter's pocket (and she's already been buried). Rather than get mum to come home, Sue Ellen fakes her CV to get a job (and of course gets a good one), while her brothers and sisters run amok at home.

Unfortunately the writers behind this film aren't as skilled as Sue Ellen is with her resumé, and this is pretty much devoid of laughs. Adults will hate it, because all the kids are unlikeable, while kids will just yawn at the dullness of it all. *X-Files* fans should note that a young David Duchovny pops up as one of Sue Ellen's weasely workmates. ★★☆☆

EDWARD SCISSORHANDS

Starring Johnny Depp, Winona Ryder (1990)

A superb left-of-centre fairy tale, this marked the first teaming of star Johnny Depp with director Tim Burton (they went on to make *Sleepy Hollow* and *Charlie and the Chocolate Factory* together).

Edward is not a real boy at all, but rather the creation of the Inventor (Vincent Price), who died before he could complete his masterpiece. Poor Edward looks human enough except for one thing – instead of hands, he has long, shear-like scissors at the ends of his arms. Since the death of his 'father', Edward has lived a lonely life in a crumbling mansion high above a neighbourhood of pastel-coloured houses. It is only when kindly Avon lady Peg (Dianne Wiest) discovers his hiding place that Edward descends to the 'real' world below, and finds himself embraced by Peg's neighbours when he displays his talent for hairdressing, dog-clipping and hedge-shaping. Of course, it's not the happy ending it seems, and when Edward falls for Peg's cheerleader daughter (a blonde Ryder), it sets off a chain of events that leads the town to turn on him.

Absolutely beautiful to look at, this skilfully blends humour with sadness and a thoroughly entertaining story. The cast are all superb, from Anthony Michael Hall as Ryder's oafish boyfriend (playing against type, as he's best known as the nerd in *The Breakfast Club*) to Alan Arkin as Peg's bemused husband. But it is Depp who steals every scene, conveying Edward's frustration with few words, his pale, scarred face showing the hurt when he discovers that even the gentlest touch with his scissor hands can cause pain. Wonderful stuff. ★★★★★

FERRIS BUELLER'S DAY OFF

Starring Matthew Broderick, Mia Sara (1986)

Musing one morning that 'life moves pretty fast. If you don't stop and look around once in a while, you could miss it,' young Ferris Bueller (Broderick) decides to skip school and, because it's his ninth absent day so he won't be able to have another without getting into major trouble, aims to make this one count. With the reluctant help of pal Cameron (Alan Ruck, who at thirty is surprisingly convincing playing a teen), Ferris 'borrows' Cameron's father's beloved Ferrari and heads for downtown Chicago, where he scams his way into a fancy restaurant, catches a game at Wrigley Field and, in one of the movie's most unforgettable scenes, performs the Beatles' 'Twist and Shout' during a town parade.

It's all deliciously good fun as the teens get to break the rules while the adults are given short shrift (Jeffrey Jones's school principal providing the laughs as he is foiled again by Ferris) and Broderick has never been better than as the good-natured, irrepressible teen we all wish we had known at school. A classic, funny and absolutely unmissable teen movie. A quickly cancelled spin-off TV series *Ferris Bueller* was made in 1990, with Charlie Schlatter as Ferris and a young pre-*Friends* Jennifer Aniston as his disapproving sister. ★★★★☆

FIRST DAUGHTER

Starring Katie Holmes, Marc Blucas (2004)

Not to be confused with the similar and marginally better *Chasing Liberty*, this stars a pre-Tom Cruise Katie Holmes as Samantha Mackenzie, daughter of the President of the United States (Michael Keaton, who surely deserves better than this). Our Sam just wants to be like every other girl and go to college without the Secret Service following her every move, and her dad finally agrees but isn't too happy when a photo of her campus exploits gets splashed across the tabloids.

It's very predictable stuff that suffers from a bland script, plodding direction and two wishy-washy leads in the form of Holmes and Blucas as her romantic interest. A tedious romantic comedy that gets a D-minus in both the love and laughs department. ★☆☆☆☆

THE FLAMINGO KID

Starring Matt Dillon, Hector Elizondo (1984)

Garry Marshall, who directed *Pretty Woman*, is the man behind the camera for this sweet comedy starring Matt Dillon. It's the summer of 1963, and young Jeffrey (Dillon) is a poor Brooklyn boy who gets a job at the exclusive El Flamingo beach club. He's soon rubbing shoulders with the rich members in his job as a cabana boy, most notably Phil Brody (Richard Crenna), a wealthy sports car salesman who befriends Jeffrey and fills his head with get-rich-quick ideals, much to the consternation of Jeffrey's hardworking dad (Elizondo).

Yes, this movie has a big old moral staring at you throughout, and a few really obvious plot twists too. But Dillon is likeable, Crenna is always gruff good value, and the summer of '63 looks warm and appealing. Movie fans should look out for Marisa Tomei and John Turturro in early roles. ★★★☆☆

FOOTLOOSE

Starring Kevin Bacon, Lori Singer, John Lithgow (1984)

This teen drama was dated even before it was released, but it has a kitschy charm nonetheless. It marked Kevin Bacon's first major starring role, as new-kid-in-town Ren, who finds that the place where he and his mum have moved is a bit too strait-laced for his liking – especially when he discovers the local reverend (Lithgow) has banned rock music. What's a spiky-haired, tight-jeans-wearing boy to do? Well, he decides he's gotta dance anyway, be it in a barn (the acrobatic dance moves clearly not by Mr Bacon, but a stand-in), lit by the headlamps of

'*Footloose* was my favourite movie as a kid, because it's all about moving. As a kid I wanted to move but felt awkward, teenage frustration, and then I felt I could burst into dance. I even demonstrated a dance from *Footloose* on the *Letterman Show* in 1998.'
CLAIRE DANES

his car, or at a cowboy bar. And to make matters worse, he also decides to annoy the local jock and date the reverend's snooty daughter (Singer).

It's all completely hokey, of course, but the soundtrack of eighties soft rock and pop ('Let's Hear it for the Boy', 'Hurts So Good', and of course, Kenny Loggins's title track) is infectious, and the story of a boy rebelling against the grown-ups is timeless. Grown-ups will get the added satisfaction of sniggering at a bouffant-haired pre-*Sex and the City* Sarah Jessica Parker, while kids will just wanna rock. Note that while this had a 'PG' certificate when it was originally released, it earned a '15' on DVD – must be all that satanic rock 'n' roll. ★★★★☆

GIDGET

Starring Sandra Dee, James Darren (1959)

One of a slew of 'squeaky clean' teen movies from the fifties and sixties aimed at teenage girls (if your 21st-century teen doesn't find this too dated, she may also like some of the beach-set movies like 1963's *Beach Party* and 1965's *Beach Blanket Bingo*, both with Frankie Avalon and Annette Funicello). Gidget (played by Sandra Dee, who was, of course, immortalised in a song in *Grease*) is a bouncy young blonde who discovers surfing and then love after she befriends cool Moondoggie (Darren) during the summer in this fun if forgettable feature.

Based on a book by Frederick Kohner, this was a phenomenal hit, not only launching many imitation beach movies, but also a Gidget phenomenon – two more movies followed (*Gidget Goes Hawaiian* (1961), *Gidget Goes to Rome* (1963), neither of which starred Dee), plus a handful of made-for-TV films, and even a spin-off TV series, which launched the career of Sally Field, who took on the role of Gidget (the name Gidget, incidentally, is an abbreviation of 'girl midget'). ★★★☆☆

GOSSIP

Starring James Marsden, Lena Headey, Kate Hudson, Joshua Jackson (2000)

Proof that a clever idea doesn't necessarily lead to a good movie. It all begins well as students Jones (Headey), Derrick (Marsden) and Travis

(Reedus) decide to start a rumour and track its progress as part of a college project. So at a party, when Derrick spots beautiful (and very drunk) rich kid Naomi (Hudson) – well known for her refusal to have sex – making out with her boyfriend Beau (Jackson), he suggests to his pals that the gossip they spread is that Beau and Naomi slept together. Soon the scandalous news explodes around campus with the story getting wilder and wilder until Naomi (who doesn't remember much of anything) believes it and accuses Beau of rape.

It's at this point it all goes horribly pear-shaped, as preposterous twists and ridiculous motives turn a potentially gripping and thought-provoking movie into an utterly daft and slightly dubious one in which any moral point is completely lost. For older teens only, but only if there really is nothing else available in the DVD store. ★★☆☆☆

GREASE 🔺 PG PG

Starring John Travolta, Olivia Newton-John (1978)

A snake-hipped, slick-haired and skinny Travolta (well, it was nearly three decades ago when this classic musical was made) shines as Danny Zuko, hip leader of the T-Birds at fifties school Rydell High, who falls for sugary-sweet out-of-town girl Sandy (Newton-John) during the holidays and is then mortified when she turns up at his school, her goody-two-shoes image threatening to cramp his style.

Because the boy-meets-girl, boy-dumps-girl, boy-shows-his-manliness-and-wins-back-girl plot was already as old as the hills when the film first came out, this has stood the test of time surprisingly well, helped by the timeless song-and-dance numbers, unashamed kitschness and spot-on performances from an ensemble cast which includes Stockard Channing (as bad girl Rizzo), Didi Conn (as beauty school drop-out Frenchy) and Jeff Conaway (Zuko's tough pal Kenickie). Girls of all ages love this movie (and much younger members of the audience probably won't pick up on the few, muttered references to sex) but even boys can be convinced to watch for the super-cool car race. ★★★★★

GREASE 2

Starring Michelle Pfeiffer, Maxwell Caulfield (1982)

This sequel to the phenomenally successful *Grease* is only worth catching if you want to see a movie that truly defines the word *terrible*. Set in the sixties, a decade later than *Grease*, this musical stars Michelle Pfeiffer (before she was a star, and on the strength of this it is amazing she ever became one) as Stephanie, the cool girl at Rydell High who doesn't look twice at new English student Michael Carrington (Caulfield). In a reverse of the original movie, it's him (not her) who has to change his image, and he does just that – donning dark-tinted motorbike helmet and biker jacket to whisk our Steph off her feet.

No doubt Pfeiffer leaves this one off her career CV, or she should following her dreadful rendition of songs like the eye-wincingly awful 'Cool Rider', while director Pat Birch – a talented choreographer who did the choreography for *Grease* – sensibly returned to her first profession and has not directed another movie since. ★☆☆☆☆

GREGORY'S GIRL

Starring John Gordon Sinclair, Dee Hepburn (1981)

Writer/director Bill Forsyth must remember quite clearly what it is really like to be a teenager – awkward and embarrassing – for he captures it all perfectly in this lovely, funny Scottish comedy drama. While the Scottish accents had to be re-recorded (softer) for American audiences, the story is universal: young, gangly Gregory (Sinclair) discovers his new-found height isn't helping his co-ordination on the football field, and he is replaced by a pretty girl named Dorothy (Hepburn), whom he naturally falls in love with. She, however, rebuffs him, while the dippy Susan (Clare Grogan) harbours a secret crush on him instead.

Sinclair is hilarious as the awkward teen who seems to be all arms and (very long) legs, while Forsyth adds to the humour by peppering the film with witty dialogue and quirky moments that truly depict the pain and sheer bloody awfulness of growing up. Forsyth returned to Gregory's tale in 1999 with the less successful *Gregory's Two Girls*, in which Gregory has grown up and become a teacher (snore). ★★★★☆

HEATHERS

Starring Winona Ryder, Christian Slater (1989)

One of the coolest teen movies of all time (but alas, one with an '18' certificate – you have been warned). Veronica Sawyer (Ryder) belongs to a popular but bitchy clique at Westerberg High called the Heathers (because the other three members are all named Heather, of course). She's had enough of their back-stabbing ways, however, so when she meets new-guy-at-school JD (Slater), it's not long before the pair of them have teamed up and 'accidentally' murdered one of the group. Getting a taste for blood, JD then wants to kill all the annoying jocks and cheerleading types, but Veronica's not sure this is such a good idea.

A bleak, dark and satirical look at teen life that's often macabre and always dripping in sarcasm, *Heathers* boasts two superb central performances from Slater (channelling his inner Jack Nicholson) and Ryder, while there is nice support from Shannen Doherty, Lisanne Falk and Kim Walker as the three Heathers. Superb stuff, but do note – owing to some rather raunchy language and the deliciously sadistic tone of the movie, you should definitely keep this hidden from younger viewers! ★★★★★

HERE ON EARTH

Starring Chris Klein, Leelee Sobieski (2000)

Klein (perhaps the blandest actor around right now) is rich, arrogant prep-school kid Kelley, who finds his softer side after he crashes his flashy car into a small town restaurant. The locals decide his punishment should be to help repair the diner, which he reluctantly does, while attempting to romance sweet Samantha (Sobieski), even though she has a boyfriend (Josh Hartnett).

Like the far superior *A Walk to Remember*, this is a weepie, so you know before long that Samantha is going to keel over, developing that strange movie disease that makes you look more beautiful as you get sicker, Kelley is going to realise What Love Really Means and anyone over the age of fourteen is going to gag at the sheer ludicrousness of it all. One for fans of Klein (are there any?), who will be the only people to believe he can change from truly unlikeable to sort of okay. ★★☆☆☆

THE KARATE KID

Starring Ralph Macchio, Pat Morita, Elisabeth Shue (1984)

A kiddie version of *Rocky* (from the same director, John G Avildsen), in which boxing is replaced by karate. Macchio is Daniel, the weedy kid who's just moved to town with his mother and spends his time drooling over gal pal Ali (Shue) when he isn't being beaten up by local thugs. The bullies, it turns out, all train in karate with the sadistic John Kreese (*Cagney and Lacey*'s Martin Kove), whose motto is 'no mercy' (though it could easily be 'beat up little guys who can't fight back'). Luckily for our hero, there's a local handyman named Mr Miyagi (Morita) who can train him in the ways of karate in time for an upcoming tournament and rousing chop-socky finale.

Packed with karate moves (great if you like that sort of thing, tedious if you don't), this film has a heart thanks to the chemistry between Daniel and Mr Miyagi. There's a solid moral, too, about strength and friendships, in between the ass-whuppin'. A fair sequel, *The Karate Kid Part II* (1986), carries on the themes of the first film while transplanting the action to Miyagi's Okinawa home, while a third film, *The Karate Kid Part III* (1989), is pretty silly stuff that has Daniel and his mentor planning to open a bonsai shop! Finally, there is the marginally better *The Next Karate Kid* (1994), with a young Hilary Swank taking over as the kid wanting to be tough and strong under Miyagi's guidance. ★★★☆☆

KUFFS

Starring Christian Slater, Milla Jovovich (1992)

Christian Slater is George Kuffs in this teen crime drama – a twenty-one-year-old with no money who leaves his pregnant girlfriend (Jovovich) to head for San Francisco, where he hopes his older brother (Bruce Boxleitner) may help him out. Unfortunately, big brother – who works as a 'Patrol Special' alongside the police – is gunned down, and Kuffs has to decide whether to track down and wreak revenge on his sibling's killer or work alongside the police.

It's like a teen version of *Beverly Hills Cop* that never quite decides if it wants to be funny or deadly serious. Certainly the language and violence is on the serious side, but Slater also has to talk directly to the audience, suggesting that this should have had some knowing funny bits, too. What happened to them is perhaps the crime that Kuffs should have been investigating. ★☆☆☆☆

LICENSE TO DRIVE

Starring Corey Feldman, Corey Haim (1988)

For a brief period in the mid/late eighties, the two Coreys (Feldman and Haim) were petite teen pin-ups, sort of bargain-basement alternatives to Michael J Fox. Haim (the squeaky-voiced, spikey-haired one) and Feldman (the baritoned one), who also appeared together in *The Lost Boys*, here star in a driving comedy that's actually not as bad as you may expect. At the beginning of the movie, young Les (Haim) fails his driving test, destroying his fantasy of being able to take hot schoolgirl Mercedes (Heather Graham) out on Saturday night. But having a licence isn't going to stop him at least trying, so he steals his grandfather's beloved Cadillac and sets off on an evening of disasters that he needs his best pal (Feldman, of course) to bail him out of.

It's like a junior *Blind Date* as everything that can go wrong does, and is very similar to another slightly more adult 1988 comedy (starring Keanu Reeves), *The Night Before*. Neither are great works of art, but they pass the time amiably enough. ★★★☆☆

LUCAS

Starring Corey Haim, Kerri Green (1986)

Odd, nerdy Lucas (a bespectacled Haim) befriends the new girl in town (Green) over the summer holidays, but when school starts she falls for the high-school jock (Charlie Sheen) and he becomes the target of bullies in this long-forgotten but well-worth-seeking-out teen drama.

It's a funny, sad tale that isn't bogged down by clichés (the high-school jock isn't an asshole – although he steals the girl away from Lucas, he still protects the boy from bullies) and features terrific performances from the young cast, especially Haim, who sadly never lived up to the potential he shows here. The movie also marked the big-screen debut of a fourteen-year-old Winona Ryder, playing a young girl who has feelings for Lucas herself. ★★★★☆

MAD LOVE

Starring Chris O'Donnell, Drew Barrymore (1995)

Matt (O'Donnell, possibly the most unlikely romantic leading man in history) is a well-behaved teenager who likes playing with his telescope, until he sets eyes on quirky new-girl-in-town Casey (Barrymore). The two fall passionately in love, but – as every romantic drama aficionado should know – the path of true love never runs smooth. Before too long, Casey is committed to hospital by her parents after a suicide attempt and Matt helps her escape, blissfully unaware that Casey's little eccentricities are in fact hints that she is a manic depressive.

This uneven, rather downbeat drama was an unusual choice as the first Hollywood movie for director Antonia Bird (*Priest*), and she doesn't seem comfortable with her surroundings. O'Donnell and Barrymore try to do the best with the material they have and largely succeed, although Barrymore's hysterical mannerisms during her depressive episodes are sometimes absurd rather than affecting. Quirky it may be, disappointing it definitely is – check out the similarly themed (but miles better) *Crazy/Beautiful* instead. ★★☆☆☆

MEAN GIRLS

Starring Lindsay Lohan, Rachel McAdams, Lacey Chabert (2004)

Heathers meets *Beverly Hills 90210* in this smartly scripted (by *Saturday Night Live* comedienne Tina Fey) and thoroughly entertaining tale of spiteful schoolgirls. Cady (Lohan) is a pretty, bright teen who has been home-schooled all her life. So the cliques and machinations of an American high school come as something of a shock when she starts attending North Shore High and discovers the most popular girls are the 'Plastics', a trio of snide, fashion-obsessed bitches led by Regina (McAdams). Befriending two social outcasts, Janis (Lizzy Caplan) and Damian (Daniel Franzese), Cady infiltrates the Plastics to report back on their antics to her new pals, but finds herself torn between the nice kids and the lure of the lip-glossed, boy-mad cool girls.

Fey's script is hilarious – as is her cameo as a bumbling teacher – encompassing every teen horror from an amorous sports coach to the pitfalls of religious home schooling ('…and on the third day, God created the rifle to shoot the dinosaurs… and the homosexuals'). And her cast are terrific too, from Lohan's innocent teen to McAdams, Chabert and Amanda Seyfried's turns as the trio of witches who rule the school. A sharp comedy that's a must for teenagers, but is pretty illuminating for adults, too. ★★★★☆

NAPOLEON DYNAMITE

Starring Jon Heder, Efren Ramirez (2004)

Teenage misfit Napoleon (Heder) marches to the beat of his own drum – a ginger, frizzy-haired teen with down-turned mouth, unattractive specs and quirky fashion sense, he lives with his grandmother and older brother in a tatty house in the run-down small town of Preston, Idaho, and sets himself apart from the cool crowd with his wild tales (when asked how he spent the summer he replies, 'I spent it with my uncle in Alaska, hunting wolverines!'). His family is equally bizarre – brother Kip is intent on marrying a woman he has only conversed with in chatrooms, while Uncle Rico dreams of building a time machine so he can go back to his teenage years and relive football glory – but Napoleon believes he is some sort of misunderstood hero, so he takes it upon himself to groom new-kid-in-school Pedro (Efren Ramirez) to run for school president.

   Often funny in the strangest of ways – you'll honestly laugh as the school bus passes a field just as the farmer is shooting a cow – this is a quirky slice of American life that hits in some terrific scenes (Napoleon dancing on stage being one of the most memorable) but occasionally misses, too: while Napoleon is brilliantly played by Heder, he's often quite difficult to like, making it hard to root for him. Nonetheless, it's an impressive oddity from writer/director Jared Hess (who wrote the screenplay with his wife, Jerusha) that will have you chortling at the sheer madness of it all. ★★★☆☆

NEVER BEEN KISSED

Starring Drew Barrymore, David Arquette, Michael Vartan (1999)

In this enjoyable comedy Drew Barrymore is Josie Geller, a bumbling twentysomething journalist who gets a chance to prove herself when her editor sends her undercover at a school to lift the lid on what nefarious activities teens get up to nowadays. A brainy geek during her own school years, Josie sees this as the perfect opportunity to rewrite history, become a popular kid and get the kiss she never had first time round, and in the process she falls for her English teacher (*Alias* star Vartan) who is, of course, unaware of her true identity.

It's a simple but fun romance in the *Clueless* vein, enlivened by a great central performance from the infectiously cute Barrymore, and a wacky supporting turn from *Scream*'s Arquette as her older brother, who fancies reliving his own high-school glories. ★★★☆☆

THE NOTEBOOK

Starring Rachel McAdams, Ryan Gosling (2004)

A very old-fashioned tale of love across the years, this drama is aimed squarely at anyone who's a sucker for slushy romance, and has already gained a cult audience among teenage girls. It's based on a novel by Nicholas Sparks, whose Mills and Boon-like stories have also appeared on the screen as the sweet teen drama *A Walk to Remember* and schmaltzy fortysomething romance *Message in a Bottle*. So get those hankies (or a sick bucket, depending on your tolerance for these things) at the ready.

In the present day, an old man (James Garner) reads a story of young love to an elderly woman (Gena Rowlands) with Alzheimer's. The story he tells is of the 1940s summer romance between rich girl Allie (McAdams) and local boy Noah (Gosling), who fall in love but are then separated when an inconvenient world war – and her parents – intervene.

Director Cassavetes – star Rowlands's son – mixes the teenage love story with the present-day relationship between Garner and Rowlands (yes, you guessed it, they are the ageing Noah and Allie, though she doesn't remember). It's extremely sentimental stuff – all luscious scenery, lakes filled with beautiful swans and glistening sunsets – that's pretty predictable in the flashback scenes, but thanks to four sweet performances from the old and young leads, a three-hankie weepie nonetheless. ★★★☆☆

PRETTY IN PINK

Starring Molly Ringwald, Andrew McCarthy (1986)

Poor Andie (Ringwald) is, well, poor – a girl from the wrong side of the tracks who wears funky clothes, hangs around with quirky guy Duckie (Jon Cryer) and is viewed as one of the social outcasts by the rich kids at school. So it's probably not a good idea for her to fall for super-rich boy Blane (McCarthy) then, is it?

Written by John Hughes, the man behind other eighties teen movies *Sixteen Candles* and *The Breakfast Club*, *Pretty in Pink* is a pure slice of teen angst as our feisty heroine decides she will go to the prom, even if it means cutting up a perfectly decent old prom dress and turning it into something far less appealing. But will she choose Blane or the ever-faithful Duckie for that slow dance? Female viewers may be disappointed by her choice, but the mid-eighties soundtrack (Psychedelic Furs, OMD, etc) and enjoyable performances are enough to keep everyone entertained until the end credits. Terrific stuff.
★★★★☆

THE PRINCE AND ME

Starring Julia Stiles, Luke Mably (2004)

Ah, the perils of being a young 21st-century woman. There you are, concentrating hard on your studies at the University of Wisconsin, determined to become a doctor and help the needy, when along comes a hunky European man to sweep you off your feet. And darn it – he turns out to be Edward, Crown Prince of Denmark (a Prince William-esque Mably). Life just isn't fair, is it?

As directed by Martha Coolidge (*Rambling Rose*), this Cinderella-style romance gets a feminist twist – young Paige (Stiles) doesn't need rescuing, nor does she particularly dream of being smothered in riches and jewels – but deep down it has a slushy, sentimental heart as an incognito 'Eddie' escapes his princely duties and playboy lifestyle for a year at an American college, finds true love there with Paige (who is initially miffed that he didn't tell her who he really was but sensibly gets used to the idea of having a princely boyfriend) and in the process grows from boy to man. Grown-ups may find it a bit too unbelievable (come on, how many girls would really be annoyed to discover their amour is a prince?) and cutesy, but a funny turn from Ben Miller as

Eddie's long-suffering butler almost makes up for the high level of silliness. A straight-to-DVD sequel starring Mably (but not Stiles) was filmed in 2006. ★★★☆☆

PUMP UP THE VOLUME

Starring Christian Slater, Samantha Mathis (1990)

Thirtysomething viewers may remember that brief moment in time in 1990 when it looked like Christian Slater was going to be the next Jack Nicholson. He brooded in *Heathers* and gave a terrific turn as a shy teen with a ruder, cruder radio alter ego in this cool drama. By day, Mark (Slater) is just another student, but at night he broadcasts on pirate radio and teens in their droves listen and call in to talk about sex, teen suicide, loneliness and fitting in. Unfortunately, Mark runs foul of the law when one listener commits suicide and the cops try to figure out who the mysterious DJ is.

Backed by a terrific soundtrack that's just as cool now as it was over a decade ago (Concrete Blonde, Cowboy Junkies, etc), this is strictly for teenagers whose parents don't mind them watching a film littered with swearing and (shock horror) teen rebellion. It's intense, funny and enjoyable though, and a good look at teen angst that never gets preachy. ★★★★☆

REBEL WITHOUT A CAUSE

Starring James Dean, Natalie Wood (1955)

Numerous fifties films tackled the then-new subject of teenage 'delinquents', but none did it better than this classic, tragic movie that has become part of Hollywood myth, partly due to the untimely deaths of its three lead actors (Dean, of course, died in a car crash in September 1955, Wood drowned aged forty-three in 1981, and Sal Mineo was murdered in 1976).

Often copied (the 'chicken race' has appeared in everything from *Footloose* to Paula Abdul's 'Rush, Rush' video, with Keanu Reeves taking on the Dean role) but never bettered, it's the story of young Jim (Dean), a confused, alienated and misunderstood teen who feels let down by every adult in his life. Befriending Judy (Wood) and outsider Plato (Mineo), and creating something of a makeshift family with them, seems to be a solution, but they are all destined for inevitable tragedy.

Superbly performed, this was a ground-breaking movie, from Plato and Jim's unspoken, homoerotic love (a kiss between the pair was apparently filmed but later dropped) to the depiction of gangs and teen frustration that hadn't truly been explored on film before. Despite being half a century old, it hasn't dated and remains as powerful now as it has always been. ★★★★★

RED DAWN

Starring Patrick Swayze, C Thomas Howell, Charlie Sheen (1984)

A film that has dated thanks to its anti-Commie politics, which won't mean much to teens watching today. They may get a kick out of seeing a group of teens taking on the world – when Soviet forces invade America, these kids, led by Jed (Swayze), band together to become gun-toting guerrillas, defending their little bit of the Midwest.

Yes, it's as silly as it sounds (think of it as a junior alternative to *Rambo*!), and violent with it (the film went into the *Guinness Book of Records* at the time for having the most acts of violence in one movie – 134 in an hour), but it does have an interesting undertone of paranoia and a bleak future that thoughtful viewers may pick up on. ★★☆☆☆

SAY ANYTHING...

Starring John Cusack, Ione Skye (1989)

If you're a parent reading this and you have a son, you'll watch *Say Anything* and hope he turns out like Lloyd Dobler (Cusack), and if you have a daughter, you'll watch and pray she gets to meet a Lloyd one day herself. For Lloyd – ambitionless though he may be – is the perfect man: sincere, determined, protective, funny, and it's pretty likely he loves fuzzy animals and small children too.

Written and directed by Cameron Crowe, who went on to make *Jerry Maguire*, *Elizabethtown* and *Vanilla Sky*, *Say Anything* is a wonderful, sweet teen movie that adults will also love – especially those who remember what being a teen was like in the late eighties. It's the story of how an underachiever named Lloyd gets up the nerve to ask out the school brain (Skye) – and how she gives him the time of day just because she has nothing to do before going off to college, never expecting this slightly awkward boy to steal her heart. There's other stuff going on too – her dad (played by *Frasier*'s John Mahoney) has a secret that could change her life, while Lloyd has a sister (played by Cusack's real-life sibling, Joan), depressed young friend (Lili Taylor) and nephew to deal with. But in the end the movie belongs to the two leads, and softies should be warned to have tissues at the ready for the pitch-perfect weepy ending. ★★★★★

SHE'S ALL THAT

Starring Freddie Prinze Jr, Rachael Leigh Cook (1999)

A slight but enjoyable comedy, *She's All That* follows popular kid Zach (Prinze) after he's dumped by his vacuous girlfriend Taylor a few weeks before the prom. Instead of moping, Zach rises to his pal's challenge of finding the most unlikely (i.e. ugly) girl in school and turning her into a prom queen to replace Taylor. Of course, the girl he picks, Laney (Cook), may look dowdy but she's an absolute stunner underneath, and it doesn't take much to turn her into a sexy babe apart from some new clothes and contact lenses.

Predictable *Pygmalion*-style stuff – of course Laney will find out she's the subject of a bet and Zack will discover there's more to life than popularity – but thanks to some likeable performances (including supporting roles for Usher, Lil' Kim, Anna Paquin and Kieran Culkin), it's fun nonetheless. ★★★☆☆

THE SISTERHOOD OF THE TRAVELLING PANTS

Starring Amber Tamblyn, Alexis Bledel, Blake Lively, America Ferrera (2005)

Based on Ann Brashares's popular US novel for teenage girls, this has 'girlie weepie' written all over it. It may occasionally look like a comedy, but you just know there are going to be touchy-feely moments that require whole boxes of hankies. Four teenage gal pals are going to be separated for the first time one summer – Lena (Bledel) is heading to Greece, where she will fall in love for the first time, Bridget (Lively) is going to soccer camp, Carmen (Ferrera) is off visiting her dad, while Tibby (Tamblyn) is stuck at home, stacking supermarket shelves and befriending a little girl. What binds them – and the various strands of the story – is a pair of jeans that the girls think are magical (they fit each girl, even though they have very different figures), and which they pass between them over the summer months.

This rises above the average junior chick flick by having some smart dialogue, realistic characters and, especially, four enjoyable performances from the leads. They're all a bit too cute for real life, of course – the film looks like a Gap ad (even though the magical jeans are actually Levis!) – but when has that ever mattered to film-makers? ★★★☆☆

SIXTEEN CANDLES

Starring Molly Ringwald, Justin Henry (1984)

A ground-breaking film back in 1984, this launched the slew of romantic comedy teen movies that followed (previously a 'teen' movie meant one of those '18' certificate films featuring busty co-eds like *Porky's* and its spin-offs). This film also marked the first collaboration between writer/director/producer John Hughes and young actress Molly Ringwald (they also worked together on *The Breakfast Club* and *Pretty in Pink*). She stars as Samantha, who is discovering that turning sixteen is anything but sweet. Her family have forgotten her birthday, the school geek (Anthony Michael Hall) is pursuing her, while the guy she has a crush on just happens to be the most popular boy in school.

A mixture of teen awkwardness and broad comedy, this is a fun little film, featuring a terrific central performance from Ringwald in her first leading role. A treat. ★★★★☆

THE SKULLS

Starring Joshua Jackson, Paul Walker (2000)

This teen thriller is one of those movies that must have sounded great when all the cast signed on, but somehow didn't quite turn out as well as everyone hoped. *Dawson's Creek* star Jackson is the poor orphaned college kid who needs to be accepted by a college secret society called the Skulls to carry on his law studies because one of the perks of being a member is that they pay your tuition. They also give members flash cars, expensive watches and strange initiations in cavernous rooms beneath the college (in a building with a skull on top, so how secret can this society be?), and soon our hero realises they may not be as nice as they seem.

A great idea (there are such societies at universities like Harvard), which gets a bit silly when it becomes a *Firm*-style thriller with lots of preposterous plot twists, but Jackson looks cool and is given nice support by older actors like William Petersen. Two very missable sequels (*The Skulls II* and *The Skulls III*) have followed, neither starring Jackson or Walker. ★★★☆☆

SLEEPOVER

Starring Alexa Vega, Mika Boorem (2004)

Julia (*Spy Kids'* Vega) and her pals want to be accepted by the cool kids in school, even if that means agreeing to a challenge set by the popular girls – to compete in an all-night scavenger hunt. Of course, numerous high jinks ensue, from Julia having to retrieve the shorts of her secret crush to getting her teacher to buy her a drink in an over-21 club just to fulfil the various tasks on her list.

Grown-ups will be reminded of John Hughes's eighties comedies like *Sixteen Candles*, while young teens watching may raise an eyebrow at the odd soundtrack (who in 2004 still listens to 'Wannabe' by the Spice Girls?), but may get some enjoyment out of Vega's exuberant performance. It's relatively harmless stuff (if you can ignore the underage drinking bit) and pretty predictable and unoriginal, with some enjoyably silly moments thrown in. ★★☆☆☆

SOME KIND OF WONDERFUL

Starring Eric Stoltz, Mary Stuart Masterson (1987)

Writer/producer John Hughes took his own plot for *Pretty in Pink* (girl falls for unattainable boy when there's a perfectly good friend right in front of her) and twisted it around for this romantic comedy – here it is aspiring artist Keith (Stoltz) who yearns for popular girl Amanda (Lea Thompson) when in fact he should really be paying more attention to his drummer tomboy pal Watts (Masterson), who is such a great mate she even plays chauffeur on his hot date.

This works well because Hughes has the ability to make all his teen characters believable, rather than clichés, so while we all hope Keith will realise Watts is the one for him, Amanda isn't depicted as a vacuous girl; she's got feelings too. The three leads are terrific, especially Stoltz (in a role written with him in mind by Hughes) and Masterson, who's the smart-talking, tough-but-sweet pal we all wish we had had growing up. ★★★★☆

VARSITY BLUES

Starring James Van Der Beek, Amy Smart (1999)

Dawson's Creek star James Van Der Beek is the school American football player who challenges the authority of his control-freak coach (Jon Voight in a hilariously over-the-top performance) when he becomes the team's star player in this teen drama.

It's basically a nineties update of eighties sports movies like *Youngblood* (dire hockey drama with Rob Lowe and Patrick Swayze), *All the Right Moves* (dire football drama with a very geeky-looking Tom Cruise) and *Vision Quest* (dire wrestling drama, aka *Crazy for You*, renamed after the Madonna theme song), with the usual mix of sports action (which may go over the heads – no pun intended – of non-American football aficionados), drinking, girls (the team discover one of their teachers is a stripper) and the odd moral tale thrown in. Predictable stuff for grown-ups but heaven on earth for hormonal Van Der Beek fans, if there are any left. ★★☆☆☆

A WALK TO REMEMBER

Starring Shane West, Mandy Moore (2002)

This whole-box-of-tissues weepie is strictly for the girls. Young preacher's daughter Jamie (singer Moore) is a nerdy good girl, endlessly teased for her frumpy ways by the cooler kids in school. When brooding Landon (*ER*'s West) is assigned after-school activities as a punishment, the pair are thrown together, and despite his protestations, she predicts he will fall in love with her. Which he does. But as anyone who has ever snuffled their way through *Love Story* or any number of made-for-TV teen movies knows, just when you think everything is rosy, something nasty happens. Could it be anything to do with Jamie's pale-as-chalk skin and persistent cough?

While it's all hopelessly predictable, West and Moore deliver sweet performances and director Adam Shankman restrains himself in the schmaltz department. And parents of preteen girls should note – because Jamie is a vicar's daughter, she's determined to stay a virgin until she's married, so there are no sex scenes in the film and it's all rather sweet and innocent. Aaah. ★★★★☆

WARGAMES

Starring Matthew Broderick, Dabney Coleman (1983)

The technology in this 1983 movie has dated somewhat (just look at the cranky old eighties computers), but this is still a cracking teen thriller. Matthew Broderick (possibly better known to younger viewers as the lead in the remake of *The Producers*) stars as David Lightman, a young whiz kid who accidentally hacks into a US government computer. He finds a game there called Global Thermonuclear War and starts to play, unaware that's it's not a game at all and in fact he has started a program that will play out a global attack for real.

It's gripping stuff, as government official John McKittrick (Coleman) desperately tries to stop the world from coming to an end, and Broderick makes for an appealing computer geek gradually realising the humongous scale of his mistake. ★★★★☆

WEIRD SCIENCE

Starring Anthony Michael Hall, Kelly LeBrock (1985)

Teen comedy maestro John Hughes (the man behind *Pretty in Pink* and *The Breakfast Club*) wrote and directed this teen fantasy that features early performances from Bill Paxton and Robert Downey Jr. It's the story of two nerdy boys, Gary (Hall) and Wyatt (Ilan Mitchell-Smith) who, sick of being bullied by boys and ignored by girls, decide to create the perfect woman using a mixture of computer science and electrical-storm voodoo. What they get is the gorgeous Lisa (LeBrock) who is happy to do their every bidding (which doesn't only include X-rated stuff – she does the cleaning, too).

For about two-thirds of the movie's running time, this is really likeable silliness as Lisa teaches the boys a thing or two about morals and growing up, but then it all goes a bit haywire as Hughes throws mutant bikers (don't ask) into the mix for the finale. ★★☆☆☆

WIN A DATE WITH TAD HAMILTON!

Starring Kate Bosworth, Topher Grace (2004)

Wholesome supermarket checkout girl Rosalee (Bosworth) has a crush on hunky movie star Tad Hamilton (*Las Vegas* TV star Josh Duhamel), so is super-excited when she wins a date with him in a competition. Her best pal Pete (Grace) is less impressed, however, having loved Rosalee from afar for years, so he does his best to convince her that Tad is a womanising cad who is no good for her.

Unfortunately, what could have been a cute romantic-triangle comedy becomes a total misfire – we're meant to want Pete to get the girl but he comes off as snide and jealous while Tad seems like a nice guy who sees Rosalee as an escape from his hard-living Hollywood lifestyle. There are some mildly funny moments – especially when Pete is upstaged by an unsuspecting Tad at a local ranch – but ultimately this is disappointing stuff, only worth watching for the sharp turns from Nathan Lane and *Will & Grace*'s Sean Hayes as Tad's wicked managers. ★★☆☆☆

Coming-of-age Movies

Anita and Me

Starring Chandeep Uppal, Anna Brewster (2002)

Meena (Uppal) is the twelve-year-old daughter of the only Punjabi family in a Black Country mining village in the seventies. She strikes up a friendship with the outgoing Anita (Brewster), the often foul-mouthed daughter of an equally plain-speaking mother (Kathy Burke) who moves in next door. Soon they are listening to pop together, reading *Jackie* magazine and thinking about boys, much to the horror of Meena's traditional parents.

Based on the novel by Meera Syal, this is packed with the clichés you'd expect from a movie that reminisces about an English summer friendship between two unlikely girls, Luckily, there's a nice amount of humour provided by the supporting cast, which includes Meera Syal and Lynn Redgrave, and kids will no doubt have a snigger at the hideous seventies fashions. ★★★☆☆

Hearts in Atlantis

Starring Anthony Hopkins, Anton Yelchin, Hope Davis (2001)

Based on a Stephen King non-horror short story, this is a touchy-feely coming-of-age tale, as a middle-aged man reflects on the summer he was eleven, when the closest thing to a bogeyman in his life was a bullying neighbourhood kid. Like *Stand By Me*, this isn't just a tale of childhood – King can't resist throwing in something slightly unusual. Young Bobby (Yelchin) also has to deal with the mysterious and wise Ted Brautigan (Hopkins) who is lodging in the apartment upstairs and asks Bobby to watch out for 'low men, fellows who are ruthless and dangerous to know'. The two develop a friendship, and Ted becomes the father figure Bobby needs (especially when you consider his mum is so mean she gives her son a library card for his birthday so she can spend more on herself).

What raises this from being more than just a sweet drama that girls cry at are the performances from young Yelchin and, of course, the veteran Hopkins, who delivers screenwriter William Goldman's hokiest lines ('sometimes when you're young, you have moments of such happiness, you think you're living in someplace magical…') as if they were Shakespeare and makes you believe them. This is definitely not for cynical teens, but those who can cast their scepticism aside will be treated to a sweet, if slightly corny, drama. ★★★☆☆

I'm Not Scared 🔞 R (MA)15+

Starring Giuseppe Cristiano, Aitana Sánchez-Gijón (2003)

The idyllic, sunny Italian countryside in 1978 is the setting for this terrific drama based on the prize-winning novel by Niccolò Ammaniti. Imaginative, independent ten-year-old Michele (the superb Cristiano) and his younger sister Maria explore the cornfields and abandoned shacks outside their small village with their young friends. When Maria loses her glasses after the kids have played at a run-down farmhouse, Michele returns to get them and uncovers a concealed well that is the prison of a young, terrified boy of his own age, chained at the ankle and almost mad from fear, hunger and dehydration. This discovery looks set to change young Michele's life for ever, as his small community provides only a few suspects, including the newly arrived, boorish Sergio, and his own parents (his mother, Anna, is played by Aitana Sánchez-Gijón, best known outside Europe as Keanu Reeves's co-star in *A Walk in the Clouds*).

A tense, disquieting coming-of-age film, *I'm Not Scared* deservedly won a handful of festival awards and nominations, including the Audience Award at the European Union Film Festival. Beautifully filmed against a luscious backdrop (the Puglia and Basilicata regions of southern Italy, in case the stunning landscapes inspire you to book a holiday), it's an atmospheric, unsentimental and utterly riveting tale for teens and adults, well worth catching for the impressive performances, most notably from the children, who give subtle turns that Hollywood child actors should aspire to. ★★★★★

Now and Then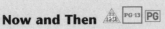

Starring Christina Ricci, Thora Birch (1995)

For some reason many coming-of-age movies are about boys (probably because most directors are men), but the girls get their chance to come over all touchy-feely in this drama set during the summer of 1970. Tomboy Roberta (Ricci), bra-stuffing flirt Teeny (Birch), tubby Chrissy (Ashleigh Aston Moore) and occult-obsessed Samantha (Gaby Hoffmann) have the whole holidays to be friends, hold seances and discover boys. They also pledge to be there for each other for ever, which leads to a present-day reunion, with the starry cast of Melanie Griffith (Teeny), Demi Moore (Samantha), Rita Wilson (Chrissy) and Rosie O'Donnell (Roberta) taking the grown-up roles.

The sequences with the adults are missable, but the teen story is quite cute, and there are good performances from the girls. It's just not that interesting though (despite a recluse named Crazy Pete wandering the streets at night just looking for a plot twist), and while it was described as a female version of *Stand By Me* at the time, it lacks much of that film's tension, warmth and heart. ★★☆☆☆

October Sky

Starring Jake Gyllenhaal, Chris Cooper, Laura Dern (1999)

Based on the memoir *Rocket Boys*, this old-fashioned movie is a true delight that first introduced audiences to talented young actor Jake Gyllenhaal. It's the true story of Homer Hickam, who as a teenager in West Virginia in the late 1950s became inspired by the Russian launch of the Sputnik satellite. Against his father's (Cooper) wishes (dad wants him to follow in his footsteps and work in the local coal mine), Homer and his friends start building their own home-made rocket with the support of their teacher, Miss Riley (Dern).

While it is sentimental in places, this is nonetheless an entertaining film throughout, a testament to one young man's spirit of adventure and invention and determination not to give up, even when his own father fails to support him. Gyllenhaal is superb as

Homer, and a bit of a cutie too, so while boys will be mesmerised by the exploding rockets, girls can drool over the young leading man (parents, meanwhile, will just be fascinated by Homer's story). Terrific stuff. ★★★★☆

The Outsiders 🔺 PG 🅖

Starring Matt Dillon, Ralph Macchio, C Thomas Howell (1983)

Rebellious teens (and those who wish they were but never will be) will love this film based on the S E Hinton novel of the same name. Grown-ups, meanwhile, will take a trip down memory lane as they watch this slice of nostalgia directed by Francis Ford Coppola featuring a who's who of eighties 'brat packers' such as Patrick Swayze, Matt Dillon, Ralph (*The Karate Kid*) Macchio, Rob Lowe, Emilio Estevez and, most hilariously of all, a buck-toothed Tom Cruise.

Set in the Midwest of the sixties, the film follows the 'greasers', a group of poor kids who are part of the local gang wars against the 'Socs'. When young orphan Ponyboy (Howell), who lives with his older brothers (Swayze and Lowe), gets involved in a murder committed by his best friend (Macchio), the violence escalates and the terrified pair have to hide out with the help of Dallas (Dillon). It's a surprisingly moving film featuring some terrific performances, and while some boys may groan at the sentimental ending (everyone else, on the other hand, will be reaching for the tissues), they'll no doubt love everything else about this classic film. ★★★★☆

Radio Flyer 🔺 PG-13 PG

Starring Elijah Wood, John Heard (1992)

A quirky gem of a movie. It's 1969, and Mike (Wood) and his younger brother Bobby (*Jurassic Park*'s Joseph Mazzello) are moving with their divorced mother Mary (Lorraine Bracco) from New Jersey to California. It's not long before Mary remarries, but her new husband – who calls himself The King (Adam Baldwin) – is a drinker and starts beating Bobby. Wanting to protect his little brother, Mike comes up with a plan to turn their red Radio Flyer trolley into a flying machine so they can leave town and never come back.

As much about the children's imagination as the abuse being suffered, this is narrated by Mike as an adult (Tom Hanks) and comes across as part fantasy, part brutal reality, which at times is an odd mix. But the performances are terrific, especially Mazzello and Wood's, and the script (by David Mickey Evans, who was the film's original director before he was replaced by *Lethal Weapon's* Richard Donner) is a lovely depiction of brotherly love. Donner's direction is sadly heavy-handed, however – perhaps this would have been an even better film if Evans had remained at the helm. ★★★★☆

Secondhand Lions

Starring Robert Duvall, Michael Caine, Haley Joel Osment (2003)

As sweetly sentimental as a Werther's Original advert, *Secondhand Lions* is the story of a fourteen-year-old boy, Walter (Osment), who is left in the care of his two eccentric great-uncles by his mother. The pair – played by gruff old geezers Caine and Duvall – live in a ramshackle middle-of-nowhere Texas farm, but neighbours seem to think the brothers have a secret fortune stashed away, apparently amassed while they were young bank robbers, mafia hitmen or wartime criminals (depending on which neighbour Walter talks to).

Often funny – the uncles fire pot-shots at travelling salesmen who try to relieve them of some of their rumoured cash – and whimsical (the pair tell stories of adventure that Walter can't be sure are true or figments of their ageing imaginations), this is a warm, nostalgic movie that features three terrific central performances and shows real heart. ★★★☆☆

Stand By Me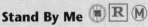

Starring Wil Wheaton, River Phoenix, Jerry O'Connell, Corey Feldman (1986)

Stephen King's short story *The Body* – a non-horror ode to boyhood friendships – was beautifully adapted for the screen by director Rob

Reiner and is a must-see not just for teens but for anyone who remembers the pain and joy of growing up. Quiet Gordie (Wheaton), the group's leader Chris (Phoenix), Teddy (Feldman) and pudgy Vern (O'Connell) are the four boys who are spending the summer of 1959 doing nothing much more than hanging out at their treehouse, until the day Vern announces that he knows where they can find a dead body. Intrigued to see what a corpse looks like, the friends set off on a long walk to find it.

A tale of friendships – related by a grown-up Gordie (an uncredited Richard Dreyfuss) – set against the beautiful Oregon scenery (standing in for the novel's Maine location), *Stand By Me* expertly depicts the fears, games, catchphrases, debates ('Mickey is a mouse, Donald is a duck, Pluto is a dog. So what's Goofy?') and secrets shared by young boys, while Kiefer Sutherland's older, meaner Ace gives a taste of what could be round the next corner in their lives. Beautifully played by the young cast, and lyrically directed by Reiner. ★★★★★

The War

Starring Elijah Wood, Kevin Costner (1994)

Long before he scaled the craggy peaks of Mordor in *The Lord of the Rings*, Elijah Wood stole this movie from his more experienced co-star, Kevin Costner. Costner plays Stephen, a poverty-stricken Vietnam vet in 1971 trying to come to terms with his experiences. His son Stu (Wood), meanwhile, has problems of his own – the impressive treehouse he and his sister have just built in the woods is under attack from mean and smelly local bullies.

While this does use the kids' conflict as a metaphor for grown-up wars and bashes the viewer over the head with the 'why can't we all get along' sentiment, there is a lovely movie beneath the preaching that is well worth seeking out. Costner gives one of his most subtle performances as the veteran suffering post-traumatic stress, but the movie belongs to the children – Wood, Lexi Randall (as his sister), and LaToya Chisholm and Charlette Julius as her friends. Even when odd plot twists come around – such as a scary bit at a water tower –they handle them with as much skill and warmth as actors twice their age. ★★★☆☆

Wondrous Oblivion

Starring Sam Smith, Delroy Lindo (2003)

A cute British coming-of-age drama that's like a cricketing version of *Billy Elliot* (but thankfully with less schmaltz). It's London in the 1960s, and young Jewish boy David (Smith) wants to be a cricketer, much to the puzzlement of his immigrant parents. When a Jamaican family move in next door, David finally gets the encouragement he needs, as neighbour Dennis (Lindo) sets up a net and stumps in the back garden and invites David to play. There's a subplot about the racism Dennis's family is subjected to, and a tentative flirtation between him and David's young mum (Emily Woof), but this is really a wistful tale of youthful dreams... and cricket, of course. ★★★☆☆

The Year My Voice Broke

Starring Noah Taylor, Loene Carmen (1987)

A beautiful movie from writer/director John Duigan, set in rural Australia, 1962. Young Danny (Taylor) is a scrawny fifteen-year-old besotted with his best friend Freya (Carmen), who has blossomed from a tomboy into a beautiful young woman. Unfortunately, while she loves Danny as a friend, Freya falls for a hunky slightly bad local boy named Trevor (Ben Mendelsohn), causing Danny to become jealous to the point that he decides to tag along when they go on a date, and tries mental telepathy to stop the two of them kissing.

There's a dark secret that, once uncovered, changes the way the three kids look at each other, but at its heart this movie is about their relationships, not some great revelation. And thanks to moving, natural performances from Taylor and Carmen (who had never acted on film before), it's well worth a look. Taylor reprised the role of Danny in Duigan's sequel, *Flirting*, in which he is sent to boarding school and begins a relationship with a young Ugandan student (played by Thandie Newton). Nicole Kidman also starred. ★★★★☆

Tiny Tots

● ●

This chapter is devoted to those films specifically aimed at very young (aged five and under) viewers. Of course, many films throughout this book – from *Cinderella* to *Stuart Little* – may be seen as perfectly suitable for such young eyes, but they're also enjoyed by older children (and grown-ups too). The films below, however, are unlikely to appeal to children older than their target audience, and so grown-ups are advised to have a good book handy while watching them with their charges!

THE ADVENTURES OF ELMO IN GROUCHLAND 🅤 🅖 u/c

Starring Mandy Patinkin, Vanessa L Williams (1999)

For the uninitiated, Elmo is one of the cutest residents of *Sesame Street*, a bright red, baby-voiced character who has his own TV show (*Elmo's World*) and is adored by babies and toddlers the world over. In his first adventure, after a tug-of-war with his friend Zoe, Elmo loses his beloved blue blanket, so has to muster up all his courage to rescue it, leading him on a journey to Grouchland, the stinky, rubbish-ridden birthplace of Oscar the Grouch, where the evil Huxley (Patinkin) keeps possession of everything he finds in the trash.

Like the TV episodes of *Sesame Street*, this is lovable stuff with a message (Elmo learns that he should have shared his blanket and not been so selfish) that's also brimming over with fun, songs, puns for parents to pick up on and general good cheer. (And in the very rare scary moments, Bert and Ernie pop up as narrators to reassure viewers that everything is going to be okay.) This is an absolute must for *Sesame*

Barbie: Movie Princess

Ah, Barbie. That blonde, all-American gal with her pink Barbie car, pink Barbie house and unattainable figure has been on the toy scene (and the wish list of many little girls) since 1959 and is still a big hit – the company that produces her, Mattel, estimate that approximately three Barbie dolls are sold every second. And don't go thinking Barbie is just a doll: Andy Warhol painted her, a section of Times Square was renamed Barbie Boulevard for her sixteenth birthday, and now she is an actress too, as the star (voiced by Kelly Sheridan) of a series of movies beginning with 2001's *Barbie in the Nutcracker*. As the title suggests, it's (loosely) based on Tchaikovsky's ballet, while 2002's *Barbie as Rapunzel* has our pretty heroine as the classic fairy-tale princess. Meanwhile, *Barbie of Swan Lake* (2003) is a nice animated introduction to the ballet for little girls, *Barbie as the Princess and the Pauper* (2004) has her singing and dancing in a musical twist on *The Prince and the Pauper*, *Barbie and the Magic of Pegasus* (2005) has her defeating a wizard with the help of a magical horse, and *Barbie: Fairytopia* (2005) has the slim-hipped one cast as a fairy who has to save her Magic Meadow home. Of course, they're all squarely aimed at very young Barbie fans (although grown-ups can at least listen out for a few celebrity voices, including Tim Curry, Anjelica Huston, Kelsey Grammer and Martin Short) and are – if you're feeling cynical – just a device to sell even more Barbie toys. But if you have a girl into all things pink, pretty and sweet, they are inoffensive films that are lovely to look at, and perfect for all wannabe little princesses.

Street fans (and who isn't one?) and features many of our favourite *Sesame* characters, including the Count, Big Bird, the Cookie Monster and Grover. ★★★★☆

BABAR: THE MOVIE

Voices by Gordon Pinsent, Sarah Polley, Gavin Magrath (1989)

A sweetly entertaining film for little tots and their grown-ups, this follows the adventures of the young Babar, boy king of the elephants, featured in the *Babar* books written by the French de Brunhoff family in the 1930s. It's like a junior *Indiana Jones* with tusks as our hero plods off to save his girlfriend Celeste's village after it is attacked by nasty rhinos and the elders are taken away.

Grown-ups may be slightly disconcerted that Celeste is a bit of a girly ninny, whimpering at the slightest sign of trouble, but that aside, this is a cute little adventure (with English-speaking voices replacing the original French ones) with some fun sing-along songs as Babar saves the day. ★★★☆☆

BARNEY'S GREAT ADVENTURE

Starring Diana Rice, Shirley Douglas (1998)

Barney, the dopey-voiced purple dinosaur first seen in the nineties TV series *Barney & Friends*, has divided adults into two camps – those who think he has kitsch charm and a sweet message for kids ('I love you, you love me…' etc), and those who think he is creepy and, in the words of one website user: 'an evil, brain-sucking alien'. Screen-savers and computer games (and numerous websites, of course) have demonstrated various ways that Barney (aka 'the purple antichrist') can be stopped (using a cannon in one online game works wonders), but while grown-ups debate his merits (and American forces use tapes of the show to get Iraqi captives to talk), tots have most likely already moved on to newer singing and dancing characters for their entertainment.

If your little one is a fan, however, this movie is a more entertaining option than the TV show, as Barney's adventure takes him out of a TV studio and onto a farm. That's where little Cody, his sister Abby and friend Marcella are staying when Cody discovers a purple dinosaur toy. Said toy turns into the 8ft purple dinosaur that is Barney, and it's he who shows the kids a magic egg which then accidentally ends up on a truck, so the kids have to go after it. It's all about believing in yourself and in others, and there are a few old-favourite songs in there too, like 'Twinkle Twinkle Little Star', to get younger viewers singing along. ★★★☆☆

THE BFG **G** PG

Voices by David Jason, Amanda Root (1989)

Made by ITV, this animated adaptation of Roald Dahl's book is delight-ful, and a must for all fans of the book. Young Sophie (Dahl naming his heroine after granddaughter Sophie Dahl) is abducted from her orphanage by the big friendly giant of the title, who lives in another world and forces himself to eat yucky food instead of the children he should be munching on. He spends nights delivering nice dreams to children, but when he and Sophie return to England, an evil giant who does eat kids follows.

It's terrific stuff – although some little viewers may be a mite scared when Sophie is first abducted – and as witty and fun as you would expect from a film based on Dahl's quirky story. The vocal cast are great, too, from Jason as the BFG and Root as Sophie to Angela Thorne as the Queen of England. ★★★★☆

THE BRAVE LITTLE TOASTER

Voices by Jon Lovitz, Phil Hartman (1987)

Based on Thomas M Disch's children's novel, *The Brave Little Toaster* is the cute tale of five household appliances – Toaster (known as 'Slots' by his pals), Blanky the electric blanket, Lampy the lamp, Radio and Kirby the vacuum cleaner – who are left abandoned in a mountain hol-iday house, so decide to go and find the Master (a thirteen-year-old boy) who makes their lives worthwhile.

It's like an animated *Incredible Journey* (except with appliances instead of animals) as the quintet head off with Kirby attached to a car battery and a chair with wheels so he can transport the troupe, and they encounter an electrical storm and other hazards such as quick-sand and a giant magnet. Little kids will probably miss the underlying messages of helping others, never giving up and selflessness, but will be enchanted by the group's colourful adventures and cute little char-acters. Aaaah. Two straight-to-video/DVD sequels followed: *The Brave Little Toaster Goes to Mars* (1998) and *The Brave Little Toaster to the Rescue* (1999). ★★★★☆

BROTHER BEAR u/c

Voices by Joaquin Phoenix, Rick Moranis (2003)

A so-so animated adventure from Disney, aimed at the most junior members of the audience. Young Native American Kenai (Phoenix) kills a bear he believes killed his older brother and is punished by the Great Spirits – they turn him into a bear so he can see what life is like for one of nature's great creatures. He will only be able to change back into a boy if he finds the place where 'the lights touch the earth', so with a new-found bear cub friend in tow, he sets off to find it, while Kenai's other brother – not knowing what has happened to Kenai – is tracking the bears, intent on killing them.

Little viewers will like the cute bears and the lovely animated landscapes, but may be scared during the tense bear hunt at the beginning of the movie. Older viewers will most likely yawn through the well-meaning message and should be warned that Phil Collins provides the soundtrack. ★★☆☆☆

THE CARE BEARS MOVIE u/c

Voices by Mickey Rooney, Jackie Burroughs (1985)

Awww. The cute Care Bears were a big hit with little kids in the late eighties, with their own cartoon series, range of soft toys and even duvet covers (they actually first appeared as greetings cards back in 1981). Simply animated and just brimming over with niceness, they are pastel-coloured bears with names like Love-a-lot Bear, Tenderheart and Bedtime Bear who live in a land in the clouds full of love and rainbows while helping children down on earth. And in this feature, they've got their eyes on Kim and Jason, who have no parents, and the trickier Nicholas, who is very lonely and under the spell of an evil spirit that wants to rid the world of caring.

While little boys may get bored as nothing gets destroyed or blown up (the Care Bears can do a 'care bear stare' that shoots rays out of their tummies when there is a bad guy around, but that only happens once in a blue moon), little girls will love the cuddly-wuddly bears and all the mushy loveliness. Do note that very little ones may be frightened by the evil spirit and Nicholas when he is in its control. Various sequels have followed to encourage the little ones to demand the fuzzy toys, including *Care Bears Movie II: A New Generation* (1986), in which they have to stop the grumpy Dark Heart from getting rid of Care Bears for ever, *The Care Bears Adventure in Wonderland* (1987), in which they meet Alice and the Mad Hatter, and made-for-TV films like the CGI-animated *Care Bears: Big Wish Movie* (2005), which parents will wish was considerably shorter. ★★★☆☆

CLIFFORD'S REALLY BIG MOVIE

Voices by John Ritter, Jenna Elfman (2004)

Clifford, the very big red dog, who began life over forty years ago in Norman Bridwell's books, here gets a big-screen adventure. Clifford (Ritter) lives on Birdwell Island with doggy pals T-Bone and Cleo and his owner, Emily Elizabeth. Worried that his voracious appetite is costing her family dear, Clifford runs away to the circus, hoping to enter a TV contest that promises the lucky winner a lifetime supply of his favourite canine snacks (Tummy Yummies).

That's about it, and this plot is stretched fairly thin over seventy-five minutes as Clifford annoys a competing ferret, is dognapped and eventually realises there is no place like home. Young viewers who have got to know Clifford via the TV series (*Clifford the Big Red Dog*) may take a while to get used to the slicker, flashily animated dog here (the budget was obviously much bigger than for the TV show) but will no doubt enjoy his amiable adventures (and laugh at the high-wire-walking cow he meets at the circus). Note that this was the last movie role for comic actor John Ritter who died suddenly in 2003, aged fifty-five. ★★★☆☆

CURIOUS GEORGE

Voices by Will Ferrell, Drew Barrymore (2006)

Margret and H.A. Rey wrote the Curious George books for toddlers over sixty-five years ago, and this traditional animated adventure featuring the mischievous monkey stays reasonably close to their original drawings and ideas. Sweet but dim museum guide Ted (Ferrell) travels to Africa to secure a giant statue that could save the fate of the museum where he works. Unfortunately, he returns with a figurine more the size of a key ring, and a stowaway cheeky monkey who has taken a liking to him, but whose antics soon cause poor Ted to lose his job and his apartment.

Squarely aimed at the littlest of viewers, this doesn't have any of that grown-up humour that's present in family films like *Toy Story* or *The Incredibles*. Instead, it's just sweet and simple stuff featuring a lovable central character and nice vocal performances from a cast that also includes Barrymore as Ted's possible love interest and Dick Van Dyke as his boss. ★★★☆☆

DUCKTALES: THE MOVIE – TREASURE OF THE LOST LAMP

Voices by Alan Young, Russi Taylor (1990)

Those adorable ducks Huey, Dewey and Louie, along with their uncle Scrooge McDuck, get their own *Indiana Jones*-meets-*Aladdin* adventure in this animated film based on the toddlers' TV series *DuckTales*. Unlike many movies based on twenty-minute TV shows, this actually has a well-developed plot that speeds by as Scrooge (Young) searches for the lost treasure of Collie Baba with the help of his cheeky nephews, pal Webby (all voiced by Taylor) and dashing pilot Launchpad McQuack (Terence McGovern). Unfortunately, when they find it, they soon lose it to evil magician Merlock (Christopher Lloyd) and find themselves with only a battered old lamp instead – which, of course, hides a wish-granting genie (Rip Taylor).

It's a rip-roaring adventure ideal for tots too young to watch *Raiders of the Lost Ark* or *The Mummy* that's packed with caverns, booby traps, chases and smart, funny dialogue. Sadly, a sequel was never made, though there are spin-off computer games including DuckTales: The Quest for Gold for kids who enjoy the movie. ★★★★☆

A GOOFY MOVIE

Voices by Bill Farmer, Jim Cummings (1995)

'Mickey is a mouse, Donald is a duck, Pluto is a dog. So what's Goofy...?' debated Gordie and his pals in Rob Reiner's movie *Stand By Me*. Well, the truth may never be known (most people think he's a dog, but the fact he can drive raises some opposable-thumb questions) but in this movie, Goofy's all grown up and is (shock horror) a single parent to son Max. Max is a teenager and doesn't have much time for his 'square' dad, so he's less than pleased when Goofy drags him on a cross-country road trip so the pair of them can bond, especially as Max would rather be drooling over a girl named Roxanne back home.

For a film aimed at very little viewers, the psychobabble bonding stuff seems a little out of place, but there are some simpler, funnier moments too, as when the pair encounter Bigfoot or visit Lester's Possum Park, a theme park where everything is about possums. It's certainly not one of Disney's better animated movies, but it's cute nonetheless. ★★★☆☆

THE LITTLE POLAR BEAR

Voices by Wesley Singerman, Brianne Siddall (2001)

A German animated movie (*Der Kleine Eisbär* is the movie's German title) based on stories by Dutch writer and illustrator Hans de Beer, this is the story of a cuddly little polar bear named Lars (Singerman), who befriends a seal pup named Robby (Siddall), only to discover the older polar bears don't usually cosy up to seals (they usually eat them).

It's all very cute and fluffy for little kids (and grown-ups will get a laugh from the neurotic lemmings who are constantly trying to off themselves), but while toddlers will love the cuddly bear and his pals, and the nicely drawn Arctic scenery, there are too many plots thrown in for them to keep up with – as well as Lars and Robby's friendship, there's an undersea adventure and a fish shortage thanks to a nasty trawler. ★★★☆☆

THE MAGIC PUDDING

Voices by Sam Neill, Hugo Weaving (2000)

The biggest animation project Australia had ever attempted, this sweet little fable is brimming over with vocal talent, from Sam Neill, *Matrix* star Hugo Weaving and Oscar-winning Geoffrey Rush to John Cleese (as the Magic Pudding of the title) and Toni Collette. Based on Norman Lindsay's 1917 novel, it's the story of a koala named Bunyip (Rush) searching for his parents, who teams up with sailor Bill (Weaving), penguin Sam (Neill) and their magic pudding Albert to find them, while nasty pudding thieves are hot on their trail.

It's all as Australian as a kangaroo, and just as bouncy, with nicely coloured (as opposed to bright and flashy) animation based on Lindsay's original drawings, a wholesome message (never stop believing etc) and a few fun songs. ★★★☆☆

MY LITTLE PONY: THE MOVIE

Voices by Danny DeVito, Cloris Leachman (1986)

Parents who find the Care Bears sickly sweet will gag on this far more sugary adventure featuring those 'lovable' (apparently) little ponies. The brightly coloured animals live in Ponyland and are preparing for their annual Spring Festival. But evil witch Hydia, who lives in the Volcano of Doom, has had enough of the ponies' happiness, and decides to cover their pretty Dream Valley in some gunk called Smooze.

It's all pretty nauseating for anyone over the age of four, but little girls who like ponies may think it's cute, and there's nothing in the film that should scare even the most nervous of small viewers. Anyone older, however, will find the animation dull (a bit sloppy too – some of the ponies change from their original colour!) and the characters annoying – especially the pony named Baby Lickety Split. ★★☆☆☆

PIGLET'S BIG MOVIE

Voices by John Fiedler, Jim Cummings (2003)

For the second feature-length movie based on A A Milne's *Winnie-the - Pooh* characters (*The Tigger Movie* came first in 2000), Piglet takes centre stage. He's unhappy because Pooh, Rabbit and pals don't include him in their hunt for honey as he is too small, so he runs away, leaving the others to use his scrapbook filled with memories (cue flashbacks of Piglet's adventures) to track the little pig down.

Clearly meant to make the littlest members of the audience feel they are important, even when they are very small, this is well meaning but pretty dull stuff – Piglet isn't really lost, and while the troupe try and figure out where he may be, the audience already knows everything is really okay, for starters. And perhaps the movie's biggest flaw is simply that Piglet is the least interesting (and most needy!) resident of Hundred Acre Wood – so couldn't the Disney animators have done *The Tigger Movie Part II* instead? ★★☆☆☆

POOH'S HEFFALUMP MOVIE

Voices by Jim Cummings, John Fiedler (2005)

Sweet if brief (it's only 68 minutes long) stuff for really little ones as Winnie-the-Pooh's kangaroo pal Roo befriends a lovable baby heffalump named Lumpy while the other residents of Hundred Acre Wood are under the misguided impression that heffalumps are evil.

Fans of A A Milne's stories will know that Pooh never actually met a mythical heffalump, so it's nice to finally see what one looks like (they're pastel-coloured elephants), but otherwise there's little here to enthral anyone but the most undemanding of small viewers. To make matters worse, over 900 children auditioned for the vocal role of Lumpy, and the child that was chosen (five-year-old Brit Kyle Stanger) mumbles throughout! ★★☆☆☆

THE POWERPUFF GIRLS MOVIE

Voices by Cathy Cavadini, Tara Strong (2002)

A prequel to the popular TV series, this adventure explains how the Powerpuff Girls came to be, and why they decided to dedicate their lives to crime-fighting. (Parents should note that such crime-fighting and 'frequent mild peril'– basically, cartoon violence that kids will be used to/oblivious to – are the reasons this is rated 'PG' and is probably best suited to the over-sixes.)

Buttercup, Blossom and Bubbles were created in Professor Utonium's lab – he was aiming to make the perfect girl when he accidentally added an extra chemical to the mix of sugar, spice and all things nice. The girls, complete with superhuman strength and flying abilities, aren't that good to begin with, so are banished to a faraway planet until an even badder dude – Utonium's monkey Mojo Jojo – decides he wants to take over the world. And of course, only the Powerpuff Girls can stop him. There are a few moments of quite subversive stuff as Mojo Jojo turns some monkeys into mutants, but littler viewers are unlikely to notice and will be cheering along as the three spunky heroines fly in to save us all. ★★★☆☆

SESAME STREET PRESENTS: FOLLOW THAT BIRD

Starring Jim Henson, Frank Oz (1985)

While not quite as adorable as *The Adventures of Elmo in Grouchland*, this *Sesame Street* adventure is a must for fans of the series, and especially fans of Big Bird, who is the star here. Although he's happy living on Sesame Street, the Feathered Friends Society has decreed that the giant yellow feathered one should really be living with other birds, so Big Bird packs up and moves to live with the Dodo family in Illinois. Of course, life there isn't all rosy, so Big Bird decides to head back home to the Street, only to find getting there won't be that easy.

Many of the *Sesame* characters pop up to find Big Bird and bring him home in this fun journey, from Mr Snuffleupagus to Bert and Ernie (Elmo, however, is absent, as he didn't become a popular character until the 1990s). It's funny and fast-paced for the kids, while adults will enjoy spotting the cameos from comic actors including Chevy Chase, John Candy and Sandra Bernhard (*Star Wars* director George Lucas also has a cameo – look into the crowd when Big Bird arrives back on Sesame Street). ★★★★☆

THOMAS AND THE MAGIC RAILROAD

Starring Alec Baldwin, Peter Fonda (2000)

Reverend Awdry's classic kids' stories about Thomas the Tank Engine got the big-screen treatment (following the much-loved TV series narrated by Ringo Starr) and a bit of a Hollywood makeover for this adventure. The plucky engine, along with twelve-inch tall Mr Conductor (Baldwin), cute little Lily (Mara Wilson) and her grandfather (Fonda), is determined to save the other engines from a bullying diesel engine.

Unfortunately, it's all a bit of a mess. Filmed mainly on the Isle of Man, the film has a very British country look to it, yet most of the (human) cast have American accents, which makes no sense. The story doesn't fare much better – there's some nonsense about magic dust and a missing train hidden on a secret railway track that is the only one who can stop the bully – while the effects are often irritating (how come the trains can roll their eyes, yet they don't open their mouths when they speak?). Older fans of the books will be horrified, while very young viewers who like the TV series will just be confused as to what on earth is going on. ★☆☆☆☆

THE TIGGER MOVIE

Voices by Jim Cummings, Nikita Hopkins (2000)

Although A A Milne's *Winnie-the-Pooh stories* have been adapted for the screen before, they were mainly made as shorts such as *Winnie the Pooh and the Blustery Day* (1968), and the 1977 collection of short stories *The Many Adventures of Winnie the Pooh*. So, technically, this was the first feature-length movie starring the characters who live in Hundred Acre Wood, and (hurrah!) it focuses on the bounciest of them all, Tigger.

It seems that the bouncy, trouncy, flouncy, pouncy, fun, fun, fun, fun, fun Tigger is too bouncy for Pooh, Piglet, Owl, Eeyore, Rabbit, Kanga and Roo – they are getting ready for winter and don't have time to bounce with him. So Tigger decides to find others like him, and ventures out into a blizzard to find his Tigger family. Delightful stuff, this really keeps the spirit of Milne's stories alive and is a great introduction to the characters for little viewers and a welcome return of old friends for adults. Following the success of *The Tigger Movie*, *Piglet's Big Movie* was made in 2003, followed by *Pooh's Heffalump Movie* in 2005.
★★★★☆

Tweenies

••

Tweenies – those kids bored with movies aimed at little tots, but too young to watch teen-oriented films – have become an important demographic for movie-makers. These are the kids (roughly aged seven to twelve) who don't only buy the DVD but also the posters, spin-off magazines and T-shirts, as well as downloading the soundtrack albums and joining the fan clubs.

They also create stars. In the sixties little girls loved Hayley Mills and in the seventies Jodie Foster was flavour of the month. In the eighties Corey Feldman and Corey Haim had a brief spell in the sun, Michael J Fox was a tween pin-up till he grew up, and in the nineties it was Macaulay Culkin and then, by the end of the decade, the Olsen twins (who remain favourites now, along with Hilary Duff, Anne Hathaway and Lindsay Lohan).

So the films here are the ones most suitable for preteens. Most of them probably aren't that fun for grown-ups to enjoy (with a few exceptions like *The Goonies* and *Spy Kids*), so for movies more aimed at you *and* your tweenies, check out the Family Movies chapter.

THE ADVENTURES OF SHARKBOY AND LAVAGIRL 3D

Starring Taylor Lautner, Taylor Dooley (2005)

Robert Rodriguez, the creator/writer and director of the *Spy Kids* movies, delivers another kiddie adventure here, which was inspired by a story his seven-year-old son Racer made up. It's the tale of a young boy named Max (Cayden Boyd) who has created another world in his mind to escape from school bullies and parents who ignore him. The name of this world is Planet Drool, and Max gets a shock when two characters he imagined, Sharkboy and Lavagirl, turn up on earth to reveal Drool really exists and they need Max's help to save it from the nasty Mr Electric (George Lopez) – who looks a lot like Max's real-world teacher Mr Electricidad – and even badder guy Minus.

It's flashy, eye-popping stuff (especially during 3D sequences, which require those irritating glasses) as the trio wander across Planet Drool through places like the Land of Milk and Cookies to the finale that pits them against the bad guys. It's nicely surreal for a kids' film, but all the brightness and rapid images may make some viewers feel as if they are stuck in some mad, loud video game. ★★★☆☆

AGENT CODY BANKS

Starring Frankie Muniz, Hilary Duff (2003)

'Save the World. Get the Girl. Pass Math.' The poster tagline for this pint-sized 007 (003 and a half?) sums up this well-meaning adventure, which was the first cinema outing for *Malcolm in the Middle*'s Muniz as Agent Cody Banks. Cody is part of a government secret-agent programme that recruits teens and allows them to drive cool cars, carry great gizmos and fight bad guys when they aren't studying. For his first assignment, Cody has to go undercover at a prep school and befriend young Natalie (Duff) in order to get close to her boffin father, who is devising some micro-robots that bad guys want to use as a weapon.

This isn't hilariously funny, but it's cute nonetheless, especially in scenes when Cody has to charm Natalie, despite being painfully awkward and shy around girls. Boys will like the gadgets, girls will like the romance, and while grown-ups would rather be watching the real James Bond than this unsubtle teen equivalent, they'll still chuckle at a few of the gags. ★★★☆☆

AGENT CODY BANKS 2: DESTINATION LONDON

Starring Frankie Muniz, Anthony Anderson (2004)

Prepubescent girls who like Frankie Muniz (of *Malcolm in the Middle* fame) may want to catch this sequel (though no one else will), in which he plays a sixteen-year-old secret agent. This time, as the title suggests, he's in London to investigate whether a music school is actually a front for something more sinister, which means plenty of clichéd shots of double-decker buses, black cabs and Big Ben, and japes aplenty.

Muniz – who was reportedly paid a whopping $5 million for his performance – isn't bad as the junior 007, but he's stuck in a film with an awful script (apparently there wasn't one when filming began and it was written as they went along), plodding direction (original director Harald Zwart walked off early on when the movie's budget was slashed and was replaced by Kevin Allen, brother of Keith, who unsurprisingly appears in the film) and a plot that is just an excuse to fill the film with shots of London landmarks and a Tony Blair impersonator. You have been warned. ★☆☆☆☆

ANASTASIA

Voices by Meg Ryan, John Cusack, Kelsey Grammer (1997)

The now-disproved legend of Anastasia, supposedly the only member of the Russian royal family to survive the massacre by the Bolsheviks at the beginning of the 20th century, is very loosely used in this animated adventure for girls from *An American Tail* director Don Bluth (if you want your tweenie to see a more serious – but not much more historical – version, search for the 1956 film *Anastasia*, starring Ingrid Bergman). In this tale, young amnesiac Anastasia (voiced by Kirsten Dunst as a girl, and by Ryan as an adult) is found by two con men, who decide to take her to meet her possible grandmother in Paris, who has promised a reward if her granddaughter is ever found.

There are a few sweet songs here, and nice vocal work from Ryan, Cusack and Grammer, plus fun from Hank Azaria as Bartok the bat. But what were the writers thinking when they made the bad guy the ghost of Rasputin (voiced by Christopher Lloyd)? A straight-to-video/DVD sequel, *Bartok the Magnificent*, was released in 1999, with Azaria's character taking centre stage. ★★★☆☆

ANGELS IN THE OUTFIELD

Starring Danny Glover, Brenda Fricker, Tony Danza (1994)

A sort of junior *Field of Dreams*, this is a remake of the 1951 film of the same name. Young Roger (Joseph Gordon-Levitt) prays that his local baseball team will finally win a few games, and that his parents will get back together. To his surprise, when he watches his team play, he sees ghostly apparitions helping them win the game, but only he can see them.

A feel-good movie for kids, this has some sweet performances from Glover (as the team coach who believes Roger has really seen angels), Fricker (as Roger's foster mother) and Christopher Lloyd (as Al the Angel), but suffers from a very twee script that tries to squeeze every last drop of sentimentality out of each frame. Even the most uncynical kids will choke on their popcorn before the end. Watch out for Adrien Brody (*King Kong*) and Matthew McConaughey in small supporting roles. ★★☆☆☆

ANNIE

Starring Albert Finney, Carol Burnett, Ann Reinking (1982)

Everyone's favourite curly, red-haired orphan – originally a comic strip that was adapted into a hugely successful Broadway musical – got the big-screen treatment here, in a movie directed by the venerated John Huston (*The Misfits*, *The Asphalt Jungle*, etc). Featuring all those Charles Strouse songs – 'It's the Hard Knock Life', 'Easy Street' and, of course, 'Tomorrow' – it's the tale of little orphan Annie (Aileen Quinn), who lives in an orphanage run by the mean Miss Hannigan (Burnett). Things get much better when she is selected to live with rich industrialist Oliver 'Daddy' Warbucks (Finney), and she charms the grumpy man and his staff, but there is trouble on the horizon from Hannigan and her brother Rooster (Tim Curry), who sense there is money to be made from Annie's misfortunes.

Huston's only musical, this is as brightly coloured as Annie's hair but somehow lacks any real joy or fun. Quinn is more irritating than she is cute, while Finney just looks uncomfortable. Young girls may enjoy the songs though (and some of them are staged very well), even if they want to strangle the saccharine lead. ★★☆☆☆

THE BELLES OF ST TRINIAN'S

Starring Alastair Sim, Joyce Grenfell, George Cole (1954)

The first film to feature the naughty girls of St Trinian's School, this was followed by three sequels (1957's *Blue Murder at St Trinian's*, 1960's *The Pure Hell of St Trinian's* and 1966's *The Great St Trinian's Train Robbery*) and a weak 1980 follow-up, *The Wildcats of St Trinian's*. Based on Ronald Searle's cartoons, the first film is a terrific slice of British camp as Alastair Sim plays not only the school headmistress (in drag), but also her bookie brother who smuggles his daughter into the sixth form so she can pick up racing tips from a schoolmate whose father is an Arabian racehorse owner.

Gambling, drinking and general misbehaviour are the order of the day – as the headmistress notes, 'in other schools girls are sent out quite unprepared into a merciless world, but when our girls leave here, it is the merciless world which has to be prepared' – and there are some classic comedy moments that will make both adults and kids giggle. Despite the girls' naughty deeds, it's all pretty innocent stuff that's perfect for tweenie viewers. ★★★★☆

BMX BANDITS

Starring David Argue, John Ley, Nicole Kidman (1983)

An Australian adventure – featuring a sixteen-year-old Nicole Kidman in one of her earliest roles – *BMX Bandits* was released in the eighties when BMX bikes were at the height of their popularity. And, er, now they're not. That wouldn't be too much of a problem if there was a decent plot to speak of, but unfortunately the one that there is (kids uncover hidden walkie-talkies and decide to sell them to buy BMX bikes, bad guys want the dated gizmos too) is weak and only serves as an excuse for lots of scenes of kids racing around on their (you guessed it) BMX bikes.

Grown-ups may watch for five minutes just to see young Nicole, while the only boys who will be interested are those with a serious bicycle obsession – and surely they'll be out on their bikes and not indoors watching this? ★★☆☆☆

BUGSY MALONE

Starring Scott Baio, Jodie Foster, Florrie Dugger (1976)

Alan Parker (*Mississippi Burning*) wrote and directed this Prohibition-set gangster movie in which all the hoodlums and showgirls are played by kids, and instead of guns the 'men' settle their differences using custard pies and splurge guns that cover the victims in a creamy goo. It's an incredibly silly (for adults) but fun (for kids) musical, as Bugsy (Baio) tries to help local tough guy Fat Sam in a gang war while romancing new-to-town Blousey Brown (Dugger) and being distracted by nightclub singer Tallulah (a fourteen-year-old Foster vamping it up).

Grown-ups provide the singing voices for the cast, which can be a bit disconcerting for adult viewers (Jodie Foster herself has said she found that a bit odd when showing the movie to her own child), but all in all this is harmless fun. Trivia fans may like to know that Baio, best known as the Fonz's cousin in TV's *Happy Days*, continues to appear on TV and was a beau of Pamela Anderson, Florrie Dugger never acted in film again and now works for the air force and, erm, Jodie Foster has a successful film career and has won two Oscars.
★★★★☆

CANDLESHOE

Starring Jodie Foster, David Niven (1977)

Jodie Foster is the young petty thief Casey Brown, who teams up with con man Harry (Leo McKern) in this fun Disney comedy. Harry thinks there's some treasure stashed at the Candleshoe estate in England, so he enlists Casey to pose as the long-lost granddaughter of Lady St Edmund (Helen Hayes), matriarch of the manor. Of course, once Casey arrives, she's torn between abetting Harry and helping the butler (Niven) save the estate, which is in financial trouble.

Foster's final family film for Disney, this is a good old-fashioned yarn, bolstered by a winning, tomboyish performance from Jodie and a tongue-in-cheek one from Niven, whose character has also been disguising himself as the gardener and chauffeur to keep Lady St Edmund from realising the estate is in jeopardy. ★★★☆☆

A CINDERELLA STORY

Starring Hilary Duff, Chad Michael Murray (2004)

The classic fairy tale *Cinderella* gets updated, with the general idea – girl wants boy, girl meets boy, girl runs off, boy finds girl – intact but the magic (both literal and otherwise) missing. Following the death of her dad in an earthquake (in an unintentionally silly scene), young Sam (Duff) is forced to share her home with his gold-digging widow Fiona (Jennifer Coolidge) and her two nasty, dim-witted daughters. When she's not slaving away at Fiona's diner, she is running after her mean stepmother and stepsisters at home, and only her fellow waitresses and geeky pal Carter (Dan Byrd) are on hand to make her feel better. The one bright spot in Sam's life is the email and text relationship she is having with a mystery boy at school who shares her dreams of escaping the town and going to Princeton – little does she know, however, that it's dreamy high-school hunk Austin (*One Tree Hill* star Murray) she's been communicating with.

While the film isn't very funny, young girls will be happy to drool at Austin, who is very pretty to look at, but also pretty dim (all it takes is Sam's eye mask for him not to recognise her). Grown-ups watching will grind their teeth in frustration over some of the plot twists that keep the two cuties apart until the end – but this movie isn't aimed at griping adults looking for a fresh take on an old idea, and the little girls who like Hilary Duff will no doubt overlook the movie's flaws and perch on the edge of their seats waiting for Cinderella to finally get her prince. ★★★☆☆

CURLY SUE

Starring James Belushi, Alisan Porter (1991)

Teen movie maestro John Hughes wrote and directed this family comedy about homeless pair Bill (Belushi) and cutesy little Curly Sue (Porter, now grown up and pursuing singing rather than acting), who live on the road and feed themselves by conning people with harmless little scams. When one such scam involves cold-hearted lawyer Grey Ellison (Kelly Lynch), they get not only a free meal, but also a possible mum for Sue and love interest for Bill (while Grey thaws and finds she has a heart).

Adults will either love or hate winsome little Sue as she charms her way across the screen, while junior viewers will chuckle at her antics but perhaps be less enthused about the potential Lynch/Belushi romance. All in all, it's sentimental but funny stuff, not a great movie but an enjoyably dippy one. ★★★☆☆

ELLA ENCHANTED

Starring Anne Hathaway, Hugh Dancy (2004)

When she was born, a fairy cast a spell on poor Ella of Frell (*The Princess Diaries'* Hathaway) that makes her obey any command. When her father remarries and her nasty stepsisters discover they can order Ella to do anything they please, Ella decides to set off on a journey to get the annoying curse finally removed.

This is a fun 21st-century take on fairy-tale adventures – this gal doesn't need rescuing from a dashing hero and is, in fact, far cannier than the movie's Prince Charming (actually called Prince Char, and the face that adorns thousands of fantasy-world teen magazines), who is being manipulated by his cruel uncle Sir Edgar (Cary Elwes). Of course, the film owes a debt to the knowing humour and adventure of *The Princess Bride* (and adult viewers will get a kick out of the fact that that film's hero, Elwes, gets to be the baddie here), and the faux-medieval settings (with modern-day references thrown in) of *A Knight's Tale* and *Shrek*, but director Tommy O'Haver adds enough of his own touches to make this fresh and fun. There are a couple of unnecessary song-and-dance numbers to endure, but tweeny audiences should be delighted by Anne Hathaway's sweet performance and nice supporting turns from a cast that also includes Minnie Driver, Jimi Mistry, Eric Idle (the narrator) and a gorgeously over-the-top Joanna Lumley as Ella's wicked stepmother. ★★★☆☆

FREAKY FRIDAY

Starring Barbara Harris, Jodie Foster (1976)

Foster's most famous movie for Disney, this body-swap comedy may be three decades old but it's still a treat for younger viewers (grown-ups may think it has dated somewhat). Rebellious thirteen-year-old daughter Annabel (Foster) and mother Ellen (Harris) each think the other has an easy life. So when they both wish they could switch places and have

Tweenies

the other's life for a while, the unexpected happens and Annabel finds herself as a middle-aged mother while Ellen gets to experience life as a teenager – if only for one very strange day.

It's over-the-top stuff (quite how one day can include a car chase and water-ski adventure is a mystery) but there are some nice touches ('mum' skateboarding past her bemused husband) and Foster and Harris pull off their impersonations of each other with aplomb. Kids will definitely chuckle. ★★★☆☆

FREAKY FRIDAY

Starring Lindsay Lohan, Jamie Lee Curtis (2003)

A remake of the Jodie Foster 1976 film (reviewed above), with Lindsay Lohan (seemingly the queen of tweenie remakes, having also done *Herbie* and *The Parent Trap*) and Jamie Lee Curtis as the daughter, Anna, and mother, Tess, who swap bodies. This time, it is a couple of Chinese fortune cookies that causes fifteen-year-old Anna (a budding rocker) and strait-laced mother Tess to find themselves in each other's bodies one Friday morning – an event they wish to alter in double-quick time, as Tess is due to marry Ryan (Mark Harmon) on Saturday.

There are a few modern twists that give this movie extra charm – mum is a psychiatrist, meaning Anna in her body has to psycho-analyse some clients, while Tess (in Anna's body) has to fend off an amorous biker boy (Chad Michael Murray) and perform in a rock audition. Curtis – who hasn't been this funny since *A Fish Called Wanda* – is a hoot, Lohan matches her scene for scene, and all in all it's fun stuff (parents of younger kids should note there are some slightly sexual situations). ★★★☆☆

THE GOONIES

Starring Sean Astin, Josh Brolin, Corey Feldman (1985)

Widely and deservedly regarded as one of the best kids' movies ever, this is a junior *Raiders of the Lost Ark* from executive producer Steven Spielberg and director Richard Donner (*Superman*, *Lethal Weapon*). And it's a riot, as a gang of kids who call themselves the Goonies (the area where they live is called the Goondocks) come across a treasure map and decide to find the loot, hoping it is the money they need to stop

'I loved *The Goonies*, which I watched every day for a whole summer as a child. I was compelled to watch, addicted to it.' JAMES MCAVOY (star of *The Chronicles of Narnia*)

their homes being demolished as part of a corporate development. The map leads them on a great adventure, through underground tunnels, into the lair of some fugitive criminals (Robert Davi and Joe Pantoliano), past booby traps and even down a water-chute toboggan ride.

All the kids are memorable, from Sean Astin's leader Mikey to Corey Feldman's smart-mouthed 'Mouth', and the action is rambunctious, to say the least. A must for all kids, thanks to heaps of action, adventure, fun dialogue and funnier characters (though parents should note there is some swearing and a few edge-of-the-seat bits), this has also gained something of a cult following among thirtysomethings who still treasure the movie they first loved when they were kids themselves.
★★★★★

HARRIET THE SPY

Starring Michelle Trachtenberg, Gregory Smith (1996)

Based on the sixties kids' book of the same name by Louise Fitzhugh, this was the first movie made by US TV channel Nickelodeon (who also made *The Rugrats Movie* and spin-offs from other cartoons). Eleven-year-old Harriet (Trachtenberg, who went on to become better known as Dawn in TV's *Buffy the Vampire Slayer*) has aspirations to be a writer. Her grown-up companion, governess Golly (Rosie O'Donnell), tells her she must jot all her experiences down in her notebook if she wants to be a good author, so Harriet becomes a spy, snooping on neighbours and friends and religiously recording everything for posterity – until the day the class goody-goody gets her hands on her notebook and reveals Harriet's thoughts (good and bad) to all and sundry. Uh-oh.

Director Bronwen Hughes (in her movie directorial debut) gets a bit carried away with jump-cuts, odd angles and MTV-style camera work that will give grown-ups watching headaches, and which also detract from the gist of the story (don't snoop on your friends etc). Trachtenberg, however, does make an enjoyable Harriet (even if she is a bit of a mean character) and there is nice kiddie support from Gregory Smith and Vanessa Lee Chester as the best pals who are horrified by Harriet's writings. ★★☆☆☆

HERBIE: FULLY LOADED

Starring Lindsay Lohan, Michael Keaton, Matt Dillon (2005)

A 21st-century update of the *Herbie* movies from the sixties and seventies (see *The Love Bug* review), starring teen queen Lindsay Lohan. She is Maggie, the daughter of a failed stock-car racing driver (Keaton) and latest owner of the VW Beetle with a mind of its own. Of course, it's not long before Maggie's doing a bit of racing herself, taking on the reigning NASCAR champ Trip Murphy (Dillon), who is none too pleased about the competition.

It's all pretty predictable stuff, but kids should get a kick out of the racing scenes, slapstick and Lohan's (and Herbie's) winning performance. Grown-ups along for the ride should keep their eyes peeled during the opening sequence for a cameo from that coolest of cars, KITT (from TV's *Knight Rider*). And parents should note that Lohan's significant post-pubescent cleavage was digitally reduced (or hidden with raised necklines) after early screenings of the movie caused concern that she looked too raunchy for small children's eyes. ★★★☆☆

IT TAKES TWO

Starring Ashley Olsen, Mary-Kate Olsen (1995)

The first big-screen movie to star the Olsen twins, made when the multi-millionairesses were just nine years old. It's a twist on *The Parent Trap*, as a rich girl named Alyssa who lives with her dad (Steve Guttenberg) and orphaned Amanda, who is looked after by a social worker (Kirstie Alley), discover they look alike and agree to swap places for a while. And if they can matchmake the two adults in their lives together, even better.

Both Olsens are enjoyable to watch here, and there are some fun moments with Alley, who displays the comic timing she perfected on *Cheers*. Adults will note that Guttenberg is miscast as the male romantic lead, but hopefully he's so wishy-washy and forgettable that the tweenie girls this is aimed at won't even notice him. ★★★☆☆

Mary-Kate and Ashley Olsen

If you have (or are) a girl of around nine to twelve years old, chances are you know who the Olsen twins are. For everyone else, here's a quick catch-up on two of the most successful girls in Hollywood...

- Mary-Kate and Ashley were born on 13 June 1986 (Mary-Kate is younger by approximately two minutes) and they won their first major TV roles less than a year later on the US TV series *Full House*, in which they shared the role of Michelle until the series finished in 1995.
- By the age of six, they had their own production company, Dualstar, making them the youngest producers in history.
- After making a series of straight-to-video/DVD movies (*Double, Double, Toil and Trouble*, *How the West Was Fun*) they made their cinema debut in *It Takes Two* (1995, reviewed above).
- You can buy a Mary-Kate and Ashley magazine, dolls in their likeness, and they have their own range of clothing.
- On their seventeenth birthdays in 2003, it was estimated they were each worth over $150 million.

JOSIE AND THE PUSSYCATS

Starring Rachael Leigh Cook, Tara Reid, Rosario Dawson (2001)

A resounding flop when it was released, this is actually a quirky, fun flick about a teen girl band (think Spice Girls but with talent), which probably only failed because it poked fun at the pop industry while still being aimed at young female viewers – and as any parent knows, young girls do not have a sense of humour when it comes to their favourite pop bands.

When hot boy band Du Jour discover subliminal messages have been inserted in their music to encourage suggestible kids to buy stuff, they are bumped off by their manager, Wyatt (Alan Cumming, in a wonderfully seething performance). He and his boss, the bonkers Fiona (Parker Posey), need a replacement group and so they recruit rocker Josie (Cook), dopey Melody (Reid) and tough Valerie (Dawson) and turn them into the hugely successful Josie and the Pussycats. But will the girls stay friends when they hit the big time? And will they uncover Fiona and Wyatt's evil scheme?

Bouncy, colourful and entertaining, this is a delightful comic update of the 1970s comic book and cartoon show on which it is based. Younger girls won't get the satirical references, of course, but they'll enjoy the girls' adventures and the infectious songs nonetheless. ★★★☆☆

THE JOURNEY OF NATTY GANN

Starring Meredith Salenger, John Cusack (1985)

A terrific Western-style adventure set in the 1930s. Twelve-year-old Natty Gann's father (Ray Wise) has to find work away from home during the Depression, so he leaves Natty in Chicago with a guardian and heads to Washington State, looking for logging work. But Natty runs away and heads off to find her dad, along the way befriending an abused wolf (played by Jed, who also starred in the movie *White Fang*) and a young drifter named Harry (Cusack) and surviving such nightmares as a train crash (in which her father is told she has died) and a nasty orphanage.

Featuring some stunning scenery (with British Columbia in Canada doubling for the western US) and a spunky central performance from Salenger, this is an interesting history lesson wrapped up in a coming-of-age story that should fascinate boys and girls and grown-ups alike. Darker than your average Disney family movie, this is a little gem. ★★★★☆

THE KID

Starring Bruce Willis, Spencer Breslin, Emily Mortimer (2000)

Unliked and unhappy businessman Russell Duritz (Willis) gets a chance for redemption in this cute Disney movie when a chubby little boy turns up and changes his life. And it's not just any young boy – Rusty (Breslin) is actually Russell's eight-year-old self, magically sent forward in time to help Russell become a better man.

Yes, this is as cutesy as it sounds, but it's also a pretty charming fantasy, as the slick, self-assured older man gets a reminder of what it was like to be a kid, and finds his inner, nicer self when the bemused pair team up to discover how this all happened and how to get little Rusty back home. There's sweet chemistry between the two leads and a superbly sarcastic performance from Lily Tomlin as Willis's assistant. One of those movies that's much more enjoyable than you expect it to be. ★★★☆☆

LITTLE BIG LEAGUE

Starring Luke Edwards, Timothy Busfield, John Ashton (1994)

When the owner of the Minnesota Twins baseball team dies, he bequeaths the team to his twelve-year-old grandson Billy (Edwards), who decides to manage the team himself, much to the consternation of the grown-up players. But it doesn't take long for Billy to overcome the odds and remind the guys how good it is to play baseball like kids – for fun, rather than for the money. (Maybe this should be remade in the UK about football?)

A simple little baseball film that's a little sugary for grown-ups, but enjoyable for younger viewers. Of course, British kids won't recognise the various US baseball stars who crop up and may get bored with the action on the field if they're not fans of the sport, but there are still entertaining moments to be had as Billy loses touch with his own friends and becomes a bit too grown up himself. ★★☆☆☆

THE LITTLE RASCALS

Starring Travis Tedford, Kevin Jamal Woods (1994)

Originally a series of black and white short films called 'Our Gang' from the 1930s, this seems an odd choice for an update, since kids – even those in America where the shorts were shown on TV ad infinitum in the fifties – have probably never heard of the original Little Rascals. Even odder is the fact that the film-makers have gone to great lengths to make sure the kids look like the thirties rascals Spanky, Alfalfa, Buckwheat and pals.

It's basically a series of comic scenes that boys younger than ten may get a giggle from if there's nothing else to watch. There's a go-kart race, pranks aplenty and a secret romance between Alfalfa and a little girl named Darla (he sneaks her into the boys' clubhouse for a romantic dinner), the only girl who gets to speak much in the entire film. Adults, however, will roll their eyes in despair at the feeble slapstick, and wonder why Donald Trump, Whoopi Goldberg, Mel Brooks and Daryl Hannah agreed to be in it. ★★☆☆☆

THE LIZZIE MCGUIRE MOVIE

Starring Hilary Duff, Adam Lamberg, Yani Gellman (2003)

A sugary-sweet tale, based on the TV series of the same name. Reprising her TV persona, Duff stars as Lizzie, an awkward young teen, who is heading off on a school vacation to Italy with her pals, including best (boy) friend Gordo (Lamberg). He, of course, harbours secret feelings for her, but Lizzie is far more interested in the handsome young Italian pop star she bumps into in Rome, Paolo (Gellman). Lizzie's adventures truly begin when Paolo points out that she is a dead ringer for his singing partner Isabella, and anyone who has ever seen a movie before in their lives can guess what happens next. (Yes, our Lizzie gets to sing, thus launching Duff's own music career.)

Duff is great at the comic and romantic stuff (although far too attractive to be the awkward girl she plays), and if you're looking for an ode to fluffy pop, teen fashion, girlish giggles and innocent romance this certainly fits the bill. ★★★☆☆

THE LOVE BUG

Starring Dean Jones, Michele Lee (1968)

The first outing for that lovable VW Beetle with a mind of its own, and still the best, *The Love Bug* remains a classic Disney live-action movie that's a must-see for all kids. In fact, legend has it that when the film was written, no one knew what car would 'play' the role – Disney apparently hired a bevy of cars which they left outside the studio for crew members to look at, including a Toyota and a Volvo. The crew members would inspect each car – but when most of them got to the VW in the line-up, they petted it instead, so the Beetle got the job.

The story is this – racing driver Jim Douglas (Jones) is best known for crashing rather than winning races. After he visits Peter Thorndyke's (David Tomlinson) car showroom, a cute white VW Beetle takes a liking to Jim and follows him home, and while Jim remains clueless to the fact the car is 'alive', his mechanic Tennessee (Buddy Hackett) figures it out and encourages Jim to race the car (now named Herbie). There's also some matchmaking for Herbie to do (between Jim and Lee's Carole Bennett) and a bad guy in the form of Thorndyke, plus some really neat races and car stunts that should thrill younger viewers. The enjoyable sequel *Herbie Rides Again* (1974) was followed by *Herbie Goes to Monte Carlo* (1977), which once again reteamed the car with Dean Jones), and the missable *Herbie Goes Bananas* (1980), while update *Herbie: Fully Loaded* came along in 2005. ★★★★☆

THE MIGHTY DUCKS

Starring Emilio Estevez, Joss Ackland, Joshua Jackson (1992)

With a plot that has some similarities to the classic kids' sports movie *The Bad News Bears*, this dumb but fun film has former Brat Packer Emilio Estevez all grown up as a hotshot lawyer who is arrested for drink-driving and court-ordered to coach a failing kids' ice hockey team, the Mighty Ducks. As memories of his own childhood as a star player resurface (he missed a winning goal and it has haunted him ever since), he grudgingly trains the group of misfits, including Charlie (an effective Jackson), the kid who most reminds him of himself.

It's a Cinderella story of sorts, as the Ducks actually get good, and it's likeable, if simple fare (cynics will see each plot development a mile off). It was pretty successful too, spawning two sequels – 1994's *D2: The Mighty Ducks*, in which the team compete in the Junior Goodwill Games, and 1996's missable *D3: The Mighty Ducks*, in which the kids get scholarships to a prep school and Estevez makes only a brief appearance. ★★★☆☆

MY GIRL

Starring Anna Chlumsky, Macaulay Culkin, Dan Aykroyd (1991)

Eleven-year-old Vada (Chlumsky) is somewhat obsessed with death. Her mother died when she was born and her father (Aykroyd) runs a funeral parlour, so it's hardly surprising. She's kept grounded by her best pal, Thomas J (Culkin), and the pair discuss life, the universe and everything – like what might happen if Vada's dad marries the beautician (Jamie Lee Curtis) who has just started work for him.

It's a very well-performed, sweet tale of kids learning about growing up (Culkin performed his first on-screen kiss in the film), but there is a tragic event at the movie's heart that may shock and upset younger audiences (a hint: those grown-ups who hated Culkin's *Home Alone* icky cuteness may let out a cheer). But if you're there with the box of tissues for your little one, they should enjoy this heartfelt tale between the sniffles. ★★★☆☆

MY GIRL 2

Starring Anna Chlumsky, Dan Aykroyd (1994)

A sweet follow-up to *My Girl*, once again featuring a cute central performance from Chlumsky as Vada. Now thirteen years old and settled with her dad (Aykroyd) and stepmum (Jamie Lee Curtis), she is given a school project to write about someone who has achieved something but whom she has never met – and decides to investigate her mother, who died during Vada's birth. Filled with misgivings, her dad allows Vada to visit her uncle in LA, knowing that she will spend the time there finding out about the mum she never knew.

With another child actress in the lead this could have been stomach-churningly sappy, but thanks to a strong performance from Chlumsky and some nice twists of the plot, it's an enjoyable if slightly slow movie. Very young viewers will probably be a bit bored, so this is best enjoyed by fans of the first movie. ★★★☆☆

NEWSIES (AKA NEWSBOYS)

Starring Christian Bale, David Moscow (1992)

A big flop for Disney (it remains one of their lowest-grossing live-action movies – costing almost $15 million to make, and making only around $3 million at the US box office), and it's not hard to see why. Originally intended as a serious drama about a group of New York newspaper delivery boys in 1899 who went on strike in protest at the unfair practices of newspaper owners Joseph Pulitzer and William Randolph Hearst, this was turned into a musical, complete with singing and dancing numbers set against a grimy Manhattan skyline.

Part of the problem here is that it's unlikely many kids will relate to a 19th-century strike (or know/care what a 'newsie' is in this digital age, for that matter). And despite some impressive choreography (director Ortega was the choreographer for *Dirty Dancing*), it all looks very dated, while young Bale, in his pre-*Batman Begins* days, looks very uncomfortable. It would all be very odd if it wasn't so dull. ★★☆☆☆

NEW YORK MINUTE 🔺 PG PG

Starring Ashley Olsen, Mary-Kate Olsen (2004)

If you are not a nine-year-old girl who thinks that twins Ashley and Mary-Kate Olsen are mini-goddesses, this vehicle for the teen queens is probably not for you. Unsurprisingly, the pair play sisters – one studious, one a wannabe rock chick – who don't get on but are forced to come to some sort of truce when a series of mishaps occur during a trip to New York and they are pursued by manic truant officer Eugene Levy.

It's extremely dumb stuff that makes most other tweenie fare seem like Kafka, as the twins try to evade Levy and some bad-guy video pirates in what is essentially a really bad rip-off of *Ferris Bueller's Day Off*. Young girls may be amused at their antics, but adults will no doubt be horrified as the girls strut around Manhattan in hundreds of different outfits, skipping school, driving without a licence and even accepting a ride from a total stranger! ★★☆☆☆

OUR LIPS ARE SEALED 🔺 G 🔺

Starring Ashley Olsen, Mary-Kate Olsen (2000)

In which the Olsen twins get a nice holiday in Australia, where this film was made. There is a plot, of sorts, as two sisters are sent with their parents to Oz as part of the witness-protection programme. The bad-guy mobsters are in hot pursuit, but the twins still have time for shopping, sightseeing and girlie bonding with their new Aussie pals. (And they talk directly to the camera sometimes, too, which is intensely irritating.)

Only of interest to young fans of the Olsens, this inoffensive but dull film will be torture for any boys or adults who accidentally end up watching it. The Australian tourist board must have been pleased, though, as this portrays the island as one big sunny beach party! ★★☆☆☆

THE PARENT TRAP

Starring Hayley Mills, Maureen O'Hara, Brian Keith (1961)

One of a handful of family films Hayley Mills made for Disney when she was in her teens (they also include *That Darn Cat!*, *In Search of the Castaways*, *Summer Magic* and *The Moon Spinners*), this is the best loved and best remembered. She plays twins Sharon and Susan, one who was raised by their father and the other by their mother after their parents divorced. Neither knows the other exists until they meet at summer camp and conspire to swap places so that each girl can get to know the parent they have never met and hopefully reunite the two adults.

It's sprightly stuff, with nice support from Keith and O'Hara as the parents (and a deliciously spiteful turn from Joanna Barnes as dad's new girlfriend), but what is most impressive here are the special effects, ground-breaking at the time, that allow two Hayley Mills on screen at once (a body double, Susan Henning, was only used in some of the shots, the rest is camera trickery). Kids now, of course, won't be impressed, but it adds to the fun of this cheery little film. ★★★☆☆

THE PARENT TRAP

Starring Dennis Quaid, Natasha Richardson, Lindsay Lohan (1998)

The classic sixties tale of twins (originally played by Hayley Mills, see review above) who swap places is remade for the nineties by film-makers Nancy Meyers and Charles Shyer, who had success with a similar revamping of *Father of the Bride* back in 1991. Identical twins Hallie (Lohan) and Annie (also Lohan) were separated shortly after they were born when their parents split up. Hallie has grown up in California with her vineyard-owning dad Nick (Quaid), while Annie has been raised by her mother Elizabeth (Richardson), who designs wedding dresses in London. Unaware of each other's existence, the pair finally meet at summer camp and then scheme to switch places so that each can meet the parent they've never known, and perhaps reunite the couple before Nick marries gold-digger Meredith (Elaine Hendrix).

While the movie is quite slow for a family film, it's saved by a thoroughly engaging cast and two fabulous performances from a young Lindsay Lohan, who carries every scene without ever being annoying.

Meant for an audience of young girls, this is nonetheless perfectly watchable for the parents-in-tow. ★★★★☆

THE PERFECT MAN

Starring Hilary Duff, Heather Locklear, Chris Noth (2005)

Tween-queen Duff stars in this girlie matchmaking movie as Holly, a teenager tired of moving every time her mother splits from her latest boyfriend. She decides to concoct the perfect guy for her mother, sending flowers and fake notes from a non-existent man, obviously not thinking the plan through and realising mum would probably like to meet him at some point.

Unfortunately for a comedy drama, this isn't very funny. Even the youngest of viewers will realise it makes no sense, while older ones will just cringe as much as the cast, who look increasingly uncomfortable as they have to perform a script that gets more ridiculous as the film progresses. One for ardent Hilary Duff fans only. ★☆☆☆☆

THE PRINCESS DIARIES

Starring Anne Hathaway, Julie Andrews (2001)

Every little girl dreams of becoming a princess, and that is exactly what happens to fifteen-year-old Californian Mia (Hathaway) in this *Cinderella*-style story. Raised by her single mother, she discovers her grandmother is Clarisse Renaldi (the wonderful Andrews), the queen of European principality Genovia, who wants Mia to take her rightful place as Crown Princess.

Of course, Mia is a gawky, modern teenager, so her transformation from average American girl to tiara-wearing princess is fraught with frustration and hilarious moments as Clarisse attempts to teach her the finer points of being a royal. Sweetly done, thanks to a classy, luminous performance from Andrews, it's a cute, amusing comedy from *Pretty Woman*'s Garry Marshall (watch out for his long-time friend, Hector Elizondo, as a co-star – he has appeared in nearly all of Marshall's films) that's especially appealing to the little girl lurking beneath the surface of all female viewers, not just the tween-age ones. ★★★★☆

THE PRINCESS DIARIES 2: ROYAL ENGAGEMENT

Starring Anne Hathaway, Julie Andrews (2004)

The Princess Diaries (above) was a cute *Pretty Woman*-style tale for young girls about a Californian teenager named Mia (Hathaway) who discovers she is heir to the throne of Genovia, and this is a passable – if uninspired – sequel. Now a Princeton graduate, it turns out that Mia has to find a husband in thirty days in order to retain the Genovian crown, so with the help of her grandmother Queen Clarisse (Andrews) she sets about finding her Prince Charming.

Unfortunately, the film feels as if it was rushed together to cash in on the success of the original before Hathaway got too old to play the role. The script is sloppy, the plot obvious and the landmark event of Julie Andrews singing for the first time on film in over twenty years is wasted. Even worse, the wit of the original is completely absent, and this will only be of interest to die-hard fans of the first film, and even then they'll be disappointed. ★★☆☆☆

THE SANDLOT

Starring Tom Guiry, Mike Vitar (1993)

When eleven-year-old Scotty moves to a new neighbourhood, he joins the local baseball team and acquires a new set of friends to play ball with, while avoiding the legendary ball-eating dog known as the Beast, who patrols the back of the sandlot where they play. Unfortunately, it's there that Scotty has accidentally hit his father's prized baseball, autographed by Babe Ruth, so the boys have to risk everything to retrieve it.

This is one of those movies spread over a golden American summer (in this case, 1962) that's aimed at tweenie boys who'll chortle at the jokes, bodily fluids and dog slobber that peppers the film. And for kids who don't know their dugouts from third base, it's not just about baseball either, but more a warm little movie about boys growing up and having a good time while they're at it. ★★★☆☆

SMALL SOLDIERS PG-13 PG

Starring Kirsten Dunst, Phil Hartman, Denis Leary, Jay Mohr (1998)

Desperate to produce a new line of toys which will meet the approval of their money-hungry boss (Leary), designers Irwin and Larry (David Cross and Mohr) come up with the Tolkienesque Gorgonites and a group of army action figures called the Commando Elite, which can move and talk, thanks to a secret new microchip which was actually designed for use in military weapons. So when the first boxes of the toys are shipped to a small-town store, it comes as no surprise that the pesky pint-sized playthings take on a life of their own – the butch Commandos declaring war on the peace-loving Gorgonites – or that teenagers Alan (Gregory Smith) and Christy (Dunst) are the only ones that can stop them.

A family film that's a mix of live action and some impressive computer-generated imagery, this is basically a combination of *Toy Story* and Dante's own *Gremlins*, which suffers from a sparse plot and scant excitement (how scared would you be of a three-inch doll?). On the plus side, there are some fun vocal characterisations of the dolls by Tommy Lee Jones, Ernest Borgnine, and *Spinal Tap*-ers Christopher Guest, Michael McKean and Harry Shearer, but that's not enough to keep adults or children entertained for the film's nigh-on two-hour running time. (Note: there are a few scenes featuring the freakier looking dolls torturing toys and humans with fire and little knives that very young viewers may find frightening.) ★★☆☆

SPICE WORLD: THE MOVIE PG PG

Starring Victoria Beckham, Geri Halliwell, Melanie Chisholm, Melanie B, Emma Bunton (1997)

Once upon a time, there were five happy, bubbly girls who sang and danced a little and wore next-to-nothing a lot. They found fame and fortune in a pop band and then decided to make a movie of their rise to stardom, which they hoped would be a bit like the Beatles' *A Hard Day's Night*. And, though it was not perhaps the best film in the whole wide world, those Scary, Ginger, Sporty, Baby and Posh Spice girls knew that every little boy and girl in the land would come from far and wide to see their movie, and then buy the soundtrack album to make them even more money.

Of course, that was then and this is now. The Spice Girls have split, attempted solo careers, appeared in the tabloids... and been replaced in the hearts of preteen girls by other, possibly more talented, pop groups. But this film remains, and while most tweenie viewers probably have no idea who the Spice Girls were, there's just about enough silliness, catchy songs and sparkly outfits to keep them amused. Adults, however, who aren't tone deaf, are advised to steer well clear. ★★☆☆☆

SPY KIDS

Starring Antonio Banderas, Carla Gugino, Alexa Vega, Daryl Sabara (2001)

An absolutely first-rate family movie from writer/director Robert Rodriguez (better known for far more grown-up films like *Sin City* and *Desperado*). Young Carmen (Vega) and Juni (Sabara) think their parents are boring. Little do they know that mum (Gugino) and dad (Banderas) were actually the world's best secret agents until they retired to raise their family. Now they've been kidnapped, and the kids finally discover from their Uncle Felix (Cheech Marin) – who isn't really their uncle – what their parents really do, and also that their parents are in grave danger. It's up to the kids to try and rescue their parents, and save the world.

With imaginative bad guys in the form of Floop (Alan Cumming), a kids' TV host who wants to rule the world, and a minion named Minion (Tony Shalhoub), and a plot that romps along at super-speed, this is fun stuff, packed with special effects, gadgets, action and adventure (none of it scary, all of it fun). Brilliant – and watch out for a brief cameo from George Clooney, who starred in Rodriguez's *From Dusk Till Dawn*. ★★★★☆

SPY KIDS 2: ISLAND OF LOST DREAMS

Starring Antonio Banderas, Carla Gugino, Alexa Vega, Daryl Sabara (2002)

An enjoyable, clever follow-up to the hit *Spy Kids*, this has the two siblings from the first movie, Carmen (Vega) and Juni (Sabara), embarking on their first solo mission as spies. The island they are sent to is odd, to say the least, none of their gadgets are working properly and there are two new spy kids to deal with too, in the form of Gary and Gerti Giggles (Matt O'Leary and Emily Osment).

The bad guy this time around is Steve Buscemi's mad scientist, who has been making mutant creatures on the island (pigs that can fly, that sort of thing), and there are some funny performances from the cast, which also includes Ricardo Montalban (as the kids' grandpa) and Bill Paxton, with Alan Cumming and Tony Shalhoub reprising their roles from the first movie. ★★★☆☆

SPY KIDS 3-D: GAME OVER

Starring Antonio Banderas, Carla Gugino, Alexa Vega, Daryl Sabara (2003)

The final *Spy Kids* movie (possibly because the two kids were getting older – Vega was fifteen when this was made), this boasts 3-D effects (3-D glasses were included with the film on DVD, though there is also a 2-D version). It's not as good as the first two films, but there's still fun and flashiness aplenty, as young Carmen (Vega) gets mentally sucked into a computer game devised by the evil Toymaker (Sylvester Stallone, who won a Razzie for worst performance of the year for his role), and her younger brother (Sabara) is the only one who can rescue her. (It's inside the game when things come over all three-dimensional.)

The 3-D effects aren't great, and the film relies heavily on the charms of young Sabara, since Vega is pretty comatose during most of the movie. But there are moments of hilarity, action and adventure, and some choice cameos from Salma Hayek, George Clooney, Elijah Wood (all of whom have been in movies made by director Rodriguez) as well as Bill Paxton, Steve Buscemi, Tony Shalhoub and Alan Cumming from the earlier *Spy Kids* films. (And if you're wondering if Stallone deserved that Razzie, the answer is, unfortunately, yes!) ★★★☆☆

3 NINJAS

Starring Victor Wong, Michael Treanor (1992)

Jeffrey, Samuel and Michael Douglas (no, not that one) are three kids who just happen to have a grandfather skilled in martial arts. It's like

The Karate Kid in triplicate as the trio – who go by the nicknames 'Colt', 'Rocky' and 'Tum Tum' – learn to ninja-kick some butt just in time to help out their FBI dad bring down a bad guy, who has done something or other that's not that interesting.

It takes a great leap of faith to believe three kids between the ages of twelve and seven could bring down the baddies that attack them, and a blind eye not to notice elderly Wong's younger (and sprightlier) stunt double in the fight scenes. It's basically eight minutes of cartoon adventure and violence (the film was cut by just over a minute of chop-sockiness to gain a British 'PG' release) that may entertain kids briefly but doesn't stand up to repeated viewings. A series of forgettable sequels followed: *3 Ninjas Kick Back* (1994), *3 Ninjas Knuckle Up* (1995) and *3 Ninjas: High Noon at Mega Mountain* (1998). ★★☆☆☆

WAR OF THE BUTTONS

Starring Gregg Fitzgerald, Gerard Kearney (1994)

A remake of the 1962 French film *La Guerre des Boutons* (which was based on a novel by Louis Pergaud), this is the simple and often fun tale of a series of skirmishes between boys of neighbouring Irish villages – the title coming from the keepsakes they take from the other child's clothes when they win (which usually leads to an interesting conversation with their parents when they get home and have to explain where all their buttons are). The 'war' is between the kids of Ballydowse and the slightly wealthier ones who live in Carrickdowse across the bridge. The 'Ballys' are led by Fergus (Fitzgerald), a boy with problems at home, while the 'Carricks' have the self-assured strategist Geronimo (John Coffey) in charge.

It's definitely a boy's-own adventure as the two groups battle each other (once in the nude, providing the hilarious sight of them charging down the hill like a collection of rabid flashers), using catapults filled with mouldy fruit and scheduling their 'fights' between school and tea so their parents don't find out. Unfortunately, because there's not much else to the movie, even the cheekiest viewer enjoying the scraps may get bored before it's over. ★★★☆☆

WHAT A GIRL WANTS

Starring Amanda Bynes, Colin Firth (2003)

A sweet (if rather implausible) comedy drama that tells the tale of Daphne (Bynes), a sixteen-year-old American girl living with her mother (Kelly Preston), who has always dreamed of meeting the father she has never known. Determined to find him, she hops on a flight to London where she discovers dad is Lord Henry Dashwood (Firth, tongue placed firmly in cheek), an aristocrat and politician who is about to marry the scheming Glynnis (Anna Chancellor) and take on her equally conniving daughter Clarissa (Christina Cole).

Girls will enjoy Daphne's adventure as her American ways raise eyebrows in English society (there's a cute little romance too, with local musician Ian, as played by newcomer Oliver James), while adults will have a snigger or two at the way the Brits are portrayed as snobby, badly dressed socialites more attached to their antique chandeliers than their children. It's all completely daft, of course, but as preteen *Cinderella* stories go, this one (loosely based on the Rex Harrison movie *The Reluctant Debutante*) is suitably fizzy and enjoyable. ★★★☆☆

WHISTLE DOWN THE WIND u/c

Starring Hayley Mills, Alan Bates, Bernard Lee (1961)

Based on a novel by Mary Hayley Bell (aka Mrs John Mills, and Hayley Mills's mum), this is a thoughtful British film that marked Bryan Forbes's (*The Stepford Wives*, *International Velvet*) directorial debut.

'My best childhood film memory is *Whistle Down the Wind* because it made me cry and made me think. I identified with the three kids so much and I wanted the murderer to be Jesus Christ.'

ANNA FRIEL

Young Kathy (Mills, swathed in a big coat most of the time to hide the fact she was sixteen but playing younger) and her two younger siblings find a man hiding in their barn. When he's discovered, he mutters 'Jesus Christ' in surprise just at the moment the kids ask who he is, so they instantly (because they are God-fearing, religious children) believe that he really is the son of God. In fact, the man (Bates) is actually a convicted murderer who is a hunted fugitive.

While Mills was already a competent and established actress, the other two children (Diane Holgate and Alan Barnes) had no acting experience, yet are both brilliant (sadly Holgate never made another film, while Barnes only appeared in 1963's *The Victors*). Bates is just right as the man who would be Jesus in what is a beautifully filmed, simple tale of childhood innocence and belief. ★★★★☆

Certificates Ratings

● ●

The British Board of Film Classification views every movie released in the UK and gives each one a certificate. To help you in your movie choices, we have noted the certificate granted by the BBFC alongside each review, and below, each certificate is explained by the BBFC. For more information, please visit www.bbfc.org.uk

 U – Universal. Should be suitable for children over the age of four. U films should be set within a positive moral framework and should offer reassuring counterbalances to any violence, threat or horror.

 PG – Parental Guidance. General viewing, but some scenes may be unsuitable for young children. A PG film should not disturb a child of around age 8 and older. Parents are advised to consider whether the content may upset younger or more sensitive children.

 12A/12 – 12A suitable for 12 years and older. No one younger than 12 may see a 12A film, no one under 12 may rent or buy a 12 rated DVD. Responsibility for allowing under-12s to view lies with the supervising adult.

 15 – Suitable only for 15 years and older. No one younger than 15 can rent or buy a 15 DVD.

 18 – Suitable only for adults. No one younger than 18 can rent or buy a 18 DVD

BBFC classification symbols are both trademark and copyright protected.

USA – the ratings are as follows:
For more information please see: www.mpaa.org

G — G – General Audiences. This is a film which contains nothing in theme, language, nudity and sex, violence, etc, that would, in the view of the Rating Board, be offensive to parents whose younger children view the film.

PG — PG – Parental Guidance Suggested. This is a film which clearly needs to be examined by parents before they let their children attend. The label PG plainly states parents may consider some material unsuitable for their children. There may be some profanity in these films. There may be some violence or brief nudity. There is no drug use content in a PG-rated film.

PG-13 — PG-13 – Parents Strongly Cautioned. PG-13 is thus a sterner warning to parents, particularly when deciding which movies are not suitable for younger children. Parents, by the rating, are alerted to be very careful about the attendance of their under-teenage children. A PG-13 film is one which, in the view of the Rating Board, leaps beyond the boundaries of the PG rating in theme, violence, nudity, sensuality, language, or other contents, but does not quite fit within the restricted R category. Any drug use content will initially require at least a PG-13 rating. PG-13 is designed to make parental decisions easier for films between PG and R.

R — R – Restricted. In the opinion of the Rating Board, this film definitely contains some adult material. Parents are strongly urged to find out more about this film before they allow their children to accompany them. An R-rated film may include strong language, violence, nudity, drug abuse, other elements, or a combination of the above, so parents are counselled in advance to take this advisory rating very seriously.

u/c — Movies with this symbol have no US rating.

Australian – the ratings are as follows:
For more information, please see www.oflc.gov.au

 G: General. The content is very mild.

 PG: Parental guidance recommended. The content is mild.

 M: Recommended for mature audiences. The content is moderate in impact

 MA 15+: Not suitable for people under 15. Under-15s must be accompanied by a parent or adult guardian. The content is strong.

u/c   Movies with this symbol have no Australian rating.

Movies reviewed that are not available on Region 2 (UK/Europe) DVD at time of going to press.

Adaptations
Anne of Green Gables (available on US/Region 1)
Courage Mountain (available on US/Region 1)
A High Wind in Jamaica (available on US/Region 1)
Little Lord Fauntleroy (available on US/Region 1)
The New Adventures of Pippi Longstocking (available on US/Region 1)
North
The Phantom Tollbooth
The Prince and the Pauper (available on US/Region 1)

Animals
Lassie Come Home (available on US/Region 1)
Alaska (available on US/Region 1)
Andre
Casey's Shadow (available on US/Region 1)
Digby the Biggest Dog in the World
Doctor Dolittle (1967) (available on US/Region 1)
Flipper (1963) (available on US/Region 1)
International Velvet
Milo and Otis (available on US/Region 1)
National Velvet (available on US/Region 1)
Rudyard Kipling's The Jungle Book (available on US/Region 1)
That Darn Cat! (1965) (available on US/Region 1)
The Yearling (available on US/Region 1)
Cats Don't Dance (available on US/Region 1)
Freddie as F.R.O.7

Fairy Tales, Fantasies and Legends
The 5000 Fingers of Dr T (available on US/Region 1)
Fairytale: A True Story (available on US/Region 1)
The Indian in the Cupboard (available on US/Region 1)
The Neverending Story (available on US/Region 1)
The Neverending Story 2: The Next Chapter (available on US/Region 1)
The Pagemaster (available on US/Region 1)
The Secret of Roan Inish (available on US/Region 1)
Three Wishes (available on US/Region 1)
Tom Thumb (available on US/Region 1)

Family Movies and Seasonal Stocking Fillers
The Bad News Bears (available on US/Region 1)

Sci-Fi and Comic-Book Adventures
Richie Rich (available on US/Region 1)
Dennis the Menace (available on US/Region 1)
Star Kid (available on US/Region 1)
Supergirl (available on US/Region 1)

Television Treats
The Addams Family (available on US/Region 1)
Doug's 1st Movie
The Jetsons: The Movie
Pee-Wee's Big Adventure (available on US/Region 1)
Pufnstuf
The Smurfs and the Magic Flute
Tom and Jerry: The Movie (available on US/Region 1)

Teen Movies
The Monster Squad
Breaking Away (available on US/Region 1)
The Delinquents
Gidget (available on US/Region 1)
Kuffs (available on US/Region 1)
License to Drive (available on US/Region 1)
The Outsiders (available on US/Region 1)
Radio Flyer (available on US/Region 1)
The Year My Voice Broke (available on US/Region 1)

Tiny Tots
The Magic Pudding
Sesame Street Presents: Follow That Bird (available on US/Region 1)

Tweenies
Candleshoe (available on US/Region 1)
Curly Sue (available on US/Region 1)
Little Big League (available on US/Region 1)
Newsies (available on US/Region 1)
War of the Buttons

Index